The French in Love and War

The French in Love and War

Popular Culture in the Era of the World Wars

Charles Rearick

Yale University Press
New Haven & London

Published with the assistance of the
Charles A. Coffin Fund.

Designed by Rebecca Gibb.
Set in Fournier and Didot types by
The Composing Room of Michigan, Inc., Grand Rapids, Michigan.

Printed in the United States of America by
Data Reproductions Corporation, Rochester Hills, Michigan.

Library of Congress Cataloging-in-Publication Data
Rearick, Charles, 1942–
The French in love and war : popular culture in the era
of the world wars / Charles Rearick.
p.   cm.
Includes bibliographical references and index.
ISBN 0-300-06433-0 (cloth)
1. France—Civilization—20th century.   2. Popular culture—
France—History—20th century.   3. National characteristics,
French.   I. Title.
DC33.7R397   1997
306'.0944—dc21   96-50287
CIP

A catalogue record for this book is available
from the British Library.

10 9 8 7 6 5 4 3 2 1

CONTENTS

INTRODUCTION

THIS BOOK is about how the French viewed life and experienced it during some of the worst times of this century—from the bloodbaths of the First World War through the nation's defeat and Nazi occupation during the Second World War. It is about ways of living, coping, and struggling that figured prominently in French culture. At the heart of this history is a national argument about the character of the French people and their responses to life's difficulties. What are the truly French ways of doing battle, dealing with disappointment, and meeting adversity? France's national culture and media proposed a mix of old and new answers, and the people made choices. In choosing they contributed to the formation of their collective identity, continuing a process that runs through the entire course of France's history.[1]

The most common answers were embodied in images and stories of ordinary people, who typically were set off against "others" in such incarnations as the foreigner, the cosmopolite, and *les gros* (big wigs). That "myth of the people" has had a long history[2] and a changing cast of characters. Scholars have given much attention to parts of the story—to Joan of Arc, for example, and to Marianne, the symbol of the Republic.[3] My book enlarges the conventional cast of characters by including such stars of show business as Maurice Chevalier and Mistinguett who, in their time, served as collective representations, defining Frenchness for many. For decades the lives of those celebrities were as familiar to their contemporaries as Joan of Arc's life was. Their publicity machines made them out to be representatives of Paris, of France, and of the French people.

In the difficult years from the First World War through the Second, representations of the people were particularly important in French culture—especially representations of the modest multitude called *le petit peuple* (the little people). Why did they became so prominent? Much of my answer centers on changes in French society—in particular the great political and economic strength attained by workers and the lower middle class between the wars. They were a critical swing group, as voters and as consumers of mass entertainment. During the 1930s their political and trade union power and their support from leftist elites reached new highs. Under those circumstances, the "little people," having a new cultural leverage, enjoyed a better image than they had a century before, when the better-off classes had viewed working people as uncivilized and dangerous, virtually indistinguishable from criminals.[4] In commercial entertainment and political culture they appeared more than before as leading figures, often as heroes. Culturally the common people, the *Français moyen* (the average Frenchman), viewed as a bedrock plurality, were more important, too, because they above all seemed to retain an essential Frenchness that elites were losing to a fashionable cosmopolitanism.

My book spotlights the "little people" as they appeared in songs and movies, which were arguably the most influential sources of images and myths then shaping notions of French identity.[5] The focus here is on established, conventional images and salient challenges to them. Commentators on movies and songs at times referred to conventional motifs as a "folklore" of the French about themselves. In my quest for telling evidence, that reference to folklore signaled that certain songs and films dealt in commonly known archetypical characters. Another marker was the description of films or songs as contemporary *images d'Epinal*, those cartoon-strip sheets of popular icons long printed in the town of Epinal and sold cheaply to the masses.

In the iconography of "the people," certain images had greatest appeal and became primary symbols, powerful crystallizers of values and experience. They were the images of such popular heroes and heroines as the tough but jovial infantryman (the *poilu*), his devoted and patriotic woman, the bantering working-class Parisian (the *faubourien*), the suntanned youth hiking to the next *auberge de jeunesse* (youth hostel), the militant demonstrator and striker, the worker enjoying a first vacation at the seashore, and the sons of the *poilus* hoping to reenact the victory of their fathers without paying the terrible costs. These were major figures in what French historians call the social imagination.

Such images of "the people" were embellished and oversimplified versions of French life. That is particularly clear when we compare those images with historians' accounts of the period, as I have done in this book. My main purpose, however, is not to treat the social imaginary as "wrong" and to correct it, but rather to present a history of its forms and their meanings during an important era. Inexact or distortional, the myths and symbols of popular culture[6] still matter historically for the part they played in organizing experience and representing identity. The popular figures whose story I tell are of historical importance for the role they played in shaping the French people's sense of itself.

At this point an old critical question arises about whether commercially produced songs and films give us anything other than the views of elites and producers. Gramsci's twofold answer, I think, is helpful: yes, the imagined in commercial forms routinely reflected the interests of the powerful, but it also communicated enough of the values and concerns of "little people" to satisfy popular consumers.[7] In a time of deep national insecurities, cultural producers sought figures with which many people could identify—characters that drew on common experiences and widely shared wishes, fears, and interests. Idealized or caricatural though they were, Julot, Margot, and other bigger-than-life characters bore some resemblance to actual people, and they pleased many. Yet they also displeased some. Disagreements about "the people" make the drama and movement of this cultural history. Rival groups battled over the myth of the people as they contended for power in the political system.

Their different stories about "the people" brought out alternative options and outcomes; so did films and songs that appeared nonpolitical. Some of the stories frightened and dissuaded. A great many of them encouraged: they depicted representatives of the society facing the challenges of the time and meeting them. Through the entire troubled period framed by world wars, the media disseminated countless stories about distinctively French ways of winning—or at least coping well with great difficulties. The French "little guy" or woman was shown facing up to the challenges with a smile or a song, resourcefully managing the adversities of the time, drawing on innate strengths of a putative national character. That is a central theme of the myth that I have examined, the one that seems (understandably) to have dominated a time when people were grappling with successive crises in their daily lives.

Through the era of the world wars, then, a Paris-centered popular culture supplied the nation with a mix of the old familiar identities and attractive new alternatives. In choosing from the gamut of cultural options and "distractions," people looked for ways of dealing with the anxieties and pains that both new and old ways of living brought. By their choices they shaped meaning for their lives in some of the most extraordinarily dangerous times of this century.

The process goes on today, with some of the reworked identities of the era of the world wars now playing the role of traditional identities. The struggles and choices of that era have their place in the making of contemporary French culture. Those responses to still familiar questions and dilemmas merit a place in the "consultable record" (Clifford Geertz's term), to which this book is a contribution.

I. FRENCH IDENTITIES
IN THE CRUCIBLE OF WAR

Mourir pour la patrie, c'est le sort le plus beau.

[To die for the fatherland is the most beautiful of fates.]

—*From a military hymn played regularly during the First World War;*
words attributed to Roland at Roncevaux

Quiconque ne maudit point la guerre soit maudit!

[Cursed be anyone who does not curse war!]

—*Soldier and scholar Paul Cazin, on the Western Front, spring 1915*

Nous en rêvons la nuit, nous y pensons le jour,
Ce n'est que Madelon, mais pour nous, c'est l'amour.

[We dream of her by night, we think of her by day,
It's only Madelon, but for us, it's love.]

—*From the song "Quand Madelon" (1914), lyrics by Louis Bousquet*

Anxious Patriots

WAR HAD ALREADY BROKEN OUT in the Balkans, but for most people in France the last day of July 1914 began as just another Friday. In the oppressive heat of the season peasants were harvesting their fields, and workers were laboring in shops and factories. Better-off Parisian families crowded into the railroad stations for long-planned departures to the seashore and the country. They were going ahead with vacations, but they could not miss the ominous signs that their normal existence was coming to an end. For days newspapers had made it clear that Europe was "on the edge of the precipice," as the mass-circulation *Le Petit Parisien* put it on 28 July. Europe was "on the eve of a conflagration which would hurl more than twenty-five million men against each other, which would be the ruin of the vanquisher as of the vanquished," the first-page article continued. Yet the same article also gave hope of mediation and a peaceful resolution. Housewives responded by going to the *grands magasins d'alimentation* with their largest baskets to stock up. By 31 July Parisians could still look for a glimmer of hope, but in the stations and on the boulevards they had to run a gauntlet of newspaper boys crying out the step-by-step approach of war. Special editions sold fast, and the news turned conversations into brooding exchanges on the conflict between Austria and Serbia and the danger of the bigger "conflagration." Everyone knew that France would be drawn into war if its ally Russia and its old enemy Germany mobilized and joined in the fighting. In the afternoon the latest worrisome news spread quickly: Germany had declared a "state of siege," a step preliminary to mobilization and a declaration of war. The late evening brought new distress of another sort: the Socialist leader Jean Jaurès had been assassinated. Now mass grief welled up, and a new worry struck: the nation was going to war with freshly inflamed political divisions.

War preparations moved forward inexorably. Vacations ended quickly on 1 August with the announcement of general mobilization. Official posters near town halls proclaimed the order to townspeople; imperious drumrolls and church bells sent the grim message through the countryside. The next day families of all social backgrounds bid emotional goodbyes to their men, now in uniform. The men took trains to join their military units, and then they were off to battle. Paris newspapers announced that Germany had already declared war on Russia, and German troops had already crossed the French eastern boundary even before declaring war on France.[1]

As they steeled themselves to meet the enemy, the French had to recast their collective self-identity. For decades before the war, books, newspapers, and popular songs had regularly served up representations of the French as leisure-loving, romantic, sentimental, and patriotic—patriotic without being militarist, in contrast to their Prussian enemy. Cultural critics had depicted the people as excessively given to pleasure and had judged them frivolous at best—or decadent. The notion that the French were frivolous was a centuries-old one; the conclusion that they were decadent, worn-out, or degenerate was a turn-of-the-century diagnosis, backed by fresh scientific argument.[2] Now the tests of war would render a verdict. As they went to battle, the French people had to abandon their peacetime habits, ingrained through the decades since the Franco-Prussian War of 1870–71. Now they had to adopt a warring frame of mind. They had to sort through their cultural traditions and decide on a fresh collective face. What character traits and attitudes would help them meet the challenge of war? Could the French retain what they considered their distinctive characteristics—that is, remain French—in a life-and-death struggle? Debate on these difficult questions went on as long as the war.

A consensus did emerge on one point at the very beginning: the immediate need for an energetic defense of the fatherland. With unexpected swiftness France's

Jovial singing soldiers march past their favorite barmaid Madelon outside her rural tavern. This sunny scene—the epitome of prewar innocence—was the original cover illustration for the music-hall march "Quand Madelon" (1914).

rival political leaders put aside their differences and joined in a "sacred union." So did the common people. Fervently patriotic observers described the people's reaction as mass enthusiasm for a long-awaited conflict, and historians long echoed that view. In such accounts nationalistic crowds greeted the declaration of war with cheers and joyful anticipation of an overdue settling of scores. Their heroic men in tricolor splendor were finally to end the "great ennui" of peacetime, at last going off to fight and vanquish the feared and hated old enemy Germany, which had inflicted defeat on France forty-three years before. Those accounts of chauvinist zeal came in part from wishful thinking during a national crisis and in part from many years of cultural priming. In the press and in literature war had been commonly viewed as a romantic adventure, a sporting game. Even novelists creating stories of future wars were unable or unwilling to imagine anything else.[3]

Research by historian Jean-Jacques Becker has yielded a quite different view of public opinion in August 1914: most people in France showed little or no enthusiasm when confronted with a real war.[4] Major newspapers of the period reported that on the day of mobilization, 2 August, Parisians hung flags out their windows as they did on national festival days, but they showed no other sign of rejoicing. The sight of departing soldiers evoked some cries of "Vive l'armée!" and here and there people sang "La Marseillaise," but more frequently they showed anxiety and reacted with sadness and resignation. People soberly prepared to do their duty. In cafés there was none of the usual laughter or loud banter, journalists noted. Tension and even anguish showed in voices and faces; tears glistened in women's eyes. Strangers stopped each other on the boulevards and exchanged reactions: "They have fired on us. . . . How could they dare do that?" In villages across France church bells and drumrolls announcing "La guerre!" commonly evoked the same responses of consternation and tears.[5]

With *la patrie en danger*, the French government declared a state of siege for the capital. The city of light, so long celebrated as a place of freedom and pleasure, became a potential battle zone. Soldiers and republican guards patrolled the streets and checked the papers of everyone entering Paris. At eight P.M. cafés had to close, tramways and the métro stopped, and outside lighting was turned off. Theaters and music halls also closed. Around town halls in all quarters crowds gathered to read official dispatches and discussed them "with emotion," *Le Temps* reported.

During the day itinerant musicians sang and hawked patriotic songs and war ballads on street corners. The country's initial cultural response was to exalt the patriot, who was so devoted to the common struggle that he or she readily gave up ordinary indulgences and pleasures. Centuries of experience had taught that war meant sacrifice. While the mobilized men risked their lives and suffered in combat, the rest of the people felt obliged to show respect by abandoning normal frivolity. It seemed best to show that they, too, were making sacrifices and were turning their energies to war. "We no longer had the heart to amuse ourselves, and nothing could distract our attention from the sublime and painful drama of which our little soldiers were the heroes," explained two chroniclers in 1915.[6]

In late September, after the French army stemmed the invasion with a victory on the Marne, the initial sense of crisis passed. In early December—after nineteen weeks of war—Paris theaters reopened, yet light entertainment still seemed inappropriate. At the end of the Comédie-Française performance of *Horace*, actor Mounet-Sully declaimed "La Marseillaise." At the Opéra-Comique, the robust diva Marthe Chenal, draped in a tricolor flag, sang the anthem with an ardor and volume unmatched in that era. When she stretched out her arms and spread out the flag, she became Victory.[7] Or so she did in the eyes of those brought up in the nationalist, republican culture that had long been propagated in public schools and civic ceremonies throughout France. The same nationalism was also well established in commercial popular culture. During the 1870s a singer named Amiati had won fame wrapping herself in the tricolor and singing "La Marseillaise" in Paris music halls.

Paris cinemas featured films with patriotic scenarios (for example, *Mères françaises*), showing devotion to *la patrie* and the moral superiority of the French cause. Weekly newsreels showed heavily censored, sometimes staged, and ever upbeat reports on the war. Music halls presented a stream of flag-waving revues. At every turn a song resounded to the glory to the Allies and the French soldiers. As a

Pour le Droit et la Civilisation
Pour l'Honneur et pour la Patrie.

A postcard tableau dressing up the war effort in the loftiest rhetoric of wartime nationalism—Right, Civilization, Honor, Fatherland. The feminine symbol of the French Republic (Marianne) stands protected between a French soldier (*left*) and a British soldier.

climax for any performance the most applauded and frequent selection was, of course, "La Marseillaise." On 14 July 1915—the first national celebration during the war—it received special ceremonial attention that honored both the revolutionary war hymn and the army. That day the ashes of the song's author, Rouget de l'Isle, were given a place of honor in the Invalides. In his speech there President Raymond Poincaré called "La Marseillaise" the cry of a "sovereign nation which has the passion of independence and whose sons resolutely prefer death to servitude."[8]

"To die for the fatherland is the most beautiful fate," so the hero Roland was said to have declared at Roncevaux. His sentiment echoed through the war in song and speeches. As the troops went to battle, army bands played "Mourir pour la Patrie"—Roland's words—and "Le Chant du départ" with its all-demanding line: for the Republic "a Frenchman must die!" A typically patriotic program in November 1914 included the reciting of the poem "Mourir en Chantant," which heaps the highest praise on the dying patriot who goes down singing. Best of all was to die singing "La Marseillaise," and according to the poem such patriotic virtue was anything but rare: "All France wants to sing and to die for liberty to the accents of 'La Marseillaise.'" The idea behind all these works was expressed most directly by a "Grande Marche patriotique" launched in December 1914: "Die for France."[9]

Ordinary Heroes, New Community

From the beginning the home-front press referred to French soldiers as brave heroes, whose devotion to *la patrie* deserved the emulation of others. They were the men rising to give might to Right, to defend civilization and liberty. Their courage and moral superiority made certain their eventual victory—so went the cheerleading editorial line of the major Paris dailies, echoing government statements on the war. At the same time, the "heroes" remained "our little soldiers"—ordinary nextdoor neighbors, dear and familiar, not aloof or socially remote.

By early 1915 the press was popularizing a new identity and name for the French soldier: the *poilu*, the epitome of the tough warrior. The poilu was above all tough and manly—hairy, literally, in the manner of a strong, mature man.[10] On the front in October 1914 when an army captain called bespectacled sergeant Marc Bloch "a real poilu," clearly Bloch, a professor of history in Amiens before that August, had doubly earned the title: he had grown a full, untidy beard and had ably led his platoon under fire.[11]

The 2,877,000 men called to arms in early August 1914—professors, merchants, clerks, workers, and peasants—within months became simply poilus, alongside the 800,000 soldiers in the active army before the war. Photographs and drawings in the press habitually depicted the poilu as a scruffy but imposing middle-aged man with a moderately unkempt beard and mustache, from which protruded a pipe. Engaged in a constant struggle for survival, he endured not only enemy fire but also mud, rain, and cold. He lived like a "primitive," burrowed into the earth. In their trench newspapers the first year, poilus called themselves troglodytes.[12]

The new soldiers quickly adopted a new vocabulary of slang that reinforced their new identity and set them apart from the civilian world. Everything important had a special word known only to the initiated: wine became *le pinard*, a Parisian was a *Pantruchard*. A shell (*obus*) was a *marmite* (a mess tin). The new language derived partly from army tradition (for example, the word *poilu*), partly from Parisian slang, and partly from new coinage. Many of the new words were amusing in their sound or secondary meaning. The bayonet was a *fourchette* (fork) or *cure-dents* (toothpick). Lice were *totos*. A rifle was a *seringue* (syringe) or *arbalette* (crossbow). To kill was *zigouiller*. A propaganda lie was a *bobard* or *bourrage de crâne* (literally, skull stuffing). Much of this new vocabulary came from Parisian workers, famous for their bantering facility with words. In the trenches peasants picked up those ways, as did well-educated city men, amusing themselves by speaking like the most plebeian of the plebs—"canaille-style." Journalists began to report the new language to the home front during the first six months of the war, when most of the slang gained currency.[13] The effect was to show that the soldiers had formed a new close community within which they playfully expressed inventiveness and lightheartedness, traits that the press was eagerly reporting.

In the tense time of a still-advancing German invasion force in September 1914, *Le Miroir* published a photograph showing soldiers fishing several kilometers from the enemy—"between two rough fights." After French victory in the battle of the Marne, the lines of combat stabilized: in muddy trenches forming the Western Front the men began to settle into a new form of combat existence. By November, the popular magazine *L'Illustration* showed that French soldiers just six hundred meters from the German trenches had rigged up a shower room with an annex that served as a barber shop; they talked of organizing and performing a music-hall revue in another room.[14] The amenities so optimistically reported remained a rarity on the front, but the hope of entertainment there did not go unfulfilled. In early December the illustrated magazine *Le Miroir* ran a photograph showing soldiers finishing a trench in the Aisne: "Rapidly our *pioupious* have be-

What it took to be a poilu: courage, gaiety, perseverance, and other virtues, forming a new set of "ten commandments." A postcard from the war years. Private collection.

come skillful excavators and they construct trenches [that are] not only good for sustaining attacks, but almost comfortable." The 14 February issue contained six photographs of "a luxury trench" that provided *le confort moderne* "six feet underground."[15] Morale boosters in the press arguably had grounds for portraying some poilus as men adapting well to working the earth and to the rigors of outdoor life—almost half the fighting troops were peasants—but none of that applied to the men from the cities. Exaggerated and selective, such reportage offered psychological comfort to the still comfortable mass of civilians behind the lines, few of whom faced new hardships. Most people wanted to believe the reports that the men on the front were managing well in the face of difficulties. In the words of the time, the poilu excelled at using what became known as "system D," meaning the ability to cope resourcefully (*se débrouiller*): the poilu was a good *débrouillard,* and that added to public admiration of him.

In late December *Le Miroir* gave its readers another upbeat news story enti-tled "Our Soldiers Remain Big Children," with one photograph showing soldiers near the front listening to a phonograph and another image showing men riding a merry-go-round as their comrades look on and laugh. In the same issue another pho-tograph of men chatting in a trench appeared with the caption, "The men remain calm under the machine-gun fire." Still another picture showed men playing cards. "The old French gaiety never looses its rights," declared the accompanying text, "and our troops excel at killing time when the enemy leaves them leisure." The mid-February issue reiterated the article of faith about "the old French gaiety" that "regains ascen-dancy." The soldiers "compose satirical songs . . . [and] write cheery newspapers like *L'Echo des Marmites;* singers sing, artists draw." In behind-the-lines camps, accord-ing to other articles, soldiers fashioned their own game of skittles from tree trunks, and some joined in a game borrowed from the British called tug-of-war.[16]

This kind of story became a staple of the Parisian press, intent on reassur-ing the home population. In February 1916, *Lectures pour tous* printed a photograph of soldiers playing football in a snowy field in the Vosges with the remark: "What to do between two attacks in the Vosges? A game of soccer is organized and the he-roes, becoming boys again, easily forget that they will soon have to resume the re-doubtable game of war." And in March the same magazine showed troops prepar-ing to celebrate Mardi Gras, improvising comic disguises, making crêpes, having a donkey race, and dressing for a costume ball.[17]

Thus the poilu was tough, but he was also boyishly playful, ever resource-ful, and irrepressibly cheerful. According to home-front opinion-shapers, he was giving his all in the exhausting deadlocked hostilities, yet he was always able to tap resources of gaiety, a natural *French* gaiety. French troops were reported to be liv-ing up to legendary models of the past, maintaining high spirits and winning bat-tles with the help of wine and song. "While bellowing [the] famous march 'Chante petit pioupiou' . . . the brave line regiment mounted an assault in the battle of the Yser and, at the price of its blood, won, gained victory while singing, just like our ancestors," reported *Paris qui chante* in late 1915.[18] The refrain of that song urges on the men with a cheery cliché: "Sing, soldier [*pioupiou*]. Gaiety, it's life."

According to the clichés of wartime songs, singing was indeed essential to poilu life. The march "Jusqu'à Berlin" (1916) has the soldiers singing "Trou la la trou la la Trou la trou la trou la la" all the way to the German capital. The song "Les Poilus" by Paul Darny described them more fully: "Always happy, never beaten, that's what we call a poilu." Another line identified the poilu as someone "who knows how to sing in pitched battle." The song "Pour Faire un Poilu" itemized the soldier's essentials as "le pinard, l'amour, et les chansons." "Eh! Ah! les poilus" described the men as "always merry [*gais*] and full of enthusiasm," as they sang their "joyous refrain". in battle and loosed their war cry, "Eh! ah! don't worry" (*faut pas s'en faire*).[19]

According to some journalists, the frontline poilus in their comfortable shelters regularly laughed at the enemy's machine-gun fire. "They're the devil in person, these French, when they attack while singing and laughing," wrote one journalist whose columns were reprinted in 1916 under the title *Le Sourire sous la mitraille*. Members of a genial fraternity, they joked and bantered and scoffed at the enemy *Boches* and the French shirkers alike. Undaunted by their ordeal and the storm around them, they drank their beloved pinard and sang gaily of love, wine, and battle. President Poincaré told the men that gaiety in the face of danger was "one of the most charming forms of French pluck." Some of the most outrageously upbeat reports on the poilus came from the ultranationalist writer Maurice Barrès. "They are all gay-hearted! They're having fun," he wrote in an article entitled "Le Gai Courage" in April 1915. At times he conceded that such descriptions could be exaggerated, and he felt compelled to point out that the men lived daily with real hardships and danger, yet those remarks did not stop him from concluding with his preferred theme: the poilus' inexhaustible capacity for high spirits.[20]

After the first year journalists offered fewer reports of the laughing poilu, but the motif of singing, jovial soldiers persisted in popular songs. The government and the public alike wanted to maintain the patriotic confidence expressed succinctly in a hit song of 1915: "We'll Get 'Em" (On les aura). The next year a widely disseminated poster showed that battle cry coming from a smiling, charging young soldier. Tension between the two poles of poilu life posed a persistent dilemma for journalists and government. It was a delicate balance. To overemphasize hardships was to risk demoralizing the rear and the front, while to stress the light side of the poilu was not to take the ravenous war seriously.

From letters, memoirs, and newspapers written by soldiers themselves a fuller picture of the poilus' life emerges. The soldier of 1914 found, a trench paper explained, that "he had to kill time before killing the Boche"; "he had to fight ennui along with fighting the enemy."[21] As the armies dug into a fixed Western Front, an insidious enemy called boredom took a mounting toll on morale. The stalemate war brought a problem that the military had not anticipated: "a certain kind of Sadness characteristic of the trench . . . the ennui of monotony," explained poilu Albert

The exuberant battle cry of 1915 "On les aura!" here illustrated on a war-era postcard, based on a war-bond poster by Jules Abel Faivre.

Thierry in March 1915. "Our days dragged on and repeated one another in meals, fatigue duties, writing and sleep. They all resembled one another to the point that we no longer knew their names."[22] As expectations of a short war were widespread, and an important region of the country had been invaded and was occupied by the enemy, the soldiers on the front received no leave for more than six months—none through the long fall and winter of deadlocked battle.

Men with a literary bent founded frontline newspapers, *journaux des tranchées*—some four hundred of them over the war years—and spent countless hours writing, editing, and publishing them.[23] Frontline soldiers, the papers reported, began organizing their own football matches by late fall of 1914; they also passed the quiet times fishing, playing cards, smoking, writing letters, and reading. Many men in the trenches occupied their hours making rings, pendants, pen holders, and medallions out of shells and scrap metal. And they drank. Wine and brandy were so integral to daily life and physical existence on the front that they were not

55ᵉ Année, Nᵒ 5   Le Numéro : 60 centimes   Samedi 3 Février 1917

LA VIE PARISIENNE

Un débrouillard ou...   le sac a Malice

A light-hearted home-front view of the Frenchman in war: the jaunty, resourceful (*débrouillard*) infantryman—the famous poilu—strides off to the front with all that he needs. This cover of *La Vie parisienne* (3 February 1917) came out only a few months before mutinies broke out in the battered, demoralized French army.

usually included in discussions of leisure activities, but the trench papers leave no doubt of their daily importance. The men also sang frequently. Some sang folk songs from back home in the village—songs in Breton or a local dialect. Some sang songs that were popular back in city cafés-concerts.

With the help of drink the joking that home-front propagandists described as gaiety surfaced regularly, but it generally lacked the lightheartedness that reporters stressed. It was more a devil-may-care humor breaking through as a reaction against the tension and gloom.[24] Much of the banter had a caustic edge—especially when it referred to civilians. Despite the joking and the pastimes as outlets, tensions often ran high: many soldiers argued and fought among themselves over practically anything.[25]

Entertainment that the poilus produced for themselves expressed discontents that went unreported in the home-front press. Within weeks after the fighting began, soldiers with a penchant for the limelight began putting on shows behind the lines for the benefit of the wounded. Even in the war zone poilus put on revues and sketches that first winter.[26] While they included some patriotic verses, the songs also presented themes not permitted by censors in Paris music halls. In a revue staged in a Pas-de-Calais village on 18 April 1915, poilu performers sang bitterly of the men who shirked military service—the *embusqués*—and of the deputies who helped them do it. One stanza targeted the *p'tit miche* ("little John," a prostitute's client), who made babies with the *filles* and "with the wives replaced the husbands away for the war." Thus early in the war frontline soldiers were voicing an identity framed by discontents: "We the little guys [*petits*], the obscure ones, the lowest

Poilus in the trenches—without the fabled gaiety, heroic élan, or even the beard and scruffy appearance. Amateur photograph. All rights reserved. Private collection.

Another image of the playful, resourceful poilu: dressed as an Alsatian woman, the soldier entertains his comrades on the front. *Le Théâtre,* September 1919.

ranks [*sans-grades*] / We who march dead-tired, covered with mud, wounded, sick."[27] Those "little guys" were creating a new poilu culture in opposition to state-sponsored official culture and its music-hall counterpart.

The soldiers' own shows dwelled not on allegorical ideals, but on down-to-earth women, figures the men dreamed of. Performers sang of *poulettes* with whom they arranged secret nighttime rendezvous in frontline villages. The lyrics often made sexual references ironically conveyed in military terms: conquests, aiming one's bayonet and penetrating with it, having a good *boyau* (hosepipe or military communication trench) for going into a little trench. These songs spread quickly via frontline newspapers and camp shows. Audiences near the front reacted with greatest enthusiasm when women—often fellow poilus in female costume—appeared in skits and revues. Men who had not seen a woman for weeks or even months wildly applauded the hammy "godmothers," Alsatian women, and stars like Loïe Fuller.[28]

While the fervent patriots behind the lines created their fables of heroics and ideological showdown, the men on the front lived day-to-day preoccupied by immediate hardships, suffering, and necessities: the cold and dampness, fatigue and wounds, lice and rats, thirst and hunger, wine, tobacco, coffee, soup. They coped: they became proficient in system D, but hardly in the perky way celebrated on the home front. Some, like Marc Bloch, resented having to cope as much as they did. Officers often resorted to the line "let them cope" instead of tending to their men's needs, Bloch observed bitterly.[29]

Early in the war the soldiers expressed disgust with the French civilians more commonly than with officers. A cartoon in the trench paper *Rigolboche* (1 June 1915) shows two angry soldiers resorting to what the caption calls "Suprême injure": the highest insult was "gueule de civil"—mug of a civilian. In fact, the poilus seem to have directed more hatred at the shirker (*embusqué*) than at the Boche, for whom they had a respect that the Paris press did not share. When they were not caught up in the immediate discomforts and tasks or in a kind of shock—an emotional and intellectual numbness—the men's minds turned to dreams of resuming a quiet life with their women back home. "To die [for the fatherland] is the most beautiful fate—that's not true," wrote soldier and former professor Paul Cazin in the spring of 1915. "The most beautiful fate is to live a long time and to be happy. Why lie?"[30]

Holding On

Combat and improvised pastimes still left the poilus plenty of hours for boredom, homesickness, and melancholy. Bouts of depression—*le cafard*—became so much a part of life in the trenches that not even the Paris press could ignore it. In 1915 soldiers' letters to editors attacked and ridiculed the journalists' image of the playful, laughing poilu. After a year of war, the press began acknowledging the men's complaints and difficulties, but it still managed to brush over them with set praise for the poilus and a simple recommendation of more recreation for the troops. Backing off from the gaiety theme, writers then stressed the poilu's intrepid individuality, toughness, and seriousness. With a sense of stoic resolve and irony, the men held on, ever faithful to their sense of duty.[31]

Popular songs were on the whole even more blinkered. Melodramatic "realism," highlighting the pains and deaths of good "little people," had long been a staple of the café-concert repertory and continued to be popular during the war. Most songs in this vein continued to center on heartbreaking domestic events far from the front: "Le Train fatal" (1916), for example, tells a mournful tale of a train wreck caused by a betrayed lover. Very few popular songs expressed the tragic side of war itself: they escaped censorship only if they ended by celebrating the poilu's heroism and some kind of victory, as "Le Petit Mécano" (1915) did. It tells of a worker of the *faubourgs* (old working-class neighborhoods just outside the central city) who whistled on his way to work every morning down the boulevard de la Villette and enjoyed "the enchanting smiles" of the "nice young dressmakers and milliners" (*gentilles midinettes*). "He was a kid without pretentions and airs, always cheerful, child of the *populo*." Everyone adored him. Then war broke out. He went to battle without fear of the machine gun, fought while scorning danger, and even captured a German flag, but then one day he fell to a German bullet. The colonel, "his voice full of tears," delivers this simple graveside tribute: "I salute this child, this hero, / Sleep forever, brave little *mécano*."[32] The praise of a war hero was commonplace, but censorship and the desire to keep up morale combined to make such pathos exceptional.

By 1915 civilians began to get used to the idea of a drawn-out war and adopted an attitude of resignation—or turned their attention from the war. Patriotic editorialists sang the praises of endurance. In July columnist Henri Lavedan urged in the popular magazine *L'Illustration*, "resist and hold on," and he devoted his column of 7 August to praising perseverance and patience. Holding on became a supreme virtue as victory seemed more and more elusive. Caricaturist Jean-Louis Forain's famous cartoon of 1915 presented the soldiers' point of view of the ordeal: two poilus in a trench conclude that all depends on whether the *civilians* will hold on ("pourvu qu'ils tiennent"). From the year of Verdun on (1916), the phrase "they won't pass" resounded in song, edging out the earlier optimistic "we'll get 'em!"

From the soldiers it is clear that some of their tenacity came from an attitude of resignation or fatalism, which they developed on the front. Upon hearing news of an order to move forward the next day, twenty-one-year-old poilu Louis Mairet wrote to his parents on 16 April 1915: "I am resigned, I have a sense of fatalism, [which is] silly and profound at the same time, which forms the most precious baggage of the soldier." He deemed "this indifference" the best of his "acquisitions" in his ten weeks of war. Then he corrected himself: it was not exactly indifference. It was a "belief in a good destiny, . . . limited by the fear of 'Nemesis.'" The following week he was still thinking and writing about "this beautiful indifference of the poilu," addressing it directly: "O blessed fatalism, subtle poison which stops the searching for what tomorrow will be, the questioning (which is in vain: no one in the regiment knows anything), the devouring disquiet! O adorable I-don't-give-a-damn [*je m'enfichisme*], which anaesthetizes the heart and leaves thought free, may you go pour your comfort in the heart of my tormented parents."[33] The men on the front told themselves: "no reason to worry. Don't try to understand [*Y a pas lieu d's'en faire. Faut pas chercher à comprendre*]," testified poilus Raymond Lefèbvre and Paul Vaillant-Courturier. Many became irritated at those who tried to reason. It was not just that the combatants were too tired to think and too sad. It was also that they did not want to lose "the sole advantage of this life which is imposed on you: the absence of responsibilities, the lethargy of initiative." Indeed, the men came to enjoy what the two veterans called a "sad passivity": "people end by taking a certain pleasure in not disposing of a single minute by themselves."[34]

The home front had no sense of the men taking pleasure in such unheroic ways. Although leaders behind the lines came to recognize the virtue of just "holding on," older images of decisive combat remained easier to glorify. To home-front patriots the hope of a bold offensive and a sudden knockout retained a powerful appeal. Advocates of this style of war held that charges and combat by bayonet were distinctively French, the tried-and-true French way to win.[35] Belief in the famous *furia francese* was as deeply entrenched as the belief in a special Gallic gaiety. The press fed such beliefs and hopes with regular accounts of advances, especially the taking of enemy trenches by fearless poilus deftly wielding bayonets. The virtue of tenacity clearly had less luster and, further, offered nothing to allay the fear that the war might go on indefinitely.

Home-Front Culture on the Front

From time to time the flag-waving jingoism of the rear was brought to the front by professional entertainers. Early in the fall of 1914 singer and songwriter Théodore Botrel, who had immediately volunteered for the infantry at the outbreak of war, began touring the front and singing his patriotic, anti-German verses to the troops. Though he was a Breton regionalist and a royalist, he was also an ardent French nationalist.[36] Botrel's central themes were the heroism of the soldiers and the patriotic devotion of all the French. His song "La Marche des Poilus" (on the familiar air of "Les Pioupious d'Auvergne") characteristically proclaimed the Patrie's pride in "its dear poilus." In "La Victoire double, double" and "En Passant par Ton Berlin" he trumpeted the glorious French cause and heralded sure victory. His most famous song sang the praises of the soldier's beloved, ferocious Rosalie, who in battle pierced and tore at the enemy: Rosalie was the poilus' name for their bayonet. Through such songs and performers, the government and music-hall culture joined in a fighting *union sacrée*. In the first year at least, the men on the front seem to have shared that mood of an aroused patriotism and nationalistic pride in the military.

Morale-booster Botrel was followed by many others. At the beginning of 1916 military authorities sent a newly created Théâtre aux Armées to the front to entertain. The director of the new venture, Emile Fabre, feared at the outset that the soldiers would not be in the mood for amusement. Before the first performance (9 February) Fabre worried, "Weren't they going to find that there was something sacrilegious in bringing comedians and singers to them, those marked by death?"[37] Acting on that worry, the entertainers at first offered only patriotic songs and "elevating" works by Corneille and Hugo. Then some dared to present café-concert acts. Journalists complained about heaviness on the one hand, indecency on the other. Finally the directors "decided to consult only the taste of our spectators." Accordingly, almost all music-hall entertainment became acceptable: "All genres were good for them, except for the bawdy kind, unless it was enveloped with wit," Fabre concluded.

From the beginning others had recognized that most poilus favored the lighter kind of entertainment. In 1915 Lucien Boyer, a well-established cabaret singer, took charge of organizing music-hall entertainment for the troops and did not bother to include a redeeming dose of high culture. Through the next three years he brought such stars as Mayol, Bach, Polin, Dufleuve, Dranem, and Eugénie Buffet to perform near the front. Their usual repertory was a standard music-hall mix of patriotic bravura, sentimental romances, and light-hearted renderings of everyday life—from "Jusqu'à Perpète" and "Ils ne passeront pas" to "Vive le Pinard" and "Quand On vient en permission," to name a few. They also included an ample measure of bawdiness, that old commonplace of barracks singing: songs about the poilu and various compliant women—camp followers, canteen keepers (*cantinières*), country girls, young urban working women, and "godmothers" (*marraines*) who played hostess to lonely soldiers on leave.

The singer known as Bach played the role of a *comique troupier,* a not-too-bright provincial infantryman who relates his misadventures and simple pleasures. One of his songs was a light, sentimental march and love song that he had tried to launch—without notable success—the spring before the war. "Quand Madelon" was about ordinary soldiers drinking in a peaceful country tavern and their play-ful, flirtatious relationship with a lovely young waitress, who only laughs when an admiring soldier takes her by the waist. The song was "launched" in the army at Fontenay-sous-Bois by the Twelfth artillery regiment, according to postwar ac-counts, but it made little apparent impression in the first year and a half of the war.[38]

During that period it was just one of many songs in this vein serving to lighten the men's mood. One that became popular among the troops as well as civil-ians in 1915 was "Le Cri du poilu," whose refrain asks the question, "What do our poilus on the front need as a distraction?" The answer was simple: "Une femme."[39] Needs and discontents were certainly more numerous and complicated than that, as letters and trench newspapers show, but clearly the soldiers' desire for women was widespread and intensifying. A song of 1916—"Tu le r'verras Paname" (You'll see Paris again)—spelled out more fully the men's longings and hopes. It, too, be-came a hit with both soldiers and civilians. Written by real poilus—one fighting in the battle of Verdun, the other recovering in a Paris hospital—this song was a re-assuringly simple message from one poilu to another, devoid of heroics or any ref-erence to the war. "Don't worry, you'll see Paname again." "Tu le r'verras Paname" focused on the simple pleasures of life back in Paris: "the boulevards and the beau-tiful ladies," "the métro, the bistro where you took the *apéro* after work," "your home, your little woman / And the kid [*loupiot*] that you made unintentionally / During the seven days [furlough]."[40] Like most popular songs of the time, this one had as its protagonist a Parisian worker—a faubourien. Like the "petit mécano," he was the good-natured little guy from Paris who was content with his small world and who dreamed only of going back to the humble life that the war had inter-rupted. Such songs, though simplistic and overly optimistic, better suited the troops in the middle of the war than Botrel's productions did. The men's own trench newspapers reflected a growing preoccupation with home and women as the confl-ict dragged on. Giving little thought to grand political objectives, the men in the trenches dreamed of resuming a quiet life after the war, and they preferred songs that evoked those dreams.[41]

Home-Front Tensions

The soldiers on the front had no opportunity to go back home or to Paris on fur-lough during the first winter and spring of the war. It was not until 15 March 1915, that the army's leaders gave leaves or *permissions* for men who could claim an im-portant family event or who had pressing farming work to do. Only in July 1915 was the decision made to grant all combat soldiers short breaks away—at first for only six days total, including travel. One of the official hopes was that the visits home would spawn a new generation. Wags called the furloughs *spermissions*.

When men on leave sought amusement in movie theaters and music halls, they encountered films and songs that presented the war in the grand rhetoric of "glorious deaths" and heroic poilus sure to vanquish cowardly Boches. The bravura and brassy patriotism irked many veterans of the front, and their complaints appeared regularly in the trench journals.[42] Songwriter Jean Deyrmon expressed some of those complaints in a song about the abuse of "La Marseillaise." Under the title "Une Soirée au beuglant" (An evening in a low-class music hall) came a subtitle that made the bitter point: "ou le sabotage de 'La Marseillaise' dans les Caf' Conc'." This protest struck a chord in many; the song was performed often in cafés-concerts during 1916 and 1917.

Censors made sure that many other grumbling lyrics were not performed. The song "Maudite Sois la Guerre" (Cursed be the war) was completely censored, and so was "Le Martyr d'un héros"—"the narrative of a maimed soldier." Also judged unacceptable were "Les Profiteurs de guerre" and "La Misère." Songs could make heroes of the working poor, but lines attacking the rich were censored. In sum, dozens of songs were denied public performance. So were particular lines judged divisive, morale dampening (lines about cuckolded husbands, for example), or immoral.[43]

The problem for movie audiences in 1915 was not simply that the patriotic films became tiresome; it was also that overall French movie production had fallen off drastically because of the war. French distributors found in the United States a large supply of fresh films unburdened by war concerns. And audiences in France quickly took to the new fare: comedies starring Charlie Chaplin, the serial *Les Mystères de New York* with Pearl White, and the westerns of William S. Hart. The furloughed men were particularly overjoyed when they found entertainment that was free of *bourrage de crâne*. One of their great discoveries of the war era was Chaplin, who became known in France as Charlot. Blaise Cendrars, for one, never forgot the first time he heard of him. Mired in mud on a rainy fall evening in the Bois de la Vache, Cendrars's patrol was rejoined by its first man back from furlough in Paris, Garnier (nicknamed Chaude-Pisse). All night Garnier told stories of Charlot to the delight of his buddies. Later each new batch of *permissionnaires* brought back new stories. "All the front was talking only of Charlot," Cendrars observed. And the men began to see something of him in each other. One day when a group of artillery men saw Cendrars approaching with his pants torn and his face covered with dirt and a two months' beard, they called out: "Hey look, there's Charlot!" They laughed and cried, "Charlot, Charlot, Charlot."[44] Fatigued veterans of the front could well appreciate the lively little guy trying valiantly to maintain his dignity and independence in the face of mishaps and repressive authority figures. The "marvelous vitality" in Chaplin's characters was also pleasing and striking, as Philippe Soupault observed.[45] When Cendrars finally got his long-overdue first leave, he hurried to a little movie hall in the Place Pigalle and saw the great comic in action. His laughing to tears prompted a civilian to complain to him: "Hey, soldier, one doesn't laugh like that. C'est la guerre!" Cendrars replied, "Merde, I just saw Charlot!" but he could not make the other understand. The clash between officially encouraged somberness and poilu preferences was only to grow.

Through 1916, the year of the great bloodbath at Verdun, the death toll mounted by the tens of thousands month after month, but civilians reading the heavily censored newspapers knew little of the real magnitude of the casualties. They went on applauding songs like "Verdun! On ne passe pas" with its evocation of the "young heroes" repelling the enemy.[46] When they were not cheering on the French cause, many people managed to put the war out of mind much of the time. They went on with their lives, but it was not always easy. Toward the end of 1916 came disturbing fresh reminders of the critical times: the government put new restrictions on civilian life, including a prohibitionist regime for alcohol and the rationing of gas and electricity. There was also talk of closing theaters—again. Such measures raised fears of going too far; it would not help if people thought that "the war is a divine punishment," as an editorial in *Le Petit Parisien* warned.[47] The balance was difficult to strike: how to make civilians feel as though their country was still facing a crisis without alienating them by deprivations? How to assure the furloughed poilus some Parisian fun without exposing them to a disgusting excess of gaiety during wartime? Those cultural tensions persisted to the end of the war.

Everyone a Poilu

To encourage wholehearted service to the nation at war, home-front leaders never missed an opportunity to extol patriotism and to pay homage to the fighting men. During the second and third years of the war, the home front enlarged its cult of the poilu by extending the fighting man's identity to many besides the combatants. The poilu became an idealized representative of the French people at its best in a variety of guises. Lucien Boyer's song "Nos Poilus" paid homage to "our poilus" first by hailing them as the grandsons of the tough, proud diehards (*dur-à-cuire*) of the First Empire, Napoleon's Grognards. Then, shifting to the present, another verse finds such heroes everywhere: "Scratch the surface of the Frenchman, there's the Poilu!" Still another verse, praising the army's officers, ends by calling Generals Foch and Joffre poilus. Meanwhile a newspaper series reporting on extraordinary civilians' service dubbed them "civilian poilus"; Lucien Boyer was one of those honored with a place in that "Galerie des Poilus civils." At the same time patriotic women came to be known as *poilues*. In a song of 1917 the leftist singer and songwriter Montéhus, for example, used that term to sing the praises of all civically virtuous French females—from the strong, proud working woman described as "queen of the factory" to the République personified by Marianne. Irked by the extreme chauvinism of right-wing women, feminist Séverine derisively called them "poilues de l'arrière," but few shared her view.[48] Anyone unwaveringly devoted to the war effort received the name of the honored warrior. By the same token it became fashionable among civilians to use the slang of the poilu.[49]

The real poilus were not impressed. They continued to express disgust with the civilians—especially with profiteers, shirkers, and seducers of soldiers' girlfriends or wives. The exchanges between front and rear did not close the gaps of misunderstanding; the longer the stalemate dragged on, the more the irritation and

Women's patriotism and sacrifice—as drumbeaters for the war effort liked to picture them. The "heroic women of France" do the plowing the hard way while the "heroic" men and horses are away on the front. U.S. National Archives and Record Administration.

The poilus' disenchanted view, captured here in a home-front cartoon in the final year of the war. The grousing soldiers, looking out on ruins, pay inflated prices and are served by a woman who is nothing like the beloved young barmaid celebrated in the most famous song of the war, "Quand Madelon." Drawing by Hautot published in *La Baïonnette,* 3 January 1918.

bitterness felt by many combatants mounted. As a character in Henri Barbusse's famous war novel *Le Feu* (1916) observed, reflecting a poilu point of view, France was separated into two countries, one too unfortunate, the other too fortunate.[50] The soldiers under fire loathed and cursed the shirkers as though they were the enemy. The poilus were also galled by bombastic heroics behind the lines, perhaps as much as by civilian indifference. In trench newspapers the soldiers expressed contempt for press accounts of the "heroes" joyously mounting assaults, always making progress against cowardly Boches, fighting on despite wounds, and knowing the joy of dying for France and Right. That home-front version of the war particularly grated on the poilus as the battles of 1916 took their horrendous toll. As one "hero" of Verdun put it to a reporter for *Le Petit Parisien* late in the year: "Let them double our wine [*le pinard*], brandy [*la gniolle*], and also leaves [*permes*] and not brainwash us [*qu'on ne nous bourre pas le crâne*] with that claptrap!"[51] As the reporting of these remarks from Verdun shows, the press began to reflect some understanding of that discontent, but the bad feelings continued unabated. Despite such reporting, the furloughed soldiers' testimony to family and friends at home, and the appearance of realistic battle accounts like Barbusse's *Le Feu* from 1916 on, poilus continued to feel that they were badly misunderstood and their life behind the lines misrepresented.

The furloughed poilu as lover, a favorite home-front subject of the later years of the war. A posed scene on a postcard of the period. Collection of the author.

Romantic Poilus and Their Women

While depictions of trench life polarized into propagandist stereotypes and disturbingly realistic exposés, the home front became fascinated with the love life of the poilu. The granting of furloughs in the summer of 1915 first opened up the possibility. An outpouring of new songs—"Joyeuse Permission," "Le Polka du permissionnaire," "Permission du repeuplement," among others—told the essential story of the happy soldier reuniting with his fiancée or wife, a reunion often resulting in her pregnancy, helping to repopulate France. The quickly spreading practice of women corresponding with lonely soldiers and treating them as their new "godsons" opened the way to fresh romance, imagined and real, between strangers.

In songs, plays, newspaper accounts, and postcards, the godmothers (*marraines*) were portrayed as consoling patriotic women, sometimes motherly or saintly and sometimes erotic—in much the same way as the figures of wife or fiancée and nurse in the imagined world of the poilus. While the moralist strain of nationalist culture focused on such remote symbolic figures as Marianne, Alsace and Lorraine, and Joan of Arc, the mass-entertainment branch put the spotlight on the marraine and her adopted love-starved poilu. In song lyrics, stories, and plays, the muddy savage of the trenches became the handsome leading man on furlough, visiting the woman who had befriended him through letters. Some narratives, the sentimental song "La Marraine des poilus," presented her as simply tenderly maternal toward a young soldier who had no mother. Other songs along with numerous plays told stories of how two strangers became lovers, happily united during furloughs.[52]

Another romantic daydream with wide appeal in the worst of wartimes came from the prewar song about the barmaid Madelon and the soldiers who loved her. By 1916, the year of Verdun, "Quand Madelon" had caught on as a favorite of the troops, and in 1917 it became a hit among civilians as well. Written for music-hall comics, it was a march with a bright, lively tune—a soldier's song in its rhythm as well as content. Each verse concluded with an exceptionally catchy chorus, culminating in a rising, triple invocation "Madelon, Madelon, Madelon." The lyrics, conjuring up peacetime military life, highlighted two favorite pleasures of the soldiers: wine and romance. To men in hard battle conditions the song offered the enticements of a delicious dream:

> The waitress is young and nice,
> Light like a butterfly,
> Like her wine her eye sparkles.
> We call her La Madelon.
> We dream of her by night. We think of her by day.
> It's only Madelon, but for us, it's love.[53]

The story of Madelon and the soldiers never comes close to being bawdy, in contrast to many other songs of that time with their clear references to sexual acts between soldiers and women. Frank eroticism was common, too, in music-hall revues and on illustrated postcards. And brothels near the army camps were enjoying a booming business: prostitutes drawn there by hopes of big earnings were working eighteen hours daily "doing" fifty to sixty men a day.[54] As the war went on, poilus showed more interest in *Rose-à-lit* (Rose in bed) than in Rosalie (the bayonet), as one wag put it.

"Quand Madelon" clearly had an appeal of a quite different kind. It evoked a fond dream of the welcoming, fresh young woman who was close to the soldiers but who was not taken by any of them. Nor was she ready to give herself to any of them. Madelon was an old-fashioned woman. Comforting and cheering, she served men in a traditional manner, unlike the numerous women moving into jobs formerly restricted to men—driving busses, running the métro, and working in mu-

A more modern and flirtatious Madelon with some poilus, relegated to the margins, as her eagerly drinking customers. Drawing by Clérice, late in the war.

nitions factories. Singing Madelon's praises, the men in the military at least momentarily allayed worries about the "new woman"—worries about whether their women would give up wartime gains of independence and go back to prewar subordinate ways.[55] From contemporary testimony it appears that many soldiers took the Madelon lyrics at face value and adopted the song as an expression of their longings. Others may have taken the lyrics as a mocking, ironic commentary on real desires and deprivations. For soldiers of both categories, the song served as a welcome alternative to official rhetoric: it was happily free of heroics and talk of the beauty of "dying for one's country."

Singing "Quand Madelon" thus became oppositional for some, but in 1917 there were far more blatantly rebellious songs in the air. Most objectionable to authorities were revolutionary and antiwar songs—especially during the crisis in the army in the spring of 1917. After the massive bloodletting of the failed offensive of General Nivelle in the Champagne region in April, morale in the army reached a nadir, and mutinies broke out in some five divisions during May and June 1917. The troops who refused to obey orders sang the Socialist anthem "L'Internationale" and angry antimilitarist songs like the "Chanson de Craonne," which was about a place on the Aisne front where in 1917 the soldiers had fought numerous murderous, futile attacks and had finally mutinied. To the melody of a prewar love song an anonymous lyricist (or perhaps several) added bitter new words describing how desperate troops struggled at Craonne, saw their comrades slaughtered, and rebelled. The song spread behind the lines quickly and made a long-lasting impression on many, even peasants far from the fighting.[56] Back on the front the shaken command soon regained control of the rebellious troops. By late June, repression in the army, the removal of General Nivelle, and the promise of longer and more regular furloughs had worked; order was restored, and the troops once more sang old marching songs—and the new favorite, "Quand Madelon."[57]

In the summer and fall of 1917 "Quand Madelon" became a hit in Paris. It peaked in popularity in Paris music halls just after the army passed through the crisis of morale and startling mutinies. The home front itself had just passed through a difficult period of strikes that broke out even in munitions factories. Female workers there took on a new role, that of strikers in a critical war industry. For the poilus in the audience (as on the front), the song about Madelon was a warm evocation of their world in better times—of peacetime camaraderie in an attractive rural setting and flirtation with an amiable young woman loved by all the men. For civilians the song celebrated their preferred image of the poilu: the playful, innocent, leisured *bonhomme*—now in stark contrast to the war-sick mutineer and the sexual predator or patron of prostitutes.

It also celebrated an image of woman that most civilians (men *and* women) favored—an old-fashioned young woman, pure and devoted. Songs evoking sexual relations between soldiers and women ran the risk of being offensive, even though censors were at work keeping that risk to a minimum. The censors decided, for example, that Bach's "Marie-Margot" went too far in describing the patriotic camp follower whom the men of all ranks "mooned over": "For the fatherland she is very hard-working, / In a day she relieves a battalion."[58] Madelon offered the same characteristics without the questionable sexual ending. She also represented a reassuring alternative to the freer, independent employed women that civilian men worried about. Certain new performers of the Madelon song in 1917 reinforced the heroine's appealing image. In 1917 "Quand Madelon" was often performed by a woman, even though the point of view of the song and its singer was clearly a male soldier's. In the tenser times of 1917 a woman singer escaped suspicion of being an *embusqué*. But more important, an attractive woman was more appreciated by the predominately male audiences, military and civilian. In effect, for those audiences she became the Madelon, the idealized young woman, whom she sang about.

By the fall of 1917 "Quand Madelon" was so familiar that new lyrics were in demand. Soldiers attending a performance of the *Théâtre au front* called for repeated singing of a new song about wine, set to the melody of "Madelon." In the better cinemas of Paris, audiences were applauding a filmed dramatization of "Quand Madelon." And music-hall revues offered parodies of the original song with fresh risqué touches—new lyrics ending, for example, with a rousing tribute not to Madelon, but to "*mamelons, mamelons, mamelons!* [nipples, nipples, nipples!]."[59] Madelon had taken on a life apart from the music-hall march and had become a favorite new mythic figure. She not only evoked roseate memories of unscathed soldiers and beloved young women from a time before the war; now she also brought to mind the front poilus who were known to be singing of her. In the dark times of 1917–18, after Verdun and Craonne, she and the song about her were in high demand.

Americans in Paris

In 1917, civilians and poilus alike had still another reason to welcome a song that highlighted old-fashioned French soldiers. Singing and listening to "Quand Madelon" was also a way of reaffirming French traditions and identities in opposition to the fast-growing American presence. In the summer of 1917 American soldiers—the French called them "Sammies"—were arriving in increasing numbers, and so were their songs. The balance in Parisian wartime culture shifted further toward gaiety. The newly arrived Yanks wanted to have fun before going to the front. The capital's cafés, restaurants, tea shops, and dance halls drew crowds night and day, and new venues opened continually in response to growing demand. Prostitutes also increased in number and found more customers.[60] The great Parisian spectacle of people enjoying themselves grew ever bigger, noisier, and bolder. Parisian entertainment became more cosmopolitan and spectacular. Nude women, filling the stage, danced and posed for the soldiers of the Allied armies. English and American stars and acts became commonplace on Parisian music-hall stages and movie screens.

As the American forces arrived, French music halls quickly added welcoming new songs such as "Vive l'Oncle Sam," "Le Drapeau américain," and "Les Sammies à Paris" to their repertories. The Americans, for their part, brought their own music—fox-trots and jazz—and quickly added it to the sounds of Paris. "'Swanee' aroused the enthusiasm of the boys in khaki and the *bleus horizons* [French infantrymen in blue uniforms] who were timidly offering 'La Madelon' in this period," Pierre MacOrlan recalled after the war.[61]

While French songs clung to old-fashioned images of women like Madelon, the American songs celebrated modern women. "The famous [American] fox trots 'Chicago,' 'Bébé' ["Baby"], 'Sweet One,' etc. sing the presence of tall lissome girls, the pride of the most tentacular commercial firms, girls who—their arms loaded with files—go up in sparkling elevators," MacOrlan noted. He concluded optimistically that women, by working, could enhance love relationships with "the intellectual possibility of a provisional renewal." Many French men were anything but optimistic. They worried about women throwing themselves at the Americans, and whether women after the war would go back to traditional submissive roles.[62]

During the very months when Americans in France were first making their mark, the performances of "Madelon" peaked. In juxtaposition to the new music from America, "Madelon" was more old-fashioned than ever, continuing an old tradition of French guardsmen's songs about a sweet maidservant and a young soldier.[63] After years of a harrowing war and profound social changes, such quaint old French types and songs offered timely reassurance: the new women and foreign ways were not sweeping the field.

War-Weary Poilus—and the Others

Worries about the men also intensified in 1917 and 1918. After three or four years of war, the soldiers' paradoxical outbursts of gaiety were less visible than in the early years, observed two psychologists in July 1918. The long war had worn down nerves, they explained. The poilus sang "very little" that last year of the war. Instead, they griped. "The poilu grouses and resists [*rouspète*] as he breathes, in all times and places." The common soldier's "spirit of opposition" was undeniably a prominent trait from the spring of 1917 on.[64] Even behind the lines the reasons were not hard to understand. During the last year of the war the Paris press regularly reported on the hardships and suffering of the poilus. Doubts about the war's outcome were widespread—at least until July, when the last German offensive was turned back.

The psychologists concluded that one of the reasons for the change in the poilu was the influence of the Parisian worker on his provincial comrades. That influence showed up most clearly in the poilus' vocabulary, above all in the neologisms, infused with "the very genius of the workshop slang, at once witty, vulgar and ribald, and prodigiously evocative." The common soldier had picked up the workers' "verve in turns caustic and bantering, this *vis comica* which assures success in popular milieus." That verve was expressed in a "catchy gab and communicative gaiety" long familiar to the people of the cities and faubourgs—newspaper hawkers, wine merchants, and employees of small shops. The Parisian worker also spread his penchant for griping, the experts reported. But counterbalancing that negativity was the workers' capacity for "coping in common," a trait that had overridden the peasants' tendency to be individualist and resigned.[65] Vivacity, high spirits, grousing, and an indomitable resourcefulness—the same general poilu traits highlighted by the press and popular songs—were now attributed by scientists to a specific source: the workingmen of the Parisian faubourgs.

Although it is difficult to determine how much the workers changed the peasants' psychological natures, it is clear that in the army peasants and urban workers came to share a new poilu culture. Altogether eight million men—one-fifth the population of France—had been mobilized and newly acculturated in a wartime military milieu. Peasant soldiers picked up the argot and songs of *faubouriens*. Provincials also learned of the newest Parisian novelties through furloughs spent in Paris and entertainers' appearances on the front. Meanwhile, civilian provincials back home were discovering the poilu-influenced entertainment of the capital on their local stages and screens, thanks to the efforts of music-hall and movie theater managers. While these new wartime spectacles spread from the capital, many traditional local dances and festivals were falling into desuetude.[66] France became more culturally homogenized.

Behind the myth of the poilu and beyond the greater cultural sharing, however, social differences remained strong. Men from the same region continued to feel common ties, which continued to inhibit relationships with outsiders. Many Bretons had a hard time communicating with comrades from other regions. Rivalries between different military units often took on a bitter edge. "Hatred between ordinary foot-soldiers [*fantassins*] and other infantry corps [*chasseurs à pied*] is great," noted peasant soldier Jean-Louis Talmard.[67] A gulf also persisted between officers and their men. And class differences made for distance between many men within those two categories. Peasants—about half the fighting troops—rarely developed close relations with workers, differences in background outweighing shared experience in the present.[68] Wartime friendships that seemed so warm sel-

Singing all the way to victory—the happy propaganda motif in a music-hall showgirl image ("La Victoire en chantant"). *La Baïonnette* cover, 3 October 1918.

dom lasted beyond the trenches. The common uniform and the trials of battle did not forge any enduring social unity.

A gulf also remained between poilus and civilians, many of whom were the despised shirkers on whom the front soldiers displaced much hostility. By the later half of the war many poilus, we have seen, rejected the same official and music-hall patriotism that glorified them. On the home front, too, cultural and political strains and divisions intensified as the war went on. As "patriots" sang of Everyman being a poilu, workers were turning against the government's economic policies and conduct of the war. Many singers and songwriters responded to the critical poilus and disaffected workers by rejecting the heroics of official culture, reintroducing ribald and silly sketches of military life, and focusing on the soldier who cared above all for home and loved ones. Censors kept busy trying to suppress songs expressing the late-war disenchantment, pacifist sentiments, syndicalist and socialist threats, and revolutionary appeals. The censors were probably far too zealous, as it seems doubtful that such songs would have found much favor with the public at large, for they did not express the views of the majority (as Becker's studies of public opinion show).[69]

Right up to the end of the war a mainstream of popular songs and patriotic rhetoric continued to propagate an image of the poilu as the simple bonhomme gaily singing, drinking wine, bonding with his fellows in the great cause, and fighting on with insouciance. In the press, music halls, and official discourse the civic religion of nationalism and republicanism persisted. As the Allies made advances from July 1918 on and the war clearly moved toward a conclusion, songs celebrating the warrior heroes and the patriotic community took on new life. Numerous songs and the press depicted the struggle increasingly in triumphal terms: by virtue of high morale and innate national character the French army and people were moving inexorably toward victory. The events of the second half of 1918 almost seemed to validate old myths of the French Everyman always coping ingeniously, united with his comrades in a boundless love of la patrie, and prevailing over adversity—and the enemy. In fact, the French people did turn out to be *débrouillard:* they coped and muddled through the long struggle. They did not, however, manifest the solidarity or good humor that the ultranationalists insisted on. Those brightly positive, propagandist depictions—a response to widespread war-weariness and worries—were in large part a response of denial.

A poilu wounded "for France" stands for a photograph with the help of a buddy. Private Collection.

Poilus in a posed photograph record their comradeship and war wounds.

When German Gothas bombed the capital in late 1917 and 1918, the Casino de Paris produced a morale-serving revue bearing the defiant title "Laisse-les tomber" (Let 'em fall). In fact, many Parisians responded to the bombing by fleeing in a mass exodus to the south. But what echoed in French memory was the courageous, cocky response. The Great War put a confirming seal on the myth of the beleaguered little guy singing his way through the worst. As the war came to a close, that fiction rendered service again when a punishing inflation and the "Spanish" flu raged. It was a cheering fiction that highlighted a way to respond to overwhelming

Dining heartily with a large bottle of wine hiding his damaged arm, the soldier seems intent on conveying that "tout va bien." Private collection.

Celebrating the armistice with patriotic songs, a woman in a tricolor sings for a relieved and joyful crowd in a Paris street. Séeberger ©Arch. Phot. Paris/SPADEM.

crises that most people could do little about. It was a myth that would enjoy fame and favor through a succession of difficult trials ahead.

On 11 November 1918—the day of the Armistice—spirited crowds filled the central boulevards of Paris and rejoiced to the strains of "La Marseillaise," played by military bands and sung by soldiers and civilians together. That evening, Marthe Chenal sang it for a jubilant crowd assembled in front of the Opéra. The warring anthem now served as a celebratory fanfare for the proclaimed victory. Other songs sounding that day expressed other emotions of the extraordinary occasion. On many corners the favorite was "Quand Madelon." Devoid of references to war and to any lofty ideal, that poilu favorite now expressed happiness with the military outcome, gratitude and relief, and an easy nonideological tribute to the common soldier. Singing it was a way of achieving solidarity with the men who had fought and suffered. In a comforting way it drew attention to their boyish good humor, asserting that those who experienced the worst of the war had somehow kept their playful prewar innocence. Singing "Quand Madelon" was a way to celebrate the "little guy" who won. Singing and sharing the joy of peace covered over wartime differences and resentments, temporarily at least.

On the occasion of what was euphemistically called victory, numerous new celebratory songs appeared, most of them merely reworking old nationalist conventions. "La Délivrance ou gloire aux alliés," for example, and numerous updated lyrics for "La Marseillaise" ran through the familiar incantations of heroism, Right, Justice, and the glory of the victorious nations. Songsmiths made the most of the rhyming of *victoire* and *gloire*. The old rhetoric persisted: the propagandistic notes that had disgusted some for years, particularly poilus, still commanded willing singers and audiences. Prewar representations of women also persisted, outmoded as they were by new social realities. Though legions of women had taken on new work roles and were enjoying greater social freedom and capacity to make economic decisions, civilians and soldiers still sang of the old-fashioned barmaid Madelon. The old images of woman as servant and sweetheart became an insistent nostalgic counterpoint to strikingly modern and foreign types. In sum, the social representations current in 1914 persisted through the war, but they became increasingly problematic. Like the French nation through the four years of once unimaginable destruction, they held on to the end (*jusqu'au bout*), but the strain was great. At the war's end they no longer commanded as widespread or as firm an acceptance as before.

The night following the armistice, songwriter Lucien Boyer had the inspiration of adapting the Madelon myth to the new peacetime. Working with composer Borel-Clerc he quickly came up with the song "Madelon de la Victoire." In this version Madelon presides at the peace celebration and fills the glasses of the joyous poilus. The soldiers not only sing the praises of the young woman, "la muse du front," but they also fête "victory, Joffre, Foch, and Clemenceau." English verses by Bill Sharp allowed the Americans to join in celebrating Madelon along with "Wilson, Foch, and Pershing." In December Maurice Chevalier launched the new song at the Casino de Paris, and Suzanne Valroger launched it at the Olympia. Like the original, the new lyrics invited audiences to identify with the poilus and to pay homage to the gentle young woman. Unlike the original, this version centered on topical political content. Singers and audience express joy over victory and gratitude to the nation's wartime leaders and the humble Madelon. They pay fresh tribute to the old-fashioned woman, muse and servant, while ignoring the worrisome recently independent women who worked in factories and ran farms during the men's absence. The Victory Madelon, in short, accommodated the official view of lofty achievement with the down-to-earth poilu fondness for a young woman and a toast to peace. It was a typical hit, taking the conciliating middle ground of popular culture. Characteristically, too, it left unmentioned the casualties of the war—including the 1,322,000 war dead. Giving them proper representation was a painful problem, one that soon began to trouble the celebrators of victory.

2 . UNQUIET VICTORY

Victoire, défaite . . . ces mots n'ont point de sens. La vie est au-dessous
de ces images, et déjà prépare de nouvelles images.
[Victory, defeat . . . these words no longer have meaning. Life is beneath
these images, and is already preparing new images.]
—*Antoine de Saint-Exupéry,* Vol de nuit

Celebration and Mourning

IN THE WEEKS AFTER the armistice when Maurice Chevalier sang the new song
"La Madelon de la Victoire" in the Casino de Paris, audiences dominated by Allied
soldiers cheered and joined in singing the chorus. "Fill my glass," the singers tell
Madelon, and "sing with the poilus." Then they exclaim: "We have won the war /
Hey, you believe that we've had them?" The song caught on, but Chevalier soon
felt uneasy singing it. He felt shame in exploiting such facile effects, he explained
later. Glorifying the victors and vilifying the defeated struck him as forced and un-
seemly. Chevalier had experienced "profound sadness" and German humaneness
in a prisoner-of-war camp for twenty-six months after being wounded in battle and
captured. Although the public clearly relished victory songs, Chevalier gave up
singing the new hit after about a week.[1]

"Profound sadness" was commonplace by the war's end. Virtually every
family in France had suffered the loss of a loved one. The dead had been buried, but
for years to come the living grappled with the pain of loss, the traumas, and the costs
of the war. How were ordinary people to deal with postwar problems? Official and

popular culture proposed conflicting answers, placing several models of behavior
and attitude in the limelight. Underlying those different answers were disagreements over the war experience—competing interpretations of the war and the
poilu, which began to show up clearly in postwar film and song only months after
the armistice.

The kinds of misgivings felt by Chevalier and the widespread sense of be-
reavement called for new representations of the war—images stripped of the bom-
bast and jingoism of wartime propaganda. The rising twenty-nine-year-old film-
maker Abel Gance and the giant company Pathé provided that kind of new view in
a mold-breaking movie that came out early in the spring of 1919. Provocatively entitled *J'accuse*, Gance's film dramatized some repercussions of the war that the victory songs never touched upon. It immediately drew large audiences and was a box-
office success.

When Gance began writing the scenario during the summer of 1917, he was
feeling anguish and rage over the number of his friends killed on the front and the
horrors depicted by Henri Barbusse's novel *Le Feu*.[2] His *J'accuse* directed a con-
suming anger at those responsible for the slaughter, as the title forewarns, echoing
Emile Zola's denunciation of the army's leaders in the Dreyfus affair. Although
Gance himself had not fought in the war, the film's point of view was that of an
alienated poilu. In the title shot the very words *J'accuse* are spelled out by forma-

The resurrected, wounded, accusing poilus in *J'accuse* by Abel Gance (1919). Courtesy of the
British Film Institute Stills, Posters, and Designs.

tions of helmeted soldiers, suggesting that it was not just a film director making the accusation, but legions of poilus.

The scenario is a tragic tale of the heroine, Edith, and her two loves—her husband, François, and a poet, Jean Diaz. While the two men are away fighting in the same battalion on the front, Edith is captured and raped by a German in the Ardennes. She has a child who François thinks is Jean's—until she is forced to explain the dreadful truth. Upon returning to the front François is killed, and Jean suffers shell shock. Back in the village where his mother lives, Jean reads the villagers a letter of accusation against them for continuing their frivolous ways without appreciating the sacrifice of the soldiers. The screen then shows Jean's vision of a battleground full of crosses and dead soldiers. The dead rise up eerily and march toward the camera and the audience. The first to be resurrected is a man with an amputated right arm (the actor was Blaise Cendrars, who had in fact lost his arm in the war). The screen then splits, and that resurrection is juxtaposed with the victory parade through the Arc de Triomphe. The fact that *J'accuse* was the first film that attempted to bring home the terrible costs of the war helps account for its impact. Further, no other film had indicted French civilians as this one did. The civilians shown, however, were not the nation's political leaders or Parisians, but villagers in the countryside. The angry poilu's bad feelings about the war were grafted onto urban prejudices against provincials, whom city dwellers considered crude and backward. The film's critical edge was deflected away from the mass audiences of the cities. At points, furthermore, the film took the official patriotic point of view, affirming the sacrifice of the war dead, and it ended by turning to an encompassing view of nature that renews itself eternally, suggesting an inevitable passing of the pain. Full of ambiguities yet distanced from the propagandist view, the movie expressed ambivalent feelings that were widely shared in the wake of the war.[3]

Popular songs of that time split more cleanly along the lines of celebration and grieving. In June 1919, as the Treaty of Versailles was about to be signed, Paris music halls resounded with a new song that posed the question "Who has won the war?"—"Qui a gagné la guerre?" The first stanza proposes various answers: America, the blockade, civilians, the poilu's godmother (*marraine*), the worker, the deputy, and leaders such as Wilson, Foch, and Pétain. Finally, the chorus spells out the correct answer: "It's the poilu, soldier of France." When Suzanne Valroger sang it onstage, she wrote the words of the chorus on a blackboard and led the audience in singing them.[4] Everyone sang the praises of the common soldier "braving struggle and suffering." With the aureole of victory added, the cult of the poilu lived on in peacetime.

Meanwhile, in the large popular music hall named the Européen, a quite different chorus "unleashed enthusiasm," noted columnist Gustave Fréjaville. It asserted the need to laugh and sing, proclaiming that war should be cursed and no longer talked about.

> Raconter les batailles,
> Malgré qu'on soit vainqueur
> C'est rouvrir des entrailles
> Et fair' saigner nos coeurs.
> [Recounting battles
> Even if one is victorious
> Reopens painful feelings
> And makes our hearts bleed.]

This bitter song, whose title in English is "People Need to Laugh," was the work of the militant leftist Montéhus, who once had supported the war but now was bent on pointing up the terrible price of victory. "If we have victory, / It is because fifteen hundred thousand Frenchmen / Have paid with their life for this glory."[5]

The retelling of battles went on, nonetheless. Over the next decade postwar memoirs and histories continued to hail the heroic victors and provided a growing number of accounts of their valor and doggedness. Some provided new versions of the old stories about French soldiers singing their way to victory, for example, soldiers singing "Quand Madelon" while retaking the fort de Vaux in November 1916 and while driving back the Boches in the battle of the Champagne in 1918.[6] Those stories, or legends (there is no direct testimony from a participant supporting those accounts), took solid anchor in postwar memory. Tales of the men singing "Quand Madelon" during crucial battles became crowning touches on the wartime myth of the poilu.

Madelon and the poilus were so well established as an anodyne war memory by July 1919 that the songs about them resounded through the celebration of the victory on the first postwar Bastille Day. Exultant crowds sang "Madelon de la Victoire" in the main intersections of Paris, and military bands played a "heroic orchestration" of the original Madelon song—with bugles dominant.[7] The day that was officially a "festival of victory" turned out to be the nation's biggest celebration of the poilus and their achievements.

When Parisians danced in the streets on Bastille Day, 14 July 1919, to celebrate the "victory," the scarcity of men in their prime years was painfully evident. Phot. Bibl. Nat. de Fr.-Paris.

Appropriately, the center of the day's events was the Arc de Triomphe. Its victory motifs, however, were overshadowed by an immense coffinlike monument placed under the arch: a giant cenotaph dedicated to the "morts pour la patrie." It was an imposing tomb, though only a discreet symbolic hint of the staggering death toll, the 1.3 million Frenchmen killed. Just a little distance away the somber mood changed abruptly. Departing from that overcharged shrine, "triumphant armies" marched down the Champs-Elysées to the wild cheering of vast crowds. At the head of the parade were "heroes" who were unable to march normally: they were the "mutilated," a thousand of them rolling along in wheelchairs and hobbling on crutches, representatives of the million Frenchmen left disabled by the war. Their presence elicited cries and cheers—and surely mixed emotions from the crowds. Nearby some two hundred disabled veterans tried to demonstrate against war, those who profited from it, and the government. They brandished signs that denounced their civilian foes and the celebration itself: "Down with the profiteers of war" and "Don't dance on cadavers." The police succeeded in keeping them away from the victory parade, but the attitudes and emotions they expressed were not so easily banished.[8] Alongside the heroic and the cheering were

A postwar "Madelon" consoles the *mutilés* with a smile and a cigarette in the Bois de Boulogne. Séeberger ©Arch. Phot. Paris/SPADEM.

the grieving and the angry, determined to make their contribution to the national memory of the war.

Government tributes to the victors even included honoring a man whose contribution to the war was his singing and songwriting. In January 1920 Lucien Boyer, the author of "Madelon de la Victoire," was named to the Légion d'honneur. Some journalists reported that the award was given to him by mistake and was intended for the author of the original "Madelon." The official dossier on Boyer, however, shows that it was no mistake. He was rewarded for his service as entertainer of the troops as much as for his songs, and officials correctly noted him as the author of the victory song.[9] Nonetheless, it is readily understandable why the two Madelon songs blended together in many minds. The sequel built on the original myth and developed it aptly, depicting the beloved woman who poured wine for soldiers before the war as the one who later presided over the drinking at a victory celebration. Her presence established a happy continuity between the fabled scene of prewar relaxation and the postwar festivities. And in a France badly wanting a

return to normal, the updated Madelon was welcome reassurance. The cheery acclamations of her admirers expressed what people wanted to believe: that France
had won a clear victory and was embarking on a postwar era of ease and success.

   The cheer dissipated soon after the victory celebrations of 1919. Entertainment producers abandoned the wartime light-heartedness about the poilus and
stopped echoing lofty official themes. The patriotic films of the war years now
seemed too much like the propaganda that had worn thin, and they vanished from
the scene. Anti-German feeling, however, did not. For years after the war, Pathé
newsreels showing German military commemorations touched off boos and hisses
in the Belleville movie house Ciné-Paradis.[10] The very sight of German pointed
helmets evoked the same responses in movie halls of Ménilmontant.[11] Reminders
of the poilus continued to evoke powerful emotions, as well, and were much more
deliberately and consistently kept in public consciousness.

Inquietude: The Dead and the Angry

The years after the armistice brought a succession of disappointments that dashed
the hopes of 1918. France the self-proclaimed victor had to grapple long and hard
with problems left by the war: difficulties of getting reparation payments from the
Germans, the threat of revanchist German aggression, and economic doldrums
brought on by scarcities, high prices, and unemployment. France also struggled to
recover from the grievous loss of so many potentially productive and reproductive
men, and simply so many loved ones. The années folles or "crazy years" were a time
of madcap living it up for some people, but for a much greater number they were a
sobering time of coming to terms with the war and its toll. Grief combined with
anxiety and what is now identified as survivor guilt. Anguish over the price paid was
made all the more painful by the lack of certainty that the peace would endure.

   For more than a decade after the war, anguish and mourning took ritual-
ized form, centering on monuments to the poilus and to the war dead. Virtually
every village and town in France acquired a monument and dedicated it in somber
ceremony. Thirty-eight thousand war monuments went up across the French land-
scape—on main streets, in central squares, at crossroads, on the edge of towns. No
other war had given rise to so many memorials. These were not monuments to
commemorate victory, but to honor the fallen. They were funereal rather than triumphant in spirit.[12] So were the new military cemeteries. In Paris the closest the
memorial creators came to commemorating the war as a victory was in choosing
the Arc de Triomphe as the site for the tomb of the unknown soldier.

New *monuments aux morts* throughout the land—solemn tributes, sad reminders of catastrophic losses: (*opposite page, top*) in Pléherel in Brittany (photo by the author); (*opposite page, bottom*) in a Paris suburb, La Courneuve (photo by the author); (*top*) in the Basque country at St.-Etienne-de-Baïgorry, with the Pyrenees in the background (photo by Anne Rearick); (*bottom*) near the Pyrenees in Sauveterre de Béarn (photo by Anne Rearick).

Although most of the monuments did not include a statue, on those that did the most common figure was of a poilu—a "Poilu dying," a "Poilu defending the flag," or a "Poilu dying while defending the flag."[13] On ceremonial occasions official and civilian speakers proclaimed that the monuments stood as lessons in devotion to the nation. War veterans dwelled on the poilus' suffering and sorrows and spoke little of victory.[14]

The anniversary of the 11 November armistice became a national holiday in 1922. Henceforth it was the high holy day in the new cult of the dead, especially the dead poilus. The central shrine was the tomb of the unknown soldier under the Arc de Triomphe, where the chosen body was laid on 11 November 1920. There a perpetual "flame of memory" was first lighted in 1923, to be relighted daily by veterans' groups. Other central memorial sites were the former battlefields to the east, now places of pilgrimage, hallowed grounds. A large and particularly moving and ghastly memorial was the Douaumont ossuary at Verdun—a glass-enclosed chamber filled with the skulls and bones of 130,000 men—dedicated in ceremonies on 11 November 1920. In the same area a smaller but much revered shrine was the trench where, it was discovered after the war, forty-seven soldiers had stood their ground with rifles and bayonets poised for combat while being buried alive in a bombardment. That *tranchée des baïonnettes* became the site of an immense monument dedicated in 1920, financed by admiring American donors. In the years immediately after the war, belief in such stories was imperative. It was not until the late 1920s that anti-war writers expressed doubts about just how the men died and attacked the heroic tales as deceptive legend.[15]

The commemorations celebrated the dead as heroes (the official view) or as victims (the disaffected poilu view), or both. Throughout the 1920s, the veterans insisted on paying tribute to the common soldier, avoiding any cult of personalities or great leaders.[16] Speakers delivered their orations as representatives of the rank and file, as impersonal voices of the poilus. The republican ethos of the equality of all citizens provided the foundation of the new cult. The rest followed from the wartime celebration of the frontline soldiers as heroes. The "little guy" as "petit soldat," celebrated in wartime as a fighting hero, was raised to new glory for having died in combat.

Civilians joined veterans in ceremonies expressing gratitude to those who sacrificed their lives for their country. The rituals no doubt assuaged survivor guilt. Perhaps they also soothed at least some of the embittered veterans. Many of those being honored for their patriotic devotion, it was well known, felt like victims.

Many of the "heroes" came out of the war angry about the carnage and angry at generals, uncomprehending civilians, politicians, and profiteers. The ceremonial tributes ignored the anger and revolt and focused on sorrow and appreciation. They enshrined a collective memory of the common soldier's unsullied valor and sacrifice—a national memory of the poilu that was ostensibly beyond politics. The cult of "the fallen" perpetuated a myth of simple patriotic and fraternal martyrs, purified of equivocal traits. Universals are the stuff of myth, and the poilu lionized by the nation was just that—the representative French soldier, undifferentiated by class or rank or regional origins, as hero. The fallen poilu was the good Frenchman par excellence.

In the face of postwar difficulties the commemorations were repeated reminders that the war's outcome was victory and that the virtues of the people had brought the victory. The government of Georges "Père la Victoire" Clemenceau held up the model of wartime sacrifice while asking people to sacrifice further for the nation's recovery from the war—to pay more taxes and to work harder—and to have more children. The cult of the poilu undergirded pleas for continuing submission to the call of duty. When discontented groups of workers and women pressed for social advancement and compensation after the long struggle, political leaders responded by invoking the memory of the fallen. As the minister of war declared during a ceremony at the tomb of the unknown soldier in 1921: "The dead—especially the dead—command the living; in the peace that they have conquered, may we obey their voices to make a France that is united and hard-working, confident and strong."[17] Selective memory of the war was marshaled to serve postwar needs. The leaders celebrating wartime patriotism were at the same time struggling to control postwar social divisions and rancor.

Restive Workers and Women

In addition to alienated veterans, two groups stood out as potential disturbers of the peace in postwar society: militant workers and tradition-challenging women. For most of the population, those types were charged with negative identities, contrasting with the models of virtue—the poilu and Madelon. That is, all these social representations existed together in a system, a mythology (of the kind analyzed so well by Roland Barthes). Working-class men and the "new" women, conspicuously discontent and combative since the last years of the war, clearly threatened the return to a prewar "normalcy."

"People scorn them and people fear them; people turn away from them with a little disgust and fright," journalist Jacques Valdour observed of the attitudes of the middle and upper classes toward workers.[18] Fear of worker insurgency and of Communists' growing strength was rife during the last years of the war and afterward. There were grounds for some concern. By the war's end some poilus, resuming their identity as workers, were eager for revolutionary change. Threats like "We'll show the bosses! Our comrades won't have died in the trenches in vain" were commonplace talk among soldiers waiting to head home in January 1919, noted Lieutenant Henri Desagneux in his diary.[19]

Conservatives like Valdour also worried about increasing numbers of foreign workers in France after the war—Communists from Italy and Spain, Algerians, and "especially Jews."[20] In the minds of such xenophobes and anti-Semites, the immigrants constituted a growing danger to the livelihood of French workers and somehow to their moral health as well.

But the first concern was the revolutionary potential of French workers. By the end of the war, workers were seething with discontent. The shared joy over victory was not enough to overcome the social antagonisms. Gratitude toward leaders and unity vis-à-vis the Germans did not cancel out anger at high prices and lowered standards of living. Prices had doubled several times since the beginning of the war, and wages had fallen far behind. In the spring of 1919 waves of strikes broke out, with traditionally militant miners, railroad workers, and metallurgical workers taking the lead. In April 1919, on the eve of what promised to be a stormy May Day of angry workers in violent demonstrations, the two chambers of the French Parliament quickly voted through a law setting a maximum eight-hour workday (a forty-eight hour work week)—in response to the International Labor Organization's urging and union demands from the Confédération générale du travail. Despite that concession to workers, May Day demonstrations in 1919 erupted into violence, and some deaths resulted.

The eight-hour-day law helped to forestall massive revolt, but it did not satisfy many workers. Prices during the postwar era continued to rise faster than wages, and to keep up with the cost of living the majority of workers worked longer hours or took on a second job. In addition, the government gave in to employer pressures and in early 1921 issued a compromise decree limiting the eight-hour day to large towns and large shops. In the Paris region in the early 1920s workers commonly worked ten hours a day.[21] Workers who found jobs in new factories in the *banlieue* and a place to live nearby were able to gain a bit of new free time at the beginning and end of the day, but for many workers the promised extra free time was taken away by longer commutes as they moved out farther to find reasonably priced housing.[22]

The granting of more leisure hours to workers, small though the gain was, quickened old fears that the workers would only misuse the new freedom by wasting more of their money and time in cabarets, aggravating the problem of alcoholism. "Organizing leisure" became an urgent concern, even at a time when productivity was drastically lower than before the war and when reconstruction needs were pressing. Government officials, academics, and social reformers advocated measures for improving workers' leisure more strongly than ever, but little was actually done by government. When the International Labor Office tried to get agreement on state protection of workers' leisure, the French government objected and strongly defended individual liberty, even the worker's freedom to work during what could be his leisure time.[23] Some mining and railroad companies set up programs for workers' instruction and encouraged gardening. The vision of the worker expending his extra energies in his garden was particularly dear to people worried about the postwar social order.

Contrary to conservatives' fears, consumption of alcohol and time spent in cabarets and cafés diminished after the reform of 1919, even though many workers had slightly more free time. And the number of workers' gardens increased sharply.[24] In 1922 a Ministry of Labor survey estimated the number of gardens at 160,000, an 80 percent increase since 1919. Abbé Lemire's Ligue française du Coin de Terre et du Foyer, founded in 1896, claimed some 50,000 "worker gardens" in 1922 and 600,000 by the late 1930s, but millions of workers started gardens on their own initiative.[25] There was little other change in workers' leisure activities, however, especially among mature workers. Fishing and the game of boules continued to be favorites almost everywhere. Many workers showed no difficulty organizing their own leisure on a Sunday as they went off fishing or hunting.

Youthful workers showed a strong interest in modern sports—football, races, bicycling, swimming, boxing, and tennis. They read *L'Auto* and were indifferent to politics. Sports organizations grew rapidly in the wake of the war: the Union des Fédérations françaises de sports athlétiques had 594,300 members by 1922—a 255 percent increase over 1913. The smaller Union des Sociétés de gymnastique de France grew from 138,250 to 225,000—a 62.8 percent increase during the same years; while the membership of the Fédération sportive catholique de France went from about 100,000 to 220,000—a 120 percent increase.[26] In the postwar years adulatory press coverage of bicycle racing champions like the Pelissier brothers, the champion boxer Georges Carpentier, and the international tennis ace Suzanne Lenglen fed the growing interest in sports. The 1924 Olympic Games, held in Paris, helped, too. As players and as spectators, the French (especially men) after the war found in sports a new sense of community and engaging struggle—often victory as well. For working men in particular, sports were a prime diversion, regularly taking attention away from political and economic struggles.

For both men and women, a great diverting interest was romantic love and sexual pursuits. The young, especially, devoted much of their free time to those interests in vicarious and real-life forms. In small towns in Lorraine, iron miners and women factory workers went regularly to Sunday dances and to movies provided by employers, who carefully eliminated all objectionable moral and political content from the films.[27] In the cities, workers had more choices, and they went most frequently to movies and dances, usually in their own quarters. Small dance halls at the back of wine shops filled up, even if the only music came from an accordion.

The postwar French woman as national sports heroine: Suzanne Lenglen in 1925. An Olympic champion (1920), she was six times champion of France and six times winner of Wimbledon (1919–22, 1923, 1925). Photo Rol. Private collection.

Georges Carpentier was both boxing champion and valiant poilu—a national hero. This studio photograph was taken in the United States in June 1921, just before his world heavyweight championship match with Jack Dempsey. Private collection.

On Saturday evenings and Sunday afternoons the movie halls were usually full, and there workers engaged in lively conversation before the film began. Youthful Parisian working men and women noisily talked and called out to others, exhilarated by the rare freedom and flirtatious repartee. In Lorraine, an investigator of workers' leisure reported that young women spent spare moments weekdays and longer periods Sundays reading inexpensive popular novels with titles like *L'Amour est maître* and *Du Harem à l'amour*.[28] Around greater Paris, bookstores and newspaper vendors sold stacks of inexpensive romantic novels with such titles as *L'Amour au coeur* (25 centimes), *L'Amour errant* (1 Fr 50), and *Les Crimes de l'amour* (1 Fr 75).[29] In films as in plays, serial stories, and novels, love stories—a mix of romantic passion, adultery, and passing amours—provided what Valdour called "the bread of illusions" for which there was an unflagging appetite.[30]

Dwelling on private life and individual relationships, commercial culture steered attention away from political or collective causes. Yet that culture, if politically prophylactic, was far from reassuring to conservatives. For in that domain of love and sexuality lurked other dangers to the established social order. One was sensational entertainment that some believed would weaken the moral fiber of the people. Surveying Parisian workers' entertainment, Valdour judged "realist" plays and café-concert acts particularly pernicious because of their overload of vice and violence. Dramas about prostitutes—with such titles as *Fleur de trottoir* and *L'Enfer des pierreuses*—provided the pretexts for titillating scenes from the lower depths of society.[31] "Everywhere the theater and café-concert are demoralizers," he concluded, echoing charges already several generations old.[32] Conservatives feared that workers would live only for immediate pleasure if given the chance.[33] In the workers' suburbs of Paris, Valdour found "loose morals," "entertainments that directly and brutally provoke debauchery," "profound ignorance," and no desire for learning.[34] Subversive, hedonist, self-centered, and indifferent to the larger community—such images made the worker everything the glorified poilu was not.

The specter of the "modern woman" appeared a similar menace in the minds of the many who wanted to stabilize postwar society. They worried about the more independent woman who had found untraditional work during the war,

A postcard (ca. 1919) featuring the marriage proposal to Madelon, a part of the song that was of special interest after the war when worries about France's recent losses of men and declining birth rate intensified. Courtesy of the Musée d'histoire contemporaine—BDIC (Universités de Paris).

who had experienced financial gains, and who enjoyed more sexual liberty. The "new woman" was in many ways the antithesis of the celebrated Madelon. While the country showered ritual thanks on the fighting heroes and the mythical Madelon, no public tributes were paid to working women for their contributions to the war effort. Those workers were too closely associated with "new women" who aroused widespread anxiety after the war by cutting their hair short, dancing provocative new dances like the shimmy, and demanding the vote.

The wartime emphasis on males was prolonged by the cult of the fallen, as George Mosse has pointed out.[35] And with that privileging of the male and fear of new female roles came a public will to confine women to traditional roles. Advocates of women's suffrage, who had hoped to have their cause rewarded by a grateful nation, were bitterly disappointed. While refusing to extend the vote to women, the nation's lawmakers took action in response to public anxiety about France's demographic weaknesses: they banned birth control information and abortion in July 1920. In that same month a new law established a national holiday honoring Joan of Arc, a symbol of old virtues and a religious and patriotic heroine long championed by the Right. Still, the specter of change would not go away. The birth rate did not rise significantly in the wake of the new law, and the "modern" women did not give up their new ways. In July 1922 a novel entitled *La Garçonne* by Victor Margueritte created a scandal with its portrayal of the sexually liberated "bachelor girl," representing the worst fears of conservatives, who knew that she was not just fictional.[36]

Taking Everything "With a Smile"

Popular songs of the time proposed several different responses to worries and sadness, responses that reveal the larger contours of popular French culture and mentalities. Songs are particularly important as historical sources for the period between the wars because they occupied such an important place in the everyday life and consciousness of the French people—even during the period just before radio and the "talkies." The music business was highly competitive, and producers who gave the public what it wanted could reap huge rewards. With those incentives, song writers and publishers paid close attention to public preferences and tried to provide songs that pleased mass audiences. For these reasons and others discussed below, the commercial production of songs can be viewed as a gauge of widely shared attitudes and changing feelings, especially after wartime censorship ended.

Ordinary people heard songs not only in the cafés-concerts, but also in the streets, where itinerant singers performed, and in boarding houses and cafés, where phonographs played on and on—as did radios later in the 1920s. Many who listened also sang for themselves while at work and in the evening at home. In a housing project in Saint Ouen, Valdour observed not long after the war, a neighbor family and their guests (relatives) entertained themselves around the table until ten o'clock one Saturday evening; each member sang a song or recited a monologue, and then together they sang the "International" and turned in for the night.[37]

"The French people are the people who always sing," wrote Léon Deutsch in 1924, quoting Rousseau: "they sing their defeats, their miseries, their troubles, as well as their good fortunes or their victories. . . . It seems that song has become the natural expression of its sentiments."[38] In content and form the songs varied enormously, as Valdour noted: rhythms brusquely changed from lullaby to rabble-rousing; sentimental notes mixed with raunchy cadences; lyrics were in turn poetic and vulgar; the mood passed from "complacent skepticism to capricious and brutal passion, from coarse joke to bitterness." To the conservative Valdour, popular songs in all their diversity were not so much a "natural expression" of the people as a major purveyor of "the bread of illusions."[39] The more sympathetic observer Pierre MacOrlan maintained that in popular music "life was expressed with perhaps the greatest force." Popular music was "a creator of images" that everyone could interpret from some degree of personal feelings and experience.[40] Songs "bring to the passions of man a simple but definitive explanation," explained André Beucler in 1928. "If a passerby meets some buddies and these people enjoy themselves, it is beyond doubt that they will end up introducing into their conversation some phrases, some verses, finally entire songs borrowed from the repertory of Mistinguett or Damia." The events sung about on stage became part of the people's daily life. Beucler put it more strongly: "One must love, live, hope, fight, grow old and suffer as in the songs."[41]

In a time of worries about postwar women and the need for "repopulation," songwriters turned out numerous romances about returning poilus marrying beautiful patriotic maidens. The hit "Choisis Lison" (1920) by Bousquet and Robert urges the beautiful young Lison to choose a returning poilu for her husband. Again and again fictional women received tributes in song for fulfilling traditional roles. New songs about Madelon continued her story. In "Le Mariage de Madelon" (1917) by Bachet-Lemonnier she marries a corporal and has a son even before the victory. According to "Madelon, c'est dimanche" (1919) she sells her cabaret, marries a demobilized poilu, and together they devote a leisurely Sunday to having "p'tits marmots." In "Madelon, j'attends la classe" (1923) by Bousquet and Robert (again), a young soldier away on duty writes to Madelon, his bride-to-be. Several lines refer to the need to repair their house and the promise of *réparation*. In sum, Madelon after the war was fiancée or wife, mother-to-be or fulfilled mother. Employment and independence were behind her.[42]

According to Parisian song vendors, in late 1920 and early 1921 the song in greatest demand was "Lison-Lisette."[43] The lyrics tell of two attractive young women on a sheep farm—a blonde and her sister, a brunette—who serve wine to soldiers marching by. The entire regiment is smitten, but soon two of the men succeed in winning over the sisters for themselves. The story concludes with the village preparing to celebrate two marriages: the blonde will marry a handsome sergeant, and the brunette will marry a lieutenant. Mythic in its essential characters and timeless concern with romance and marriage, the song made no reference to the recent bloodletting or changes in women's work.

When the "new woman" appeared in songs at all, the lyricists avoided the serious worries about her and instead focused on new behaviors that allowed listeners to smile, trivializing and dismissing her threatening aspects. The newest dances and short hair were the most obvious focal points. "Dansez le Shimmy," launched by Suzanne Valroger in 1922, depicts a contemporary young woman—*un p'tit trottin*—passing over the traditional criteria for accepting a suitor, his economic and social qualifications.[44] Instead, she asks him insistently: "But do you dance the shimmy?" She explains, "It's what is making a furor in Paris." In the song "C'est la Faute au Shimmy" (1922), the first stanza describes a woman finding "the best of husbands" in a dance hall ("it's the fault of the shimmy"); in the second stanza she turns away from her husband in bed—a little fagged (*flapi*)—again due to shimmying; and in the third she has a child who resembles "astonishingly the handsome Negro who played so well in the dance hall." The song sums up, "All that, it's the fault of the shimmy." At the end the problem of replenishing France's population comes up again: "Do you want to repopulate France? / Dance the shimmy, but yes, dance the shimmy."[45]

Songs about the new women's fashion of short hair similarly amused and trivialized social changes. A song entitled "Elle s'était fait couper les cheveux" (copyright 1924) told of all kinds of women, from young maiden to grandmother, now boasting closely cropped hair. Each one is simply taking up a new fashion, for none of the women utters the slightest hint of a desire for more freedom or of any social criticism. A year later, "Elle s'est fait repousser les cheveux" (lyrics by René Sarvil) carried the story further. The young woman grows her hair out to get a job as a department store clerk, and then a new boss comes along and disapproves of her long hair. Next she lets her hair grow long again to be presented to her fiancé's parents, only to experience more bad fortune: her fiancé is killed by a taxi. By reducing women's desires for change to a matter of feminine whim and fashion, popular songs played to the tradition-bound many and lent support to the old social order.

Up-to-date and controversial images of workers were also avoided. The postwar years produced no successful new songs praising the workers for their contributions to the victory. Most songs depicting working people were about the contented artisan and his virtuous young love in the faubourgs and their melodramatic foils, the hood that the French called an *apache* and his lover the prostitute (fictions to be examined in chapter 4). Song after song exalted the simple honest apprentice and his equally simple and pure sweetheart. The rich *rentier* often tried to win over the young woman but usually failed. The common wisdom imparted was to marry the honest but poor man, for "money doesn't make happiness," as Louis Bousquet's "Marie! Marie! Marie!" concludes. Together with the cult of the poilu, those predominant themes helped to prolong the war-caused loss of memory of earlier collective struggles.[46] While tenderly depicting the undemanding old-fashioned workers, the song industry generally ignored industrial workers and strikers. References did appear, however, when a joke could be made of them. In 1920, when general strikes were a bitterly controversial and explosive social reality, the song "Les Bienfaits de la grève générale" by George Merry concluded that the strike would permit the country to repopulate itself "in one swoop" (*d'un coup*). Demands for a five-day work week—"the English week"—were ridiculed in a song entitled "Pour Avoir la Semaine anglaise," which conjured up scenes of the woman in charge of public toilets taking the day off, and the not-quite-born child doing the same.[47]

That was the perspective of Paris' Tin Pan Alley. The workers' point of view came out in militant leftist songs, including some by local amateurs, like one entitled "Grève des Tramways de Lille—février 1920," set to the tune of "Quand Madelon." Addressing the citizens of Lille, the lyrics attack the tramway company for having ignored the workers' claims for eight months. Speaking directly to the workers—"Soldiers of yesterday, you will understand us well"—the chorus concludes by damning the bosses as the "others," those recently most despised by patriotic Frenchmen: "These cowardly assassins have remained shirkers, shirkers" (*embusqués*).[48] The wartime conflict of poilu and "cowardly" civilian still simmered away in peacetime, even though much of official and mainstream popular culture tried to deny it.

After 1920 those wartime terms of reference faded away, and labor militancy died down. Union strength declined, and strikes dropped off sharply, in large part because of the militants' lack of success. Although the emergence of the French Communist Party and Communist general trade union kept alive old fears on the Right, commercial popular culture paid scant attention to such troubling specters. Instead it continued to concentrate on images of unthreatening workers, civilian counterparts to the jovial poilu. In the movies, as in songs, industrial workers rarely appeared. The few films that did feature them and their factories and railyards—Henri Pouctal's *Travail* (1919–20) and Abel Gance's *La Roue* (1923) were notably popular—focused on melodramas of love and suffering that end with the happy resolution of both personal and class conflicts—usually by a marriage.[49]

Through the difficult postwar years, producers of popular music pumped out steady doses of reassurance in songs that made light of the gravest problems of the time: painfully high prices and taxes and inflation (*la vie chère*), the need to "repopulate" France after the bloodletting, and the difficulties of making the Germans pay war reparations. Mistinguett's hit of 1924 "La Belote," about a popular card game, is a telling example. It first describes the craze for the new game: people everywhere were abandoning other games and pastimes like dancing; now all that counted was playing belote. Conveyed was a view of the French people as essentially whimsical: they throw themselves mindlessly into the latest collective fixation, particularly in social relations and romantic situations (the first two verses). The last two verses suggest playing the game as a way of resolving disputes, instead of fighting with knives (as hoods did on the Butte Montmartre) and instead of fighting with national armies. The case of German war reparations owed to France comes up as a final problem for trivializing treatment: "But if it's with Germany that one plays, it's prudent—in order to get anything when one wins—to get yourself paid in advance."[50]

Popular songs, while making light of many issues, did not simply urge compliance with those in power. Numerous lyrics described popular strategies of resistance. The hit of 1920 "Cach' ton piano," for example, told of ways to avoid new taxes like the one on pianos by the old ruse of hiding the assessed objects. Maurice Chevalier's hit of 1921 "Avec le Sourire" included a verse that told how to take the heavy tax bills "with a smile." The singer's response to the state is that he wants to pay, but in forty annual installments. He also announces that he intends to do as the Germans do—resist payment as far as possible—concluding, "you have to take everything with a smile . . . and tell yourself that if we were the defeated surely we

During the 1920s, music-hall and recording star Maurice Chevalier, originally a resourceful "little guy" from a working-class neighborhood, excelled at playing the character who knew how to take all manner of postwar problems "with a smile." Sheet music cover (1921) by Charles Gir ©SPADEM, Paris. Private collection.

would not pay a *sou* more." It was the same unflappable, indomitable spirit of the poilu, now defending himself in the no-man's-land of the postwar economy. The song expressed the oppositional "little guy" viewpoint of hostility to the state and taxes and the Germans. Yet it also concluded with an accommodating acceptance of the inevitable "with a smile."[51]

These were songs aimed at the general public by songwriters who generally wanted to create a hit. As so many songs expressed opposition to government authorities and the rich, one can conclude that those attitudes were widespread and that audiences were known to be receptive to those themes. The song "Si Vous avez du pognon" (If you have some dough) concludes with a chorus that declares: "if you have much money, you will always be right, but if you don't have a penny, then you'll always be wrong." One verse applies that conclusion to a poilu who lost his right arm in battle: a government official awards him a simple Croix de guerre, explaining that "we keep the Légion d'honneur to reward our military contractors." Bitterness about the war and distrust of the government ran particularly high in working-class quarters of Paris. In a café-concert in Popincourt, Valdour heard a female singer remark: "They've told you: 'make children'; we'll make as many kids as you want if war never comes back to take them from us."[52] In such quarters the messages of government and mainstream songs—to take problems "with a smile"—were most clearly contested.

The Left took up antiwar songs with steadiest fervor, but it was far from monopolizing them. Since early in the war, topical patriotic songs had frequently expressed the hope that the current conflict would bring an end to all war. "Henceforth no more war" was the hope held out by a song of 1915 about the predicted glorious return of the French soldiers upon achieving victory. In 1919 Lucien Boyer and Vincent Scotto's "Marche des hommes bleus" portrayed the scene at the Arc de Triomphe on 14 July when the crowds cheer and thank the poilus as the "vanquishers of all wars." The last verse pictures Madelon as a spectator mounted on the shoulders of a Zouave (an Algerian infantryman). With a tear in her eye she cries the refrain, "Wars—there won't be any more, thank you, valiant poilus." That antiwar theme became a mainstream standard for several years after the armistice. In a successful song of 1921 entitled "Ne Jouez Pas aux Soldats" a mother begs her young boy not to play soldiers because the toy guns and sabers remind her too much of the war and the sorrows it brought: "They make the hearts of poor mothers cry too much / Mothers whose children died playing soldiers." In the last chorus she pleads with other parents:

> War and combat should horrify [the children].
> In the name of our heroes killed in the bloom of youth,
> In order that this dreadful drama not begin again
>
> . . . .
> We must never play soldiers.

One of the most enduring and popular songs of the period was "La Butte rouge" (first recorded in 1923). On the "red hill" where postwar lovers embrace and vineyards grow once more, the singer tells us, he once heard the cries of his fellow soldiers and saw their broken skulls. Evoking the bloody battlefield of Bapaume, the song combines outrage at the slaughter with sad remembrance of fallen comrades.[53]

Antiwar songwriters commonly took aim at sinister big businessmen

men. He also recalled people saying that the only thing known about the unknown soldier was that he had sung "La Madelon." Then Bach fell silent, and with an abrupt "au revoir" he quickly got up and left.[62] The satisfaction of victory had faded, but the pain of the losses had not.

Troubling Memories and War Movies

By the Pact of Locarno, signed on 16 October 1925, Germany accepted defeat and the boundaries assigned by the peace treaty. In France anti-German feeling subsided, and antiwar feeling grew stronger—or at least showed itself more clearly. After years without films about the war, during late 1926 and early 1927 the Great War came to the screens of France in the American film *The Big Parade* by King Vidor. This was a love story as much as a war story: the son of a rich American industrialist volunteers to fight in France and falls in love with a villager named Lisette. He goes into battle and loses a leg; after the armistice he hurries to his beloved's village and finds it devastated. He goes back to the United States but eventually returns to France and finds Lisette.

An early advertisement for the film called it "a homage to French women" and proclaimed it "not only a masterpiece, but also a great lesson which must impart to all people the horror and hatred of fratricidal struggles."[63] Some reviewers hailed it for showing the happy partnership—the fraternity—of the French and Americans (*Comoedia, Le Journal*). Others sharply criticized the depiction of the alliance. The movie wounded French pride in some quarters: journalists complained that the film showed too little of the combat of French soldiers and made it appear that Americans alone won the war (*L'Echo de Paris, Le Petit Parisien, Candide*). With wrangling over the question of war debts still going on, *Candide*'s reviewer René Jeanne saw in the film special pleading for the American position. In *L'Avenir* Marcel Espiau lamented that the French woman was symbolized by "a peasant woman who fastens herself on to the thighs of an American." Several articles in *Le Journal* called for censorship of war movies with the argument that "Our war . . . does not belong to the Americans." Another piece added, "It is France that has suffered 1,500,000 war deaths."[64]

The depiction of combat evoked equally polarized responses. Some admired the skill and the realism of the fighting; some documentary footage had been included along with the daunting noises of battle, actually made by men behind the screen striking drums and wooden instruments. "The reconstitutions of battle give, for the first time, a truly tragic impression," wrote Jean Chataigner in *Le Journal*.

Other spectators found the fighting and devastation falsely depicted or not shown fully enough to give an accurate impression. The battle scenes struck *Volonté* critic Jean Monda as "stupid" in their portrayal of "a joyous sport." They perpetuated "the fable of the smiling and facetious poilu who fights as one plays football, only with a little more joy." The film was a "sentimental story of a quite American puerility." In short, *The Big Parade* struck many as too much like the old bourrage de crâne.[65] Protests broke out, and while some simply booed and whistled, others lacerated movie screens and attacked theaters as well as the policemen defending them.[66] The time for exulting over heroism and victory had passed. Reminders of the war's novel love relationships, propagandist images, and cruel battles still troubled and divided the French.

During the late 1920s the war came back as a central topic of official and popular culture in France. It was a time when veterans' organizations were building up to a peak of strength and influence. Ten-year anniversaries of great battles, especially Verdun, and then of the armistice brought home the fact that the war had slipped into the ever more distant past. The funerals of the war leaders—one national hero after another—also returned attention to the war. In March 1929 huge crowds, including many thousands of veterans, poured out their grief in the funeral ceremonies for Marshal Foch, the "author of the victory, the one who saved the French nation," as one veteran put it.[67] It was "the greatest mourning event held in Paris since the nationalization of the death of Victor Hugo," wrote correspondent Janet Flanner.[68] The funeral procession passed the Arc de Triomphe, stopped for a service in Notre Dame, and then proceeded to the Invalides for the general's entombment alongside Turenne and Napoleon. When Clemenceau died later that same year (21 November 1929), no ceremony was held, in accordance with his instructions (the body was quietly taken back to his native Vendée for burial), but the press and the people gratefully pondered the memory of his war leadership. When Marshal Joffre died a couple of years later, his funeral on 17 January 1931 followed the pattern of Foch's, with a similar emotional outpouring from a mourning public that jammed the streets, squares, and bridges of central Paris. Joffre was not only the "victor of the Marne," he was also beloved as a kind of grandfather. Death once more was the victor over men long cheered for their victories.

With revived memories of the war came outspoken revulsion against war. Antiwar feeling had long been prominent in the 1920s during the armistice commemorations: year after year veterans spoke out against the "horrors of war," while pouring scorn on chauvinist rhetoric.[69] Through all the seasons and years, antiwar sentiment simmered away in leftist strongholds like Belleville, where movie audiences came alive during the newsreels to protest any appearance of financiers, priests, cabinet ministers, or generals. The sight of parades and large maneuvers provoked what Eugène Dabit described as "the same cry that we made in 1917."[70]

A wave of new films reproduced those horrors on screens throughout France. *Verdun, visions d'histoire* by Léon Poirier premiered during the week of 10–18 November 1928, the tenth anniversary of the armistice. Its use of documentary footage made the depiction of battle more authentic than any movie seen before, even though the film was silent. Focusing on such "symbolic characters" as the French soldier and the mother, it showed the war experience as one of tragic suffering. Although some critics considered it weakened by a facile symbolism, the film succeeded in stirring up strong feelings of disgust and sorrow over the slaughter of ordinary Frenchmen.[71]

In June 1929 a German novel published in France had a similar effect on readers. Already a runaway best-seller in Germany, Erich Maria Remarque's *All Quiet on the Western Front* enjoyed immediate success in France as well. A new

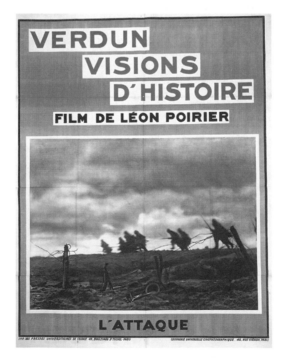

Poster for the movie *Verdun, visions d'histoire* (1929) featuring "the attack." Phot. Bibl. Nat. de Fr.-Paris.

stream of books and films on the war soon appeared in its wake.[72] Thanks to the new technology of sound, these war movies brought the awful din of battle to audiences that had known only silent images. And threats of new war—by Mussolini in Italy and Germans demonstrating on the Rhine—made the French freshly sensitive to the subject. In late 1930 the American film version of *All Quiet on the Western Front* came to French screens as *A l'Ouest rien de nouveau*. The French flocked to see it at the very time when Hitler's militants were disrupting screenings of it in Germany, prompting the German government to ban it. In the same winter the German film *Westfront 1918* directed by G. W. Pabst also appeared in France under the title *Quatre de l'infanterie*. Both not only kept alive the memory of the war, but also fed antiwar sentiment.

A reporter who saw *All Quiet* in a neighborhood cinema on the edge of Paris noted a wide range of reactions. The audience laughed at the horrifying adjutant Himmelstoss as though he were a caricature by the turn-of-the-century comic writer Courteline. Then scenes of a fierce attack—"from bombardment to the spectacle of the most frightful butchery"—caused an unforgettable "stupor, a distress [*bouleversement*]" visible on faces through the hall. A young woman seated near the reporter cried and cried. On the whole, though, *All Quiet* was "less harsh" than *Quatre de l'infanterie*, which introduced four Germans living happily in peacetime and then showed how their lives were ruined by the war. The American film came closer to what most people felt about the war, this reporter maintained. It mixed a little "good humor" in with "the tragic quotidian." The character Katcinzsky best expressed the values and attitudes shared by French spectators. The audience responded with bravos to his forceful remarks expressing "horror at the massacre," his knack for getting around obstacles (system D), and his belief in better times.[73] That is, the audience recognized in him the same kind of soldier that they knew as the disenchanted and down-to-earth poilu of the latter war years, and they shared his views. Another reaction, distinctively French, was the nationalist one of feeling slighted and insulted by the suggestion (even in the title) that the French were not fighting hard and lacked courage. This view, voiced by reviewer Clément Vautel in *Le Journal* (December 1930), does not appear to have been widespread. The most common response to the film was anguish and disgust with jingoist optimism and bourrage de crâne in general. The attitudes of the disenchanted poilus had spread to the general public.

In 1931 Léon Poirier brought out a new version of his account of Verdun, this time with sound. Entitled *Verdun, souvenirs d'histoire*, it follows a French veteran as he takes his children to the battlefield fifteen years after the battle and tries to explain what happened there. This version with spoken words and realistic cannon fire seems to have had less impact than the silent film and decidedly less than Raymond Bernard's *Les Croix de bois,* which appeared the following year.[74] An adaptation of the 1919 novel by Roland Dorgelès, Bernard's work was hailed in France as the French war film par excellence; it won critical acclaim and box-office success in France as well as abroad, especially in the United States.[75] Bernard had been a soldier briefly, and his film seems to have best captured the experience of French veterans. It showed "all the war *à la française,*" wrote veteran José Germain, with neither "American naïvetés" nor "German morbidities."[76] The contrast with "German morbidities" is less clear, for the spectator cannot miss seeing death shadowing the poilus throughout the movie. An opening shot shows lines of soldiers dissolving into rows of white crosses (*croix de bois*), and at the end—in a hallucinatory vision—the soldiers are shown carrying large crosses on their shoulders. After witnessing expectant joy during mobilization, the spectator sees the superior officers senselessly expending the lives of their men and prolonging the suffering. Times of tense waiting precede grisly attacks in hellish wastelands that become killing fields. Songs and games of soldiers in a rest area are abruptly interrupted by a convoy of cadavers. A small community of French types—a solid peasant, a complaining and wisecracking Parisian workingman, a law student—is progressively reduced to a sole survivor. Meanwhile, people back home are unfaithful to the combatants and cannot begin to understand what life on the front is like.

In an interview Bernard described his intent as one of trying "to show a troop of average Frenchmen launched in the ordeal of war—which was not the object of Pabst or of Lewis Milestone [director of *All Quiet*]." The personage of the Parisian worker ("le Sulphart"), for example, allowed Bernard to "sum up in a single figure, without falling into symbolism, the spirit of gaiety of certain soldiers of ours, heroism with a smile—or sarcasm—which was the characteristic nuance of French heroism."[77] The poilu, Bernard understood well, was a figure of tensions, an unstable compound of cheery courage and disenchantment. Audience responses revealed a similar rift. The scene that evoked the greatest response was one in which the battle-weary company parades through a village to the applause of the villagers. Spectators often joined in the applause. Some spectators, however, hissed at the scene, sensing some glorification of war. Overall, that disapproval of military values seems to have been the dominant reaction evoked by what a leading film historian has called France's most powerful pacifist film prior to *La Grande Illusion* (1937).[78]

Even if the old tales of heroism and glorious sacrifice sometimes met with objections, scenes of war still pleased many as entertainment—or even as inspiring demonstrations of martial values. Surveys and observers reported sharply divided opinions about the war movies.[79] Journalist Jacques Perdu, for example, complained that even movies with a pacifist message managed to "exalt courage, sacrifice, patriotism." In his view they were in truth bourgeois apologies for war camouflaged as "pseudo-pacifist." *Verdun, visions d'histoire,* he charged, was especially guilty of perpetuating notions of heroism and military glory.[80] Bordeaux film critic Marcel Lapierre saw *Quatre de l'infanterie* with a former poilu, who came out talking proudly of the war he had known as a participant. Reportedly women especially liked films about aviators—such movies as *Les Ailes* [*Wings*], *Ciel de gloire, La Patrouille de l'aube,* and *L'Escadre volante.* Interviews of schoolchildren showed, not surprisingly, that *All Quiet* evoked antiwar feelings, Lapierre noted. But he went on to report that young spectators seeing *Quatre de l'infanterie* manifested quite mixed reactions. Some boys viewing the film cheered the French soldiers and urged them on to kill and win, whereas girls grew pale and reticent. Observing adults' responses to the movies of Pabst and Milestone, lycée professor and veteran Emile Moussat noted that some people reacted with silence, most seemed moved, and many went out of the theater with reddened eyes. Yet Moussat also reported hearing some in the audience murmuring about taking "the Boches," and he heard some spectators exult when they saw French troops overrun German lines. Such moviegoers took away not horror of war but a memory of victory.[81] Moussat saw *All Quiet* with an audience that he thought was mostly pacifist: spectators were clearly moved by the suffering endured on the front. Yet when the newsreels came on with scenes taken at the funeral of Marshal Joffre and some earlier scenes from his career, the audience "applauded the victor of the Marne with fervor."[82]

The French were not only deeply divided about war, but also deeply ambivalent. As postwar understanding of the carnage strengthened, the old images of the comic soldier and the victorious hero lost some of their old appeal. Neither, however, disappeared completely. The comic soldier and the military hero continued to hold a place in the French cast of beloved characters. They reappeared in numerous movies through the thirties, but as prewar or postwar characters, not as poilus. The old figures, the nineteenth-century types, did not fit the poilus' experience of the Great War any more than the war monuments did, but they lived on as an alternative to the nightmare that the war films of 1928–32 brought to the home front. They lived on as just one of many ways of dealing with (and not dealing with) troubling memories during the 1920s and into the 1930s.

3. PARISIAN MODERN

Those who have survived the cataclysms of stupidity (which it seemed to them could never be ended) have turned with a kind of fever towards life.

—*Philippe Soupault*, The American Influence in France *(1930)*

Dans la vie faut pas s'en faire.

[In life you mustn't worry.]

—*Maurice Chevalier, in* Dédé *(1921)*

Paris Qui Jazz

THOSE WHO WANTED TO FORGET the darkness and pain and sacrifices of war flocked to alluring bright spots in Paris. Dance halls and music halls were especially popular in the months following the armistice. Bouncy music and big colorful revues at the Casino de Paris, the Folies-Bergère, and the Olympia drew unremitting crowds of the war-weary. A large and steady part of the crowds consisted of idle British and American troops. As the Allied soldiers departed in 1919, foreign tourists flooded in and joined with French patrons to create a postwar boom in entertainment. The shows and settings that attracted them most were fresh, upbeat, and marked by Anglo-American touches—places expressive of a bright new era.

The music hall emerged from the war as the showcase of Parisian life in its most spectacular forms: brilliant costumes and lighting effects, the latest songs and dances, and fashionable people of many countries. Above all it provided "pleasure for the eyes," reviewer Gustave Fréjaville observed in 1920:[1] a brilliant stream of dreamlike tableaux and processions of glamorous women—some in exotic, erotic costumes, others mostly nude, sparkling with jewelry and sequins and crowned with high-plumed headdresses. "For three hours each new entry eclipses the preceding one, without respite," Fréjaville summed up, "and each costume is a masterpiece of ingenious extravagance and Parisian taste." Typical revues presented forty-five or fifty tableaux in two acts—bright kaleidoscopes of flamboyant dress and settings and comic and dramatic sketches. The music hall was a dream factory full of behind-the-scenes machinery and lighting systems, a technological complex producing the magical succession of scenes and bathing them in rainbow hues and bright whites. It was also a showplace of the experimental and novel in fashion and morals, music and dance. Nowhere else did postwar France show more capacity for creativity and energy.

The leading music halls displayed the modern face not only of France, but also of the world. In the 1920 revue *Paris qui jazz* at the Casino de Paris, for example, a colorful prologue featured the biggest movie stars from America—with Douglas Fairbanks and Mary Pickford impersonators at the head. Then the stage became a fashionable beach, followed by an orientalist extravaganza entitled "The Harem," and dozens of songs, dances, sketches, and processions. The music hall gave spectators a surreal trip around the world in a couple of hours. Its productions

A postwar *grand spectacle* at the Moulin Rouge—dreamlike distractions of bare-breasted women in colorful plumage. Photo Waléry. *Paris Plaisirs*, November 1926. Courtesy of the Bibliothèque Forney.

Parisian music halls as dream machines: a living Leda and Zeus in the form of a swan. *Paris Plaisirs*, February 1931. Courtesy of the Bibliothèque Forney.

celebrated luxury, cosmopolitan sophistication, and eroticism. They enacted vivid daydreams. Sketches like "Une Nuit de Don Juan" and revues entitled *Mieux Que Nue* (Better than nude) put the spotlight on hosts of bare-breasted beauties and simulated lovemaking. For hours the music-hall stage brimmed with brilliant scenes of life liberated from bourgeois moral constraints, reinforcing the tourists' image of Paris as a haven of erotic freedom and fulfillment.

Altogether the sights and sounds on stage formed a discordant whole bursting with movement, a flux of incongruous happenings barely controlled. "We see a kind of tamed catastrophe dancing on a hurricane of rhythms," wrote Jean Cocteau about an early jazz and dance act at the Casino de Paris. "The music-hall is the place of clashes where a curious harmony through contrasts establishes itself"—like the music of a jazz band, observed critic Legrand-Chabrier.[2] It struck many as delightful and fresh. After a while it became too much for some. "From dazzlement on dazzlement, one loses the capacity to admire," Fréjaville observed;

"One leaves the show with eyes tired, mind confused, and of all these splendors, one's memory retains only a brilliant chaos of agitated images, of the gold of jewels, of feathers, of pearly flesh, of shimmering swirls of fabrics and colors."[3] Tired or not, spectators left with a sense of having witnessed an extraordinary spectacle. In producing what the French called *la féerie*, a fairy-tale show of visual marvels, the music hall easily outdid its popular rival, the cinema, still silent and still only black-and-white.

In the 1920s even the architecture of the great music halls, both inside and out, took on a fresh look of modernity. On 29 February 1924, a redesigned Empire opened (39–41, avenue de Wagram) with three thousand seats and a huge stage measuring thirty by twenty-three meters, sufficient to accommodate circus acts of forty horses, musical elephant acts, and a large ballet, as well as such stars of song as Maurice Chevalier, Damia, Yvette Guilbert, Ouvrard, and Sophie Tucker.[4] A renovated sleek and cool Moulin Rouge reopened in early 1925, and the Folies-Bergère put on a striking art deco façade in 1927. At the end of the 1920s, the Lido on the Champs-Elysées added an artificial beach to its swimming pool and Turkish baths, a beach illuminated by bright lights and mirror effects in what the French knew as *un décor de féerie*. In the spring of 1930 the Zig-Zag opened on the boulevard Haussmann, billing itself as "the five-o'clock-tea music hall" (*le music-hall de cinq heures*), offering "élégance moderne."[5]

In clientele and performers these were among the most international enclaves in Paris. Performing for spectators of many lands were Russian dancers and Spanish dancers, jazz bands (among others, a Chinese jazz band from San Francisco), and gymnasts and jugglers from Eastern Europe and the Far East. At the Casino de Paris in May 1926, the main attractions were the Dolly Sisters, the Lawrence Tiller Girls, and the Rowe Sisters. At the Théâtre des Champs-Elysées the American Elsie Janis sang and imitated a music-hall cowboy. At the Empire a horse wearing a black wig, "Gee-Gee Chaplin," did a Charlie Chaplin routine. At the Olympia the burlesque dancers Harry White and Alice Manning of the Ziegfeld Follies performed. Paul Whiteman and his orchestra starred at the Théâtre des Champs-Elysées in July 1926. All those entertainments were primarily visual and musical, well suited to cosmopolitan audiences. Most of the foreign performers did not even try to communicate in French. Certainly the slangy popular French that flourished in the old café-concert had little place in the leading music halls.

Mistinguett was a representative of both the chic *Paris qui jazz* and the working-class faubourgs where she seemed equally at home. Sheet music cover of "Ça . . . c'est Paris!" (1927). Private collection.

nothing forbids a golden future." After the war "Miss" was a glittery exemplar of the lowborn woman who had risen to success and was fully enjoying a golden time.

Year after year in revue after revue at the Casino de Paris and the Folies-Bergère, she was the queen of the show. Her place was at the center where, surrounded by a host of adulating "boys" and show "girls," she stood out in the spotlight with the brightest-colored dress and most eye-catching plumage. Her classic entry was a climactic walk down glittery stairs, her famous shapely legs in full view and her outsized smile dominating the entire scene.

As a modern and glamorous Parisian woman, Mistinguett often sang the praises of the modern Paris that drew sophisticated visitors from all the world. Her hit of 1927 "Ça . . . c'est Paris!" presented the essential themes.[7] She hailed the city as "the queen of the world," but the rest of the lyrics described the city as more plebeian than regal. Paris is "a blond" with "a turned up nose, a mocking look, and ever laughing eyes. All those who know her, intoxicated by her caresses, go away but always come back." The quintessential Paris is "the little woman" of modest circumstances who excels at knowing how to use her attractions and has perfected her way of giving herself—"that's Paris!" In all the verses the capital is a center of love, lightness, sexual savoir-faire, and sophisticated "little women." With no references to the traditional city the cityscape remained vague, as though Paris were a sleek homogeneous whole, not the collection of provincial towns or the distinct *quartiers* that locals knew and celebrated. The sheet music cover of "Ça . . . c'est Paris!" featured the tourists' landmarks: the Eiffel Tower, the Arc de Triomphe, Sacré-Coeur, the Seine, and a busy boulevard. The song was a paean to the visitors' Paris—a city like an irresistibly attractive woman, whom all the world admires and seeks out. Such terms also described the music-hall persona of Mistinguett. In the heyday of the postwar music hall, Mistinguett personified the bustling, cosmopolitan Paris that exuberantly lived the present and showed no signs of suffering from the wounds of war.

"Oh! Maurice"

Maurice Chevalier also emerged as an embodiment of the modern on postwar stages. Before the war he had established himself as a comic singer like Dranem, a skinny, awkward, Chaplin-like figure, a ragged dandy who provoked laughter with his smooth slinking and epileptic acrobatics. The war changed him, as it changed France. Early in the war he was wounded and captured. In a German prison camp where he spent twenty-six months, he learned English from new English friends. With them he produced shows for the camp, until he managed to escape in late 1916 by posing as a Red Cross worker. He resumed his music-hall career now as the handsome debonair partner of Mistinguett. Just after the armistice while on tour in London music halls he learned an English dance style, marked by a precision and what a Parisian reviewer called a "brutal lightness." Back in Paris the new style delighted audiences. With striking ease and skill he danced the tango, the shimmy, and the fox-trot—ever a master of the latest steps. He did just enough to show off his skill and versatility and then went on to unexpected moves, switching "from classical step to parody with a brutal nonchalance."[8] While performing in England the year after the war he also picked up the habit of wearing a smoking jacket on stage. It made him a proper gentleman, up-to-date and stylishly correct in dress. In England, too, he adopted one of his trademarks: the straw boater, which for the rest of his career epitomized his leisured, playful persona. While such clothes made for a certain distinction, his strong plebeian accent and big easy smile countered any impression of putting on airs. "I have tried to appear like a man of today, without special costume, without any extreme characteristic, a man similar to all others," he explained in 1926, but he added that he "wanted to make that man, as much as possible, exceptional."[9]

He was young and handsome enough to be a leading man, a romantic figure for women and an admired model for men. His physique was fine, even athletic. In his every move he projected grace and cool sophistication. The press portrayed him admiringly as a *sportif*, a man who did a half hour of *culture physique* every day, played golf and tennis, and swam. He was also known to be a formidable boxer. Before the war, he told interviewers, he boxed daily with a former French middleweight champion. Publicity photos in the press regularly showed him practicing these sports in his private life, always smiling and enjoying himself in the same manner as his stage persona.

As a music-hall singer his performances were strongly visual, appropriately so for audiences now thoroughly accustomed to the movies. "Cinema has spoiled us: our eye no longer is content with the theater of simple conceptions that delighted our fathers," observed critic Max Viterbo in 1922. Chevalier understood well the new demands. He devised his costume, the stage set, and the lighting to suit the lyrics of each song he sang. He often surrounded himself with young women to form a series of tableaux as he performed each number. And he dramatized his songs with a virtuoso range of expressions and gestures—from the legs and hips to his lips and eyes. "A well-made song is a veritable scenario," Viterbo observed of the new style.[10]

His songs had an American sound, marked by rhythms that were lively, loose, and syncopated, but the lyrics and the tone were strictly Parisian. Alternately bantering and mocking, he performed the false delicacies of "Faut jamais dire ça aux femmes" and "Quand y a une femme dans un coin." Continuing an old tradition of popular nonsense songs, he also sang an absurd, tongue-twisting ditty "Pruneaux cuits, figues crues," which "touched off storms of laughter in the halls."[11] Old and new melded smoothly in the delivery of this disarmingly friendly man who seemed so natural in everything from his voice and popular accent to his streetwise humor.

In March 1921 Chevalier was starring in the revue *Avec le sourire* at the Casino de Paris, singing the hit by the same title—"You have to know how to take everything with a smile." The way in which Chevalier sang and spoke such lines was the

key to his popularity, maintained the critic Fréjaville. It was "his habitual roguish-
ness and this air of good-faith nonchalance which makes him so likable to the public."[12] Irony leavened the whole, keeping his romantic roles from being too serious
and his comedy from being too simple. Everything was fair game for parody—certainly the hits and conventions of the music hall. In 1921 he was quick to parody Mistinguett's "Mon Homme," for example, the hit song of the preceding revue. In the
song "Oh! Maurice" (1919) he both mocked and celebrated even himself:

> Oh! Maurice! oh! Maurice, oh! Maurice, oh!
> Tell me why your mother has made you so handsome?
> I'm not a man, I'm a bird, a bouquet, a flower, a reed [*roseau*]!
> Oh! Maurice, oh! Maurice, oh! Maurice, oh!
> All the women want my skin.
> And me—I glide along like a butterfly passing by.
> In love I'm an ace!

Repeatedly proclaiming himself an ace in love, he vowed to accept his destiny: to attract and to love women—even to the point of drowning "in floods of
love."[13] A journalist concluded in 1922, "He's the very type of the modern man
such as the war has made him," the type "who takes nothing seriously but applies
himself to what he does with a rude and smiling conscience. And then, when the job

Leading man Maurice Chevalier and his partner Yvonne Vallée performing a routine like their song
"Dit's moi M'sieur Chevalier" (the French version of "Mister Gallagher and Mister Shean")—she
the childlike questioner and he the droll, worldly respondent. Photo Waléry, *Paris Plaisirs*, August
1926. Courtesy of the Bibliothèque Forney.

is done, well done, he pirouettes on himself and sings 'In life you mustn't worry!' [*Dans la vie faut pas s'en faire!*]"[14]

With regard to women he was not entirely a modern, as his big hit (later his signature song) "Valentine" demonstrates clearly.[15] He performed it first in 1925, when recent controversies about "new women" were still at the fore of public consciousness. "Valentine" was a man's woman in very old-fashioned ways. "One always remembers his first mistress," the singer begins. Then he recounts how he met and pursued her as she walked home each evening on the rue Custine near Montmartre. The refrain enumerates her charms: her "tout petits petons" (little feet) and her "tout petits tétons" (slang for breasts) "que je tatais à tâtons [which I felt gropingly]" and her "tout petit menton" (chin) and her hair curled like a sheep [*mouton*]. She wasn't very smart, he remarks, but "in the sack [*plumard*] that's not important." At eighteen, he reminisces, he wasn't demanding. She didn't even have a good disposition: she was jealous and authoritarian, but he was crazy about her. He liked her a lot especially because (the chorus explains) "She had tout petits petons," and so on. In the last stanza he tells about something that happened just yesterday on the boulevard. He came across a large lady—with the figure of a hippopotamus—who eagerly threw herself on him and called him "mon chou." Noting her double chin and triple chest, he remarks "full of fright" on how she has changed, and then he repeats the chorus describing her appearance years before: "Elle avait de tout petits petons, / Valentine, Valentine." This patronizing, superior attitude toward his women partners became his cachet. In each act he was the one who charmed and seduced and mastered the beauty he wanted.

Chevalier displayed a strikingly nonchalant attitude toward sexuality and love, refusing to take them as pivotal life experiences that make or break happiness. In 1927 he married Yvonne Vallée, an actress, but regretted it within a few months, feeling stifled and unable to sustain interest in her. He described himself as one who does not believe in taking emotions and declarations of love so seriously as they once had been. From the war, he explained, "we have learned the vanity of words and fine pretexts." "Today we have so many diverse interests, we are solicited by so many things that, like a chameleon, we change continually. The sexual problem, consequently, has diminished in importance and is not more grave in our view than any other purely material need, and we like to forget whom we have loved without feeling any sting, without there being any impression of loss."[16] With such published bits of philosophizing and commentary on his times, Chevalier demon-

Maurice Chevalier, postwar star of the music hall, the "modern" and elegant "titi." Bibliothèque de l'Opéra.

strated that his stage persona as the winning postwar man, taking it all "with a smile," was grounded in his personal convictions.

In addition to his Paris music-hall performances, Chevalier made movies regularly from 1922 on. That year he traveled by ocean liner to America and appeared onstage in *Dédé* in New York. Fulsome publicity regularly spread news of his big earnings and his good life as well as his successes in the limelight abroad. In the mid-1920s he was known as a star who offstage always drove a new car and enjoyed an estate in the Paris suburbs and a vacation villa on the Côte d'Azur near Cannes. In 1927 he published his first memoirs, signaling his status as an established star and furthering it at the same time. He was "the incarnation, if not the symbol, of the modern young leading man, formed by boxing, the automobile, [and] jazz," wrote one reviewer in 1927.[17]

He confided to the press in 1927 that he wanted to play alternately Paris, London, and New York.[18] As the rare *faubourien* who could speak English, he could and did flourish in those great cities abroad. He recorded many of his hits of the 1920s in English and French, sometimes mixing the two, as in "Wait 'til you see ma chérie." Appearing as resourceful and unflappably good-humored as the fabled poilu, he was publicly the master débrouillard, moving with enviable ease between worlds.

In 1928, writer Louis Léon-Martin summed up the psychological process that bonded a large public to the star who was eminently "of today": "He is elegant, he likes to dress well. He has a magnificent appearance of health, a fresh complexion. . . . He is sportive, he is casual. He belongs to the times of the automobile, boxing, and rugby. On stage he is better than what we are, he is what we would like to be. Intimately, we thank him for so well representing us."[19]

In 1928 Chevalier left for America to a fanfare of publicity about his commanding the highest salary of anyone in the world. That fabulous income served as the conclusive proof of his success, and his press agents kept it before the public for years. He became the most spectacular incarnation of the myth of upward mobility during the 1920s and the one that most appealed to the mass French public. By going to fabled Hollywood, fount of the newest and most glamorous of lifestyles, Chevalier was going to modernize the image of the Frenchman in the world, sympathetic journalists reported. Urbane cosmopolitan that he was, however, he insisted to reporters that he was still "of Ménilmontant." He made a point of telling the press about going out for drinks with backstage workers from the music hall. While retaining the distinctive charms of the little man at one with his *quartier,* he was the little Parisian modernized—successful in the big new cosmopolitan world.

Black Magic: Josephine Baker

The most sensational display of the modern burst upon the Paris scene in 1925 in the city's most modern music hall, the Théâtre-Music-Hall des Champs-Elysées. Both its architecture and its performances—most notably the premiere of Stravinsky's *Rites of Spring* in 1913—had made it a temple of the modern. There in the evening of 2 October 1925, another epoch-making performance occurred in a new show from the United States. *La Revue nègre* created extraordinary excitement and the requisite level of controversy for anything daringly new to Paris, and it catapulted one young American dancer to French stardom. It was not the first African-American or jazz spectacle to have such an effect in Paris; in 1903 a black American dance called the cakewalk had made a strong impression. But the 1925 act was much more than a dance. *La Revue nègre* startled French audiences by taking the modern in several sensational directions at once.

It was both refreshingly non-French yet cleverly Parisian. *La Revue nègre* offered frenetic pacing and dancing in a style invented by Parisian impresario Jacques-Charles. He called it the "danse sauvage." The performers also danced the Charleston, then virtually unknown to Parisians. One lead dancer in particular, nineteen-year-old Josephine Baker, caught the public's attention. Her narrow head with flattened, waxed hair had an androgynous look that was also the look of the modern woman. At one point Baker wore a men's suit; at other times she appeared with only some feathers over her coffee-colored skin. Her broad smile, large rouged cheeks, and svelte figure were stunningly feminine. At times nearly nude, she moved like "a perpetual paroxysm" with strongly erotic effects.[20] To French spectators she seemed to display untrammeled instinct, an animality that they were unaccustomed to seeing onstage.

Baker's costumes and sets placed her in a variety of exotic frames of reference. Naïvely painted backdrops represented distant places both simple and ultramodern: a steamer race on the Mississippi, a skyscraper in New York, a village in Louisiana. She was a new woman, freer than Mistinguett. She was a modern yet also a "primitive," an exotic flourishing in a European hothouse, competing well even with "Miss" the *faubourien* on the latter's home turf. Her uninhibited sexuality as she danced both pleased and troubled, but its disturbing effects were mitigated by

Josephine Baker in the revue of the Folies-Bergère—the "savage" who became Parisian. Photo Waléry. *Paris Plaisirs* (August 1926). Courtesy of the Bibliothèque Forney.

the French readiness to view her as a specimen of the African savage, the Other, whose wildness could never be matched by the civilized—by French women in particular.[21]

In the decade after *La Revue nègre* Baker recorded hit songs and made movies in French. She was sexy and a romantic figure but also a comic, adept at self-parody. She became a star all across Europe. Yet she remained unpretentious and good-natured, another easygoing, big-smiling commoner. She became "French"—a French star making her home in Paris, but she remained marked by her American accent as one of the Other, someone who could not be neatly located in the French social structure. An adopted Parisian, she became another exemplar of the poverty-to-riches legend and proof of the great capital's world-inclusive, assimilationist, ever-renewing spirit. In 1930 she adopted a song that proclaimed her special bond to Paris, "J'ai deux amours," written expressly for her by leading songwriter Vincent Scotto by order of the director of the Casino de Paris. She sings that she has two loves that ravish her heart: "mon pays et Paris." With no further reference to her country she declares that it is Paris that enchants her, and "to see it one day is her beautiful dream." This became her signature song, which she recorded and which she sang again and again in concert—and when crowds of fans greeted her in the train station upon her return to the capital. Like Mistinguett, Josephine Baker identified herself with the myth of Paris that at once flattered Parisians and denied their postwar troubles in the changing city. Initially disturbing, she became another familiar, comforting star with a smile. "In Paris . . . [Josephine Baker] has been created spontaneously of the essential elements of our postwar 'disquiet,'" concluded a French reviewer in 1934. "She was born probably of a jazz band, pushed to its maximum tension—and has exorcised us of this anguish."[22]

Moderns Beyond the Cosmopolitan Centers

Beyond the expensive, cosmopolitan music halls were several venues of modern entertainment that were regularly accessible to working people. The most important was the movie theater, which offered an ever-fresh stream of comedies, adventures, and melodramas, a high proportion of which were American. For Belleville youth around the time of the war, movies took the place that the cheap local bar (*l'assommoir*) and the theater had occupied in the lives of their fathers, Eugène Dabit recalled. "Like the bistrot, like sleep and love, the cinema was part of our existence. . . . At the movies, one loses himself in the dark, one dreams as in childhood. . . . One is what fate has not let you be: lover, conqueror, criminal. All desires float up, in a collective intoxication [*griserie*]."[23]

"The movies transport . . . [the working people] into a world of riches and pleasure," Valdour observed of the laboring poor in the thirteenth arrondissement.[24] In the years from the Paris Exposition des Arts décoratifs of 1925 to the late 1920s—boom times for the well-off—a wave of movies showcased the world of cool modern art deco, sumptuous apartments, luxurious hotels and casinos and villas of the Côte d'Azur, Paris nightclubs and bars filled with the cosmopolitan rich and fashionable. Some of the more notable and commercially successful of those movies were Marcel L'Herbier's *Le Vertige* (1926) and *Le Diable au coeur* (1928), Julien Duvivier's *L'Homme à l'Hispano* (1927), Maurice Gleize's *La Madone des sleepings* (1928), and above all L'Herbier's lavishly produced *L'Argent* (1929).[25]

Critics on both Right and Left lamented that filmed display of elite lifestyles. The movies, they charged, stimulated unhealthy appetites for luxury, sybaritic sloth, and vice. The instructive influence of the screen seemed beyond doubt. From the movies young people regularly learned up-to-date ways of behavior. Bigger-than-life models taught them how to dress, talk, move, drink, and kiss. In a Belleville foundry in the early 1920s, Valdour observed of a woman worker responsible for coring molds: "the poses, her facial expression, her way of laughing, her way of presenting looks and playing her eyes are copied from the attitudes and actions of young leading movie actresses."[26] As up-to-the-minute entertainment, the movies gave the plebs almost everywhere the opportunity to see the most fashionable people of cities near and far. After sound films came to France in 1929, people throughout the country could find the latest songs, dances, and music performed in their neighborhood cinemas. There the humble of France found the most striking spectacles of modernity that Paris, Berlin, and (increasingly) Hollywood could produce.

The latest entertainment from central Paris traveled to the periphery in other forms as well. During intermission, music-hall acts filled the stage in front of the darkened screen. In the poor thirteenth arrondissement, workers packed into a vast new movie theater not just to see films but also to hear live singers, whose performances they clearly relished. Frequently a singer was billed there as "a star of the great Parisian *concerts*." At the Casino-Montparnasse in 1920 an audience comprised mostly of young workers and their wives took in the revue *Fais-Moi Shimmy* (Make me Shimmy), featuring *petites femmes* "highly made up and quite undressed."[27] In humble neighborhood halls the traditional set of songs—"tours de chant"—increasingly gave way to racy vaudevilles, operettas, and revues fashioned after the prestigious music-hall shows. Hit songs were no longer born in the café-concert. "Now it's the *caf'conc'* which takes over songs launched in the revues of the Casino de Paris and makes them known to the faubourgs," noted Fréjaville in 1921.[28] In local street fairs like the fête of Petit-Montléry, Dabit recounted, "the band played well-worn tunes [*rengaines*] made famous a year or more before in the Parisian music-halls"; "people danced under a large tent until 2 A.M., turning in a deliberately 'canaille' manner."[29] Often the music played was the foreign import known as jazz. In the wake of the war it was woven into the fabric of life of even unprivileged untraveled Parisians. There was a "jazz band everywhere," as a well-known song of 1920 put it. In the working-class quarter of Charonne, two cafés at the same intersection were featuring an "orchestra jazz band," Valdour observed in the mid-1920s.[30] Stars of screen and stage began showing up in all manner of humble venues—or, rather, their impersonators. Ordinary little circuses had their own Charlot. Imitators of Maurice Chevalier and Mistinguett found ever-receptive audiences deep in the poorer suburbs and provinces, where the people had never seen the stars themselves.

From the First World War to the Second a singer named Georgius carried to the popular halls of the faubourgs much of the same revitalization that Chevalier brought to the major music halls. He had the *bon enfant,* cocky, and bawdy spirit of the Parisian working-class kid even though he had not been born or raised in the faubourgs (his parents were bourgeois provincials living in a town sixty kilometers from Paris, Mantes-La-Jolie).[31] In the 1920s he brought the distinctively modern to faubourg stages with his troupe, *Le Théâtre chantant de Georgius.* To plebeian halls he introduced music-hall-style lights, decors, costumes, and dancers, making songs into highly visual acts, dramatic sketches with colored lights changing to match the mood of each one. Georgius modernized the café-concert, as a journalist put it in 1927.[32] His movements and songs radiated sensuality and verve. His renditions of old hits slipped into parody without warning. After giving audiences a dose of the Parisian populist genre, he would suddenly caricature it, allowing listeners to feel

"Jazz Band Partout!"—the 1920 fox-trot hit of "all the Parisian *dancings*"—proclaimed, "day and night there's a jazz band everywhere." Private collection.

Georgius, madcap comic and favorite of faubourg audiences. Private collection.

superior and to share laughs at the excesses of the popular sentimental or "realist" songs. He mixed new songs with old—some of them political, many of them re-stating the folklore of the faubourgs (to be examined in chapter 4). He was "fre-netic and riotous" (*dechaîné*), ever energetic and sportive.[33] He was "a Maurice Chevalier of our faubourgs," a reporter remarked in 1926.[34]

In the mid-twenties as he performed in some higher-class music halls, Georgius curbed the bawdiness that marked his songs as "popular." By 1928 when he took his troupe to the famous central Paris music hall the Scala, he was wearing black tails (*habit*) instead of the blue suit that he had worn for performances in the faubourgs. He even presented foreign singers and songs along with his Parisian standards.

Yet he never abandoned the plebeian audiences. Georgius often played the Européen in the Place Clichy, where Chevalier never appeared. He also made the rounds of the Théâtre des Bouffes du Nord, Folies-Belleville, the Eldorado, and the Royal-Variétés in the Faubourg Saint-Antoine. He toured the provinces, too, starring in such venues as the Alcazar Marseilles and Nice's Casino de la Jetée-

Promenade. In 1933 when writer Eugène Dabit heard Georgius perform in what had long been known as the Gaîté-Montparnasse, he described the show as "popular, rapid, Parisian." It "transported" him back in time thirty years, so old-time Parisian did it seem. Yet Georgius could not have been more up-to-date in his language: he used "the vocabulary of sports papers and popular dailies, 50-centime novels, crime reportages"—above all "the vocabulary of the people in the streets." He communicated and amused with a rapid-fire stream of "puns, obscenities, and a variety of slang"—all with an air of cheery don't-give-a-damn about troubles: "on s'en fout."[35]

In the 1930s Georgius appeared even in the remotest corners of France through the medium of film. So did fellow stars Maurice Chevalier, Mistinguett, and Josephine Baker. By way of the movies, Parisian gestures and accents, styles of singing, and knack for repartee became regular entertainment fare for ordinary people in towns all over France. Filmed versions of music-hall events brought the latest song-and-dance acts and the showiest spectacles of Paris to sleepy burgs throughout France. The movies also brought America's musical follies to provincials and Parisians alike. Although musicals did not become as predominant on the French screens as in the United States, Ziegfeld's extravaganzas played a part in widening the gap between familiar French productions and cosmopolitan modern ones. The French who went out on the town were becoming "denationalized," remarked journalist Louis Roubaud in 1928. They were losing their parochial mentalities and were subjected to "Anglo-American morals, tastes, and pleasures." Using a modern industrial term that had an ominous ring to the French, he described these changes as a process of "standardization." "By the screen, by the stadium also, by the radio, by the illustrated magazine, a soul of the denationalized spectator is being fashioned."[36]

Roubaud neglected to mention another source of cosmopolitanism: fashionable new dance halls. In the summer of 1919 the magazine *Paris qui chante* reported: "Currently it is the *One Step*, the *Two Step*, and especially the *Fox-trot* which obtain the favors of the public in the large Parisian dance halls [*bals*]." At that time it was necessary to explain: "The fox-trot is an American dance"—to "very rhythmic, gay, and cadenced music like a festive march." A couple of years later the shimmy was the exciting new dance from the United States. Almost any novelty from America appealed to those wanting to be in vogue. In early 1922 a song entitled "Kiss Me" (the words in English) appeared in *Paris qui chante*, promoted as a "New American Song and Dance." In the refrain a young "Negress" dances and

constituted an "invasion." That was the term commonly used—among a people all too familiar with aggression from abroad.

The "invaders" were a mixed lot: workers from poorer countries and tourists and expatriates from rich countries. The area around the Opéra, which well-off foreigners frequented, was scarcely French any longer, complained outspoken Parisians. But it was Montparnasse that was the "hottest" cosmopolitan quarter, a cultural crucible of immigrant artists, writers, and tourists. "Suddenly" after the war, with Scandinavians and Americans pouring in, writer André Warnod remarked, "the little cafés of Montparnasse grew like monstrous plants, devouring all around them until they became enormous and sole masters of the terrain, after having absorbed all the shops that were their neighbors."[45] In the cabaret Les Vikings, customers drank Akavit and ate red caviar sandwiches. In a Montparnasse boîte called Le College Inn in 1930, patrons sipped cocktails and socialized on the main floor and played ping-pong in the basement.[46] Expatriate British writer Sisley Huddleston called Montparnasse a "horizontal Tower of Babel," teeming with visitors and immigrants from every corner of the world. "At the Closerie des Lilas you will find mostly Poles. At the Rotonde you will find Italians, Spaniards, and Balkanics—with a sprinkling of French. At the Dôme there are Scandinavians, British, and Americans. At the Coupole, a great Munich café . . . you will find Germans and Russians."[47]

Foreign presences in Montmartre, too, evoked strong reactions. Already in 1924, in his book entitled *Coins curieux de Paris*, Charles Fegdal warned that changes underway there would end in an "assassinating cosmopolitanism, in the furor of builders of giant apartment buildings." Long notorious as an unsavory pleasure district, Montmartre held more dangers than Montparnasse and fell more under the sway of vendors of vice. Just off the *grands boulevards* the siren song began: the rue Montmartre blazed with multicolored neon lights beckoning pleasure seekers to jazzy boîtes and cabarets. Just after the war, Americans with money had flooded in. Following an economic crisis in 1920–21 the influx had picked up again with Latin Americans and the English predominating. Francis Carco recalled how "old rustic houses and arbors that made the charm of this little village so far and so near to Paris" disappeared and were replaced by nightclubs and restaurants for tourists, chiefly Americans. He recorded it as a terrible loss.[48] Illicit trades thrived: cocaine was the drug of choice, and prostitution became an instrument of the drug dealers.[49] Parisians readily linked all these evils to the foreigners, as a reviewer of Lucien Boyer's show *Montmartre en balade* did in October 1928. The revue made him fondly recall "the Montmartre of the old days, the one before the annexation by Cossacks and Negroes—in a word, the French Montmartre."[50] Nostalgia and xenophobia formed a strong compound of bitter resentment.

The resentment was laced with volatile fears, many of which came out in newspaper attacks on the dance halls. "Les dancings" proliferated in postwar Paris and were "an epidemic as dangerous as the Spanish flu," asserted journalist Adolphe Aderer in 1919. In the view of such observers the danger came from the foreign-born dancing instructors and pick-up artists who were suspected of seducing all comers and spreading drugs. The "professional dancer," who was usually from Latin America (especially Argentina), took on new importance in a society that had just lost more than a million men in war. Alarmed critics considered the professional dancer nothing but a corrupting, despoiling gigolo who contributed to the lamentable decline of marriage and motherhood. Two authors of a documented study on dancing reported that "our dancings are used conveniently by the Germans to spread another vice: the use of cocaine for the purpose of weakening and diminishing our race." The president of a large anti-alcoholism organization reported that liquor merchants also used the dancings to sell their products to youth—to the detriment particularly of young women, more of whom had become alcoholic since the war. The women, he explained, were drowning their sadness. What the editor of *La Revue française* found intolerable was that whites danced to the music of "Negroes" and to the direction of "Negro" orchestra leaders.[51]

The dances themselves were held to be pernicious in a startling number of ways. In 1920 the new archbishop of Paris condemned the latest dances as immoral, including not only the shimmy, but also the java—a plebeian syncopated waltz. Other critics deplored the new dances as a "means of more or less hypocritical sexual pleasure," or even "vertical lovemaking." Novelist Victor Margueritte maintained that girls who were fond of the "demoralizing dances" (the tango, the foxtrot, and the shimmy) were seeking "a kind of precocious and dangerous 'virginal' deflowering." Some observers warned that the dances were contributing to France's depopulation—by causing impotence and exhausting women, bringing on sterility, when not simply killing the maternal sense. A gynecologist, Dr. Pagès, enumerated more dire consequences: dancing was linked to "insomnia, wasting away and loss of appetite, circulatory troubles, dizziness, migraines, phenomena of autointoxication by over-exertion, then tics, more or less generalized spasmodic neuroses, trembling, sometimes also troubles of arterial tension, memory, speech difficulties, anomalies of salivation, indeed even sphincteral accidents, etc." The

In response to worries voiced about the new dances, Georgius, quick to mock every commonplace idea and fad, sings, "it's the tango that makes him neurasthenic" (1922). Private collection.

doctor added that the excitement contributed to "venereal abscesses," which he called "the great physical ailment [*mal*]" ravaging France. The president of the Société des Amis de la France expressed alarm in more general medical terms: the Argentine dances, he declared, were "a true sickness" attacking the social body, already debilitated by the war.[52]

"Dancings," like music halls, were the haunts of a demimonde of nouveaux riches and foreigners of dubious character. Famous foreign women including Josephine Baker and Barbara Hutton seemed to many to epitomize loose morals. So did cosmopolitan travelers like the fictional heroine of novelist Maurice Dekobra's *Madonna of the Sleepings* (1925)—a sexually liberated woman who throws herself into affairs as she travels on luxury trains across the continent.[53] The "new woman," in herself menacing enough to traditionalists, was all the more threatening in the guise of a foreigner or the accomplice of one.

After the crash of 1929 the floodtide of moneyed visitors dwindled to a trickle. And the music halls that had put big spotlights on foreigners began to disappear. But the images of "the other" remained prominent in France: more than ever before they filled the movie screens. The aura of danger did not diminish when the economy stalled and began to decline in the early thirties. Social critics recognized cinema as a source of influential foreign models, perhaps the most powerful of all sources. "Cinema today imprints life" and "imposes its 'standards' on it," observed José Germain in 1931. In particular, he noted, the movies were changing French ideals of beauty and morals. "The French woman americanizes herself to attract and provoke desire," he summed up. "She changes her hair, figure, and hemline to keep up with American fads, and she abandons demure ways of attracting men's attention; now it's no longer the man who takes the woman, it's the woman who chooses, captivates, and masters [*s'empare*] the formerly strong male." To describe the new manners taught by the silver screen, the French in the early thirties adopted an American phrase, "sex appeal," which Germain described worriedly as a new weapon in the war of the sexes.[54] During the period around 1930, too, American crime movies filled with scenes of violence and underworld vice came into vogue. A chorus of critics, particularly on the Right, immediately attacked them as baleful and a danger to French society. Thus foreigners and cosmopolites long provoked a heated debate in France. They impressed some of the French as models of energy and the new, but to others appeared to be sources of corruption and decadence. The outcries continued through the thirties, along with the widespread presence of Anglo-American culture in songs and movies.

It was not until France was defeated militarily in 1940 that a French government undertook an all-out offensive against foreign culture and a program of strictly French renewal. Before that catastrophe and change of program, those who disliked the foreign found solace in viewing some large groups of modest Parisians still solidly rooted in a distinctly French way of life. These were the "little people" of the old working-class quarters, the *faubouriens*, to whom I now turn.

4. FOLKLORE
OF THE PEOPLE'S PARIS

Ah! qu'il était beau—mon village,
Mon Paris, notre Paris
On n'y parlait qu'un seul langage
Ça suffisait pour être compris!

[Ah! it was beautiful—my village,
My Paris, our Paris
People spoke only one language there
That was enough to be understood!]
— *"Mon Paris,"* lyrics by Lucien Boyer

WHEN THE PARISIAN "little people" made appearances in the great music halls, they had to share the stage with an array of cosmopolitan acts. Their main stage was elsewhere, in quite modest venues throughout France, where they were consistently the lead characters. In old-fashioned cafés-concerts, on street corners where itinerant singers performed, and in cheap lodgings where phonographs played favorite tunes over and over, audiences composed largely of "little people" regularly heard a repertory in which the *petites gens* reigned supreme. A few types dominated the repertory: above all, the humble inhabitants of the Parisian *faubourgs*, old working-class neighborhoods just outside the central city. In most songs the leading characters were Parisian shop girls and apprentice mechanics—young women known as *midinettes* and *trottins* (young milliners, dressmakers, and errand girls) and their favorite *mécanos*. Other standard figures were pimps and prostitutes, the latter depicted either as poor girls who were victims or as bold lovers devoted to their men. Ballads about such types had become a favorite folklore of popular audiences during the late nineteenth century. The

"O, Viens ma gosse" (1921) was one of countless songs focusing on an old-fashioned working couple, young faubouriens in love, posed outside the essential local dance hall. The lyrics begin with the couple blissfully going to the nearby *fortifications* for a time of love in springtime. The ending is realist heartbreak: one evening the young woman doesn't show up because she went off with another man who offered "gros sous," and her lover becomes a wandering crazy man. Private collection.

French song industry, centered in a couple of Parisian faubourg *passages* near the *grands boulevards*, sent that Parisian folklore out to the many "consumers" of new songs in the industrial suburbs, provincial towns near and far, and the entire countryside. In spite of postwar changes in French life, France's "Tin Pan Alley" of composers and music publishers persisted in turning out its traditional staples, prudently sticking with what was known to be popular, producing variations on familiar themes.[1]

Those songs focused on the people's leisure times without mention of long, grinding workdays or cramped, miserable housing and nights of sleepless torment when hundreds of bedbugs attacked and neighbors quarreled loudly.[2] Lyrics recounted workers' strolls down the neighborhood streets, dances on Saturday nights the Parisian faubourien was a cheerful good nature—a bonhomie—which Chevalier exemplified through his career. His hit of 1921 "Avec le sourire" highlights what became his trademark: his unflagging smile was as essential to his persona as the straw boater he adopted about the same time. In the first verse the singer tells of learning from his neighbor in the stairway that his wife is deceiving him at 26, rue de la Pompe (in the chic sixteenth arrondissement). Immediately the narrator wisecracks that what his neighbor says is shameful, adding: "It's at 22!" Then he breaks into the refrain:

> You have to take everything with a smile
> And for consolation tell yourself all men are [cuckolded].
> There is no reason for me to be an exception.
> Believe me, you have to take everything with a smile
> And even with satisfaction tell oneself: between us it's flattering.
> That proves after all
> That I have a woman who is very pleasing.[5]

The main character's occupation and class position remain vague, and the wife's infidelity is presented as a universal male fate, but the attitude described is classic faubourien.

Other hit songs played a lost love for laughs by transferring the female role unexpectedly to a pet. In "Titine, je cherche après Titine" (1917), the "frivolous" female (dog) left, just as "Petit Loulou de Poméranie" did in the hit of 1925. Satirizing the romance, the narrator cries out his desperate desire for her and provides an admiring description of her all-too-human ways. Maurice Chevalier was a master of those portrayals of mock anguish, maintaining an amused nonchalance through every misadventure.

As Robert in the operetta *Dédé* (1921), Chevalier sang his public persona's philosophy in the most direct expressions: "In life no need to worry. / Me, I don't worry. / These little problems are short-term. / Everything will work out."[6]

The unflappable faubourien of popular culture was satisfied with his lot in life and with the little that he had materially. "Small" was a word of endearment, embracing the humble familiar. The song "Petit ménage" spelled it out: the narrator sings contentedly of his or her little household, little bed, and little sofa—and happily the *grand amour* that accompanies them. "The rest isn't necessary, provided that someday we have a little boy."[7]

Many songs portrayed the little people in a favorable light by graphically contrasting the humble with the rich. Mistinguett's hit of 1922 "En Douce," for example, spelled out those differences from the vantage point of a poor woman who is singing about herself.[8] Unlike the privileged, she was born on the quiet—*en douce*—without a doctor and without knowing her mother. She received her education by hard knocks, she tells us. She didn't have a single professor, but she learned from a former burglar how to pilfer bread. Some "chicks" (*poul's*) have a big wedding ceremony and luncheon, she notes, but when she gave herself to her man, there weren't any bells ringing. She "lost her flower" on the grass behind the fortifications, and no one bothered with the mayor. Finally, unlike those who have big fancy funerals after having "kicked off" (*claqués*), she will have a burial that won't stop traffic; she'll do it on the quiet (*en douce*). "No need for costly bouquets / I'd rather see, when spring comes, / A flower or two growing in my little corner on the quiet."

Another notable example is "Dans Mon Quartier," often sung by Parisys and other popular stars working the populist vein. In it the singer begins with the news that he has become rich and must move from La Villette to a better neighborhood. He finds a fine apartment in the rue La Bruyère, but the concierge tells him that neither cats nor dogs are permitted. Then the narrator sets forth the contrast: in his neighborhood "Madam', people don't give a damn about that [*on s'en fout*], / in our families there are always very nice little cats and dogs everywhere. / . . . / If they deposit some delicacies [*douceurs*], the little piles [*crottes*] bring good luck." Finally he finds a magnificent little apartment on the boulevard des Capucines and rents it for 3,000 francs. The old landlady tells him, "fine," but that he can't have many kids. He tells her that she is going too far. "In my quarter, you see Madame, / *on s'en fout, madam', on s'en fout.* / There are seven, eight, per household / And sometimes more." Finally he finds a closed-up place in a rich neighborhood. A child informs him that the place has been left by "people who took fright of the Boches and fled France." The narrator concludes: "In my quarter, you see madam', / *On s'en fout, madam', on s'en fout,* / It's not the Kronprinz and his clique who will give [*fich'ra*] us the colic. / *On s'en fout, madam', on s'en fout.*"[9]

Despite some grievances and resentments, the faubourien depicted in most songs was peaceable and easy to get along with. His social superiors could laugh and take comfort in his casual acceptance of whatever happened. With his nonchalance and surprising humor the faubourien was a model of a "little man" who has little or no control over events but takes well whatever comes. He lives philosoph-ically with an attitude of resignation.

He was tough in adversity and ever resourceful. The song of 1923 "Viva Mussolini" made the point by describing the débrouillard ways of a Frenchman vis-iting Italy. Upon arrival, the narrator tells us, he sought a room in a hotel and was told that there was none available. Thereupon the narrator relates having sung: "Viva Mussolini, he's the greatest man there is in Rome! / Bring the Chianti, we'll drink to his health!" Immediately the hotel keeper said with a confidential air: "You'll sleep in my bed / Viva Mussolini!" In a restaurant in Florence, the waiter served raviolis without meat inside; when the customer complained, the waiter told him to go elsewhere if he didn't like it. Then the visitor began humming "Viva Mus-solini!" and immediately the waiter brought what the customer wanted. In the third verse the narrator tells of making the conquest of a brunette in Naples when sud-denly her jealous husband appeared, armed with a big knife. The visitor then be-gan to cry out (of course) "Viva Mussolini!" The husband then embraced him and offered him a room. Celebrating the cleverness of the Frenchman while mocking the Fascists went over well with Paris audiences. The popular singer Perchicot made "Viva Mussolini!" one of his standard numbers.[10]

The world of the populo was one of familiar everyday life in the modest, long-established neighborhood. The quartier was home and village to the "little people," the center of their existence from which they rarely traveled far. Within that world they were secure and confident. Some of the poorest and most visible people of each quarter were those who spent most of their time in the streets. Most songs about the populo focused on a cast of such characters—the *filles* and *voyous* of Aristide Bruant's songs, the prostitute who had her sidewalk and her pimp not far away, the newspaper boy his corner, and the workers their bistros and work-shops. Geographically, linguistically, and socially, these people enjoyed a special community, a subculture resistant to international influences so conspicuously shaping the culture of the well-to-do.

Postwar Memory of Prewar Paris

Much of that world of artisans and midinettes in old settled neighborhoods was dis-appearing in postwar France. Crafts continued their long decline as production in factories, greater division of labor, and mechanization advanced. Although artisans as a whole continued to be numerous and some trades flourished (bakers and hair-dressers were actually increasing in number), other important trades went into decline. The number of dressmakers, tailors, and blacksmiths diminished, and so did the total number of apprentices.[11] In short, the times provided no basis for any sense of security among the little people, songs to the contrary notwithstanding. In the face of these changes and brutal challenges to old ways of life, the populist songs kept alive a sense of tradition. The mythology contained in the songs presented images of stability—stoic continuation of old work rites, social exchanges, and pleasures. Light songs about the little people entertained with colorful scenes of ordinary life, leaving out the daily grind, depicting old character types largely at leisure where changes were smallest—in the streets, dance halls, or Sunday outings to woods and riverbanks. That stable world was utopian—desired and ideal. To the well-off, those songs offered reassuring images of good-natured, content, peaceful *petit peuple*—a relief from news of worker militancy and anger over inflation and high prices. The common people, for their part, found a flattering self-image in lyrics about iconic types of *le bon peuple*, lead characters in pleasantly romantic fables.

Populist songs served up vignettes of a prewar life that was morally uncomplicated, full of simple enjoyments, and emotionally satisfying. Alibert's song "En Suivant la Retraite aux flambeaux" (Following the torchlight parade), like many others, appealed to nostalgia for the supposedly simpler life before 1914. When Alibert performed it in January 1926 at the Olympia, it was not just the song that played on nostalgia; it was also the singer himself, as reviewer Fréjaville noted: "The jovial youth of the artist, his light sincerity, his faubourien *gentillesse* [niceness] which knows how to avoid being *canaille* revives for us naive forms of feeling and honest pleasures whose good-natured simplicity seems lost today."[12] Fondness for those "naive forms of feeling" helped make a hit of the sad plea for loving words, "Parlez-Moi d'Amour," that Lucienne Boyer first sang in 1929 and recorded in 1930. Rejecting the cool, fast ways of the 1920s moderns (the song is set to a slow waltz), she asks her lover to speak of love and say "tender things" to her, but she also tells him that she does not believe any of his love talk. "Being a little crazy" is "so sweet," she explains. "Life is too bitter if one doesn't believe in chimeras." Through the heart she attempts to "heal [her] wound" and attempts to find consolation in a kiss. "In spite of" herself, she admits, she wants to believe in the old words and feelings.[13]

The most explicit and resounding lament for bygone days was the 1925 hit song "Où est-il donc?" The song begins by disparaging all talk of "magnificent America." At the end of a day in New York, the narrator predicts, the French visitor will be hungry and broke in the midst of "tramps [*gueus's*], outcasts, / immigrants with bruised hearts"—and, missing Paris, will think the following thoughts (the chorus):

> Where is my Moulin d'la plac' Blanche,
> My tobacco shop and my corner bistro,
> Everyday was Sunday for me there,
> Where are my friends, my buddies [copains]?
> Where are all my old bal musettes [with]
> Their javas played on an accordion?
> Where are all my meals that didn't cost a fortune,
> With a cornet of fries for ten centimes [ronds]
> So where are they?

The second verse tells of Montmartre seeming to disappear as old houses are torn down to make way for big bank buildings. "While mourning the old days / We'll sing... Montmartre, your 'De Profondis.'"[14] Georgel and Fréhel popularized this humble elegy and performed it for years.

In their homes, a large nostalgic public nourished memories by endlessly playing phonograph records of the old songs. People sang along, as they knew the words by heart.[15] Out on the town such enthusiasts found the old-fashioned singers and songs in some music halls and caf's-conc's, but not many. In 1924 Aristide Bruant enjoyed a comeback, singing his old hits at the Empire, but he died several months later. Aside from a couple of large Parisian music halls, generally small caf's-conc's catered to audiences' fondness for prewar numbers. After the war such establishments still had a turn-of-the-century air about them. Cafés-concerts were regularly going under, failing in the competition with movie-houses and music halls. Those that survived lived on in the faubourgs—concerts de quartier they were called—and in the provinces. The prewar venues could be found best preserved in the back streets of port towns: the Concert Alexandre in Saint Malo, the Bijou Concert in La Rochelle, Le Petit Casino in Lorient. In contrast to the international atmosphere of the Parisian music halls, these venues were entirely French—the performers, the audience, and certainly the language. Entertainers there either dated from before the war or were younger singers who imitated the old-time stars. The songs performed were old ones or variants, about traditional types—artisans, pimps and prostitutes, wholesome midinettes and honest apprentices—familiar to everyone, whether known primarily from life or from entertainment. These were the icons of a familiar, safe past.

The Poor and the Broken

Though resourceful and tough, some of the little people, of course, were desperately poor, and some suffered disastrous bad luck. Their misfortunes and tragedies formed the narratives of hundreds of *chansons réalistes* and *chansons vécues* (lived). In the tradition of fin-de-siècle cabaret singer Aristide Bruant, such songs told of lives undone by drugs, poverty, and faithless lovers. "Plaisir qui tue" (1915), for example, is about a twenty-year-old female worker (*ouvrière*) who seeks forgetfulness with Gypsies in Montmartre, takes ether and *coco,* and is found drunk and dying. A song entitled "Le Marchand de cocaïne" (granted a police visa on 9 December 1915) tells of the same ruin befalling victims in Montmartre and the Latin Quarter.[16] "L'Hirondelle du faubourg" (1917) relates the story of a "poor *fille d'amour*" who is in the hospital, weak from knife wounds; she takes a turn for the worse, develops a fever, and dies. In the final verse an attending doctor sadly tells his story: he so desperately tried to save her life because he had loved her mother and was in fact the girl's father. With similar effect the song "Fleur de misère" recounts the short life of an abandoned girl who was raised by Bohemians and was beaten by them. She became a dancer at fairs and eventually married a clown, but she did not live long. At her grave the mournful clown ends the story with the sad fatalist conclusion: "Happiness on earth is not made for the poor."[17]

During the war, songs about the poor were censored (as "La Misère" was in 1915, for example) if they played to resentment of the rich or the bosses, but a story of heartbreak without social accusations was quite acceptable.[18] Stories of this kind, old favorites in France, probably took on more than their customary emotional charge during the war years. To some extent, no doubt, those tales of the luckless and of death, featuring traditional figures of pity, also expressed grief from battlefield losses during a time when grief was not yet fully acknowledged or vented in public ritual.

Dressed in black, with dark circles around her eyes and expressions of pain and grief, Damia was the "sonorous and magnificent interpreter of the perpetual song of death," wrote critic Legrand-Chabrier in *La Presse*. Like a Cassandra of postwar Paris, she told her audiences "in every tone: Brother, you have to die." By addressing fate in her lyrical and direct way she offered her listeners the consolation of confronting their fears in sympathetic aesthetic forms. After the war Damia made a hit of the song "Dans les Fortifs," which evoked a poignant and colorful poverty on the margins of Paris. The narrator recounts her infancy: an abandoned child found by old people on the edge of town—the "barrier"—she grew up wild and without fear. At sixteen the handsome Julot took interest in her and proposed

Stereotypical patrons of a *bal musette*. Drawings by J. Bonnotte. *Paris Plaisirs*, September 1926. Courtesy of the Bibliothèque Forney.

Residents of "the zone" just outside Paris—the poor, Gypsies, and migrants—with their tents and trailers, ca. 1920. Songs told of the *fortifications* and undeveloped lands beyond—"la zone"—as playgrounds for faubourien lovers and colorful criminals, passing over prosaic reality. *Le Journal.*

Turcy sang some of Pierre MacOrlan's songs in a major Parisian music hall, MacOrlan himself noted the audience's keen appreciation of the slang of pimps. He also sensed that people savored the irony of a strong morality existing in such a notoriously immoral world.[27] While moral in their way, the pègre also demonstrated a flair for pragmatic ways of coping, a capacity for débrouillage, important to the many trying to survive. Altogether, those stories of strong characters living beyond the bourgeois pale made for piquant melodrama.

In working-class quarters the pimps, prostitutes, and petty criminals were part of the everyday scene. Yet like the world of the good "little people," some of the low-life world was disappearing. Right after the war, the fortifs were razed, and the marginal people living in shanties nearby were dispersed. Dark and sordid dives frequented by the "dangerous classes" took on a brighter, cleaner look with the installation of new electric lights and well-nickeled bars. The shady habitués of such places spoke less in their distinctive slang and dressed more like those in the mainstream world. Montmartre, too, was no longer what it had been in the heyday of Bruant. The old picturesque argot of Bruant's songs was gone, and so was the colorful dress of the apaches—the three-cornered cap (*casquettes à pont*), the curl of hair near the ears (*guiches*), and the chaplinesque moustache under the nose (*les crottes sous le nez*).[28] But the folklore lived on, savored by listeners who knew that its stylized characters inhabited a quickly receding past.

Georgius—the bantering, cocky, ebullient Parisian. In "Eh! Dis! Mimi tu t'rends compte!" (1925) he tells Mimi repeatedly to realize how great he is. Characteristically, the last verse tells about a time on a Paris boulevard when he was doing what the Manneken Pis does in Brussels. A police dog, he recounts, came along and with steel jaws "cut off [the singer's] . . . desire to sing." Private collection.

to remark on "the smell of an old rancor that was too obvious." And he made fun of the "social songs" of the Socialist militant Montéhus. In October 1929 he performed a sketch entitled "Cinq Minutes chez les Juifs"; its details have not been left in the records, but one can surmise from Georgius's work as a whole that it was a play on stereotypes and prejudice. In the early 1930s he went on creating new songs lampooning politicians, snobs, rude wedding night initiations and their homosexual analogues ("Imprudente"—ca. 1932, one of his most frequently performed), and nostalgia for the belle époque.[31]

With his strong Parisian accent and *titi* manner, this master showman who was a native of the provinces became a leading representation of Parisian spirit and wit. Reviewers acclaimed him as "le grand comique Parisien" and "ce chanteur

populaire de Paname." To some he was even "our *grand comique national.*"
Georgius skillfully exploited so much that was perceived to be distinctly French
that his songs were hailed by critics throughout the 1920s as a sign that the traditional French popular song was not dying. Assuming the role of defender of the
French song, he played to his audiences' critical sense of what was French and what
was the Other offstage, too. In the early twenties he organized and led a "Union in-
dépendante" of café-concert singers in a campaign of opposition to German performers (and indeed to all foreign acts, except Belgian ones). This "counteroffensive of the caf'-conc'," as reviewer Fréjaville termed it, was a struggle to stem the
tide of exoticism and cosmopolitanism engulfing the music halls and even threatening the more distinctively French venue of songs, the caf'-conc'. His songs were
like *images d'Epinal* of the old caf'-conc', noted Legrand-Chabrier. In short,
through his colorful dramatizations Georgius kept alive songs of the pre-1914 era
and new ones continuing the tradition that reviewers characterized as the "folklore
of the faubourgs."[32]

The populist genre readily played to xenophobia and nationalist pride.
Georgius responded to the crisis of the franc and cabinet instability in 1926 with
"the new popular cry" of "Attache-toi . . . il y a du vent!" Georgius' lyrics remark
that the French people's "legendary gaiety" in stormy times often surprises foreigners. "The alien residents [*métèques*] who lie in wait for us remain flabber-
gasted!" Georgius exclaims coolly, "Hold on tight, there's some wind!" suggesting
that no more serious reaction is appropriate for the French. Things will work out;
France will return to normality, and people will once more say, "Tout va bien!" In
the proverbial manner the crisis will end with a light song, he adds, "for to make
jokes about oneself is truly French!" A similar mix of feelings about the French and
the others appeared in some sentimental populist songs. The singer Perchicot's performance of "Mon Paris" in 1926 is worth another look in this context of Parisian
folklore. Perchicot, the well-informed Fréjaville remarked, was a type that had become rare: the true popular singer—that is, someone who spoke to and appealed
most to the Parisian little people. He sang such old hits as "Dans la Rue" and "Le
Couronnement de la Rosière," along with new ones about the common people. In
the nostalgic verses of "Mon Paris" the clichés describing the prewar city could
hardly be warmer or softer: "my Paris" used to be beautiful, it was like a village, and
a Parisian "cultivated his garden . . . or the wife of his neighbor." "People had contented hearts / And when spring came again / Everyone was a twenty-year-old!
/ Ah! it was beautiful—my village, my Paris, our Paris!" The sharp edge of pop-

ulism came to the surface only occasionally, as in the line evoking a lost paradise that was strictly French-speaking: "People spoke only a single language, / That was enough to be understood!"[33] The strains of "Mon Paris" did not fade quickly; the song was performed for years not only by Perchicot but also by other leading singers, including Jane Pierly, Alibert, and Maurice Chevalier.

A distinctly female perspective came out in Mistinguett's hit "Gosse de Paris" (1929). The singer tells us that when she walks around Paris, foreign men— an Englishman, a Spaniard, a German, "a rich Brazilian"—call to her and make their propositions in heavy accents. To their offers of luxurious gifts she simply responds: "I was born in the Faubourg St. Denis / And I've stayed a true *goss'* [kid] *de Paris*." As a real Parisienne she knows how to adorn herself with almost nothing (*un petit rien*). She adds that she doesn't hear any marriage proposals from the for-

In Mistinguett's hit of the late 1920s "Gosse de Paris," or "I was born in the Faubourg St.-Denis," boasts the simple, resourceful Parisienne who knows how to deal with foreign men. Private collection.

Street musicians playing and selling songs to an ideal(ized) audience, one fully participating and socially diverse but united in singing, 1926. Composer F. L. Bénech and lyricist Ernest Dumont were prolific specialists in sentimental populist songs. Private collection.

eigners. As a "gosse de Paris" she will give her heart only for love—not to deceitful and corrupting foreigners, but to a "simple and honest" (hometown) man who offers her violets just to make her happy. The song ends by proclaiming a flattering fiction: "the *p'tits goss's* of Paris will not sell themselves."[34]

The idealizing nostalgia and the resentment expressed in such songs were not simply reactions to the weak franc and to the multitude of foreign tourists in 1926–27. They also stemmed from longer-term population changes. During the decade after the war cities and industrial areas were absorbing a massive wave of foreign workers and newcomers from the countryside (85 percent of the small towns and villages were losing population). Foreigners grew conspicuously numerous not only in the chic places of Paris but also in working-class quarters like Belleville, which before the war had been the preserve of old-stock French workers. Most of those workers were strictly Parisian; they considered themselves comrades, and their memories went back to the time of the Commune (1871). Since 1914, however, foreigners moved in and changed the character of the neighborhoods—for the worse, in the view of native Parisians. Since the war, "foreigners have come to settle there [Belleville]," Dabit remarked of his former quarter, "not country people, but Jews, Poles, Algerians, and their gangs ended up giving this place its sinister character."[35] Growing numbers of immigrant workers were a troubling presence for several reasons. Conservative workers like Valdour feared for their jobs, resented the new competition in labor, and took alarm at the danger of "Reds" gaining strength. The foreign poor and "dangerous classes" did not fascinate the public and evoke the mixture of admiration and fear that the old apaches had.

By the end of the 1920s, the apaches had become passé for the public, but more up-to-date forms of low-life continued to fascinate. Toward the end of the decade a fresh stream of books took the reading public further into the world of the less than respectable. In the style of popular journalism, novelist Guy de Téramond described the shady world of fashionable dance halls in his *Les Bas-fonds: Dancings!* and the brothers Tharaud gave detailed accounts of diverse low-life milieus in their *romans documentaires*. Novels about the old-fashioned lower depths also attracted a following and sold well (for example, Thierry Sandre's *Mousseline* and Edmonde Bernard's *Agnès, Bouboule et quelques autres* [1929]).

Stories about the good ordinary people flourished at the same time. Literary populism found manifesto-issuing champions in Léon Lemonnier and André Thérive, who urged fellow writers to turn from the *beau monde* and to depict the "little people." Attacking literary pretentiousness and cosmopolitanism, they called for an end to snobbism, bourgeois preoccupations, and elite settings.[36] Their kind of work was Eugène Dabit's bittersweet story about his own parents and the cheap hotel they ran and the hard, often disappointing lives of the people who found lodging there: Dabit's *L'Hôtel du Nord* appeared in December 1929. The caring couple running the hotel, like the changing cast of unfortunate young maids and the uncaring tenants in the small rooms, made do with the little that life dealt them. They were the kind of French people whom admiring foreigners like Ford Madox Ford saw as a model of "how to be happy": "people intensely individualistic who intend to remain intensely individualistic; . . . small shopkeepers who intend to remain and only to deal with small shopkeepers; . . . people with adequate means of living who intend to retain adequate means of living but to leave it at that; . . . a people of some culture who get enough pleasure out of their culture to remain a people of some culture."[37]

Old-Fashioned Parisians and the (Singing) Talkies

By the late 1920s, then, populism was a budding literary movement, but one in danger of becoming quaintly irrelevant to the life of a majority of the French. Then the Depression lowered economic expectations, giving stories of the "little people" new relevance. It also brought new vitality to the places of amusement frequented by the humble. As the economic crisis made itself felt and big spenders began to falter, the glitzy entertainments suffered most. The expensive music halls were the first to show the effects of the downturn. In late 1929 the Olympia, Paris' first "music hall" back in the 1890s, was converted to a cinema. In May 1930 Fréjaville reported that another great "music-hall de variétés," the Empire, was threatened by "the disturbing invasion of the talking cinema," and in 1931 it became one. So had the Moulin Rouge in May 1930. Meanwhile, low-budget entertainments flourished at neighborhood movie-houses, street fairs and traveling carnivals (*fêtes foraines*), and inexpensive dance halls.

With the 1920s-style music hall in crisis, new attempts were made to revive the turn-of-the-century programs of strictly French song entertainment, the café-concert. Already in 1927 concerts of belle-époque songs reappeared at the Olympia, Scala, Eldorado, and Parisiana. Of the larger halls, the Européen did the best at keeping alive old-fashioned *caf'-conc'* performances. *Etablissements de quartier* also kept up traditions.[38] Halls like the Bobino, the Petit Casino, the Eden were the places where nostalgia for prewar Paris, a seemingly less troubled period, found sustenance around 1930. They were scattered, increasingly rare memory sites where some of the fabled modest Parisians seemed to be ever-present—both onstage and in the galleries.

In the movies, scenes of that humble life showed up in the 1930s more than ever before. Cinema producers in the 1920s had worked the other extreme, bringing moviegoers many narratives that were remote from the humble. Spectaculars about historically distant heroes included Abel Gance's three-hour *Napoléon* (1927) and Carl Dreyer's *Joan of Arc* (1928). And there were, as noted in the previous chapter, many scenarios about the rich and their luxurious lives, movies that by the end of the decade no longer enjoyed fashionable novelty. Early in 1930 critic Louis Le Sidaner wrote that "audiences are beginning to be tired of these advantaged and richly adorned princes toward whom women throw themselves like flies around a lamp; they are also tired of these cabarets in which grave men, encircled by paper ribbons and seated at tables before an open bottle, nonchalantly toss a golden glass in the direction of a sleeping woman friend, [who is] as drunk as [she is] décolletée."[39]

The new populism was also a response to a flood of foreign culture. Producers, directors, and audiences were ready for alternatives to American comedies, westerns, and gangster films. Spurred by stiff competition from abroad, French moviemakers turned with tenderness to stories of the Parisian humble people, including la pègre. Those characters were distinctively French, and so was the setting of their dramas, in addition to being close to the largest part of the audiences. In the wake of singers and writers, filmmakers like René Clair began presenting sympathetic images of the "little people" around 1930.

A favored figure in such films was the popular singer, particularly the itinerant street singer, the *chanteur de la rue*. On screen as on the street corner, he was a comforting link with a past of simple pleasures and intimate neighborhoods. Now the talkies made it possible for the singer to sing to movie audiences and to be a part of the filmed gatherings of neighbors on a street corner. The singer of the people became a frequent leading film character. In one of the earliest French talkies, *La Route est belle* (1929), a humble singer played by André Bauge becomes a star and wins the love of a rich woman. In *La Chanson de Paris* (the American title was *Innocents of Paris*) (1929) Maurice Chevalier played a flea-market dealer who sings; he has an opportunity to be a star but in the end gives up his show-business career with all its temptations to please the woman he loves. This film aroused great interest because it was Maurice Chevalier's first feature film for Paramount, as well as one of the first sound movies in French: it premiered in Paris in July 1929, only six months after the epoch-making talkie *The Jazz Singer* came to France. For the French version Paramount added a prologue delivered by Chevalier in his own persona as a popular singer of Paris. Speaking from Hollywood, Chevalier warmly assured his fellow Parisians that he was still a "little guy" from Ménilmontant—a *gars du faubourg*—who missed his hometown very much.

A singer for the common people was also the hero in René Clair's first talkie, *Sous les Toits de Paris,* which came to Paris movie theaters in the spring of 1930. All of the characters featured were Parisian "little people." The sympathetic protagonist was a street singer named Albert, who lives and performs in a humble faubourg on the hilly north edge of the city where the entire story takes place. The atmosphere of that old-fashioned corner of Paris became a character, reinforcing the spirit of its inhabitants. The tall, close buildings lining narrow, quiet streets sheltered layer upon layer of families, their lives joined by common roofs and stairways,

In René Clair's *Sous les Toits de Paris* (1930) the neighborhood gathers in the street and on balconies to hear the itinerant singer's love song about Nini, a twenty-year-old in springtime (of course)—a scene of social harmony soon marred by a few delinquents. Courtesy of BFI Stills, Posters, and Designs.

streets and cafés. It was a comfortable, small-scale environment in which people came together naturally, singing on a corner like a church choir, passing each other on daily rounds, and dancing together in the well-lighted local *bal*. The story was about a young woman from Romania, Pola, a "little *poule* [who] is wooed by a pimp" (*barbeau*), and who is "protected by a street singer," as the reviewer for *Le Crapouillot* recounted. "Finally, it's a third thief, a street hustler, who gets her." The film took spectators into "a whole world of young men in caps and young women in long hair and silk stockings" and into "the poetic and tender atmosphere of small *bals musettes,* of small bistros, of popular quarters."[40] In the end the two friends, each of whom wanted Pola for himself, accept her decision and maintain their friendship. Albert, the good guy who does not win, goes back to his street singing.

However tender much of the story was, there were enough shady characters, robberies, and fights to disturb nervous conservatives. One such reviewer inveighed against what he considered the film's "repugnant population" of streetwalkers (*pierreuses*) and apaches. The leading lady, pursued by three men and encouraging to all three at times, was deemed by another critic to be "a future *belle de nuit*." The more common view, however, appears to be that the movie was a picturesque evocation of the little people of Paris, "a true slice of life, rendered simply, humanly," as the critic for *Paris-Soir* put it. Further, it stood out favorably as a "one-hundred-per cent-French talking and singing film," as the advertising boasted. Its tenderness and charm brought relief from "mechanical comedies, ill-mannered businessmen, cowboys, gangsters and the eternal vulgar detective chomping his cigar," declared *Comoedia*'s reviewer. *Le Crapouillot*'s critic Jean Oberlé called it "the best film of the month," noting that it was rare that such a distinction could be given to a French film. He also judged it the best French sound movie to that time, a judgment that audiences evidently shared.[41]

That same year Dimitri Kirsanoff's *Ménilmontant* gave a more somber

René Clair's film *14 juillet* made popular the old-fashioned waltz, "A Paris dans chaque faubourg," illustrated here with a street scene of the Paris dear to the populists—Montmartre, its steep hill and stairs, and a woman dreamily gazing from her window one quiet spring evening. Private collection.

view of the faubourgs, dwelling on the poverty and difficulties of life there. While it pleased better-off audiences, it was booed in the cinemas of the popular quarters, Louis Le Sidaner reported. "The crowd of workers, merchants and petits bourgeois," he observed, prefer *Minuit, Place Pigalle*—a story set in a main crossroads of glamorous and criminal night life. The plebeians preferred the showy life and glitzy places to the mundane. Only Charlie Chaplin had succeeded in making populist films that reached the masses, he observed, and Chaplin did it by being "genial" and comic, showing the disinherited people's "timid desires, always unsatisfied," and "their ferocious resignation" in the end.[42]

After making the satirical and not enthusiastically received *A Nous la liberté* (1931) (a musical fable about industrial regimentation), René Clair returned to the populist genre with a light touch, though not in the comic way of Chaplin. Clair's film *14 juillet*, which appeared in late 1932, was set in the same old-fashioned faubourgs featured in *Sous les Toits* with quintessentially Parisian characters. It was the love story of a taxi driver and a florist, with complications from villains who were local petty thieves, not effective gangsters. The French public flocked to the film, and it was a hit in foreign capitals as well. Critic François Ribadeau Dumas explained Clair's appeal by declaring that the director was "of his time" and knew how to "look at life." That time was one "of transition, of waiting in view of signs and anxieties," and French life then was typically "resigned, smiling, weak and often laughable."[43] Others were most struck by a feeling that Clair was not depicting the present at all. Increasingly critics expressed unease with the falseness, the anachronism, of his representations.

Mass audiences, siding with the positive reviewers, were willing to indulge in the fictionalizing. In the face of the American successes and growing economic worries, images of the "little" Frenchman's grit and coping had great appeal. The new technology of sound made movies even more enticing: French audiences now heard the faubourien-accented conversations of sympathetic French characters in French settings and the singing of a Parisian chanteur de la rue. So at the movies millions of people entered into stories of French "little people" sharing everyday sociability and festive highs in their close, old-fashioned neighborhoods—homegrown dramas that concluded with familiar, manageable arrangements of imperfect life instead of the too-neat "happy ending" of Hollywood.

As the Depression deepened, it became ever clearer that the soft images of popular life were backward-looking and anachronistic. In the early 1930s up-to-date criminals and other low-life characters gained new prominence in films, magazines, and popular novels (those of Georges Simenon, for example). "The crime and detective film [*policier*] seems to know its golden age in Europe at a moment when America, after having given it a lightning start, tires of it and abandons it," declared Paul Bringuier in 1932.[44] Crime and detective stories strengthened their hold on a large public that had enjoyed the movie *Fantômas* and the silent-movie serial *Mystères de New York* two decades earlier. American movies like *Underworld* (*Nuits de Chicago*) enjoyed so much success that it seemed doubtful that the French could compete. How could they? France lacked organized gangs, bootleggers, and gun-toting hoods driving around in big luxury cars. Individualism reigned in France's criminal world, movie critics pointed out. In 1932, nonetheless, a series of well-crafted new French policiers appeared, featuring ordinary but likable police officers and outlaws and plots that were logical but not too simple. They included Jean Renoir's *Nuits du carrefour*, Jean Tarride's *Chien jaune*, and Maurice Tourneur's *Au Nom de la loi*, which the magazine *Pour Vous* declared in 1932 "the first great French film policier."[45] The contrast with René Clair's scenarios was stark. Whereas the populist genre was sentimental and ultimately utopian, those crime and police movies made the most of the ominous and disturbing elements in city life. The policier dramatized fears and anxieties, expressing them in tales of distressing mysteries involving bloodshed and murder. It dealt with dangerous conflict, which populism muted and showed handily resolved.

Both populist works and the policiers assumed an ultimately stable order, and that assumption was increasingly false. To some in 1933 it was unacceptable. In October of that year Eugène Dabit wrote warmly in his journal about the appeal of the old-fashioned songs still heard in faubourg halls and still so vivaciously performed by Georgius. Those acts radiated a bygone freshness and innocence, the spirit of another time. Yet the critic lashed out at the lure of such daydreams. It was time to face current realities, he insisted: "The illusion must end—people must know that we are in 1933, with Montparnasse and *boîtes de nuit* nearby, and war and revolution or fascism before us. Life is not easy, sure, slow, and men [are] ever more beastly to each other, and more sick in their joys or their hatreds."[46]

Dabit, the author of *Hôtel du Nord*, understood the charms of nostalgia as well as anyone, and he perceived the dangers of the present just as clearly. But his protest, timely though it was, simply updated a position that had been part of an ongoing cultural debate for years. The disagreement went on through the rest of the 1930s. For some, populism provided consoling icons and myths; for others (on the Right and Left), it was no longer satisfying or appropriate to the troubled thirties, and it was morally suspect. With the deepening of the Depression more up-to-date myths and heroes emerged (they are the subjects of the next two chapters). Yet alongside them the old-fashioned fare continued to appear in song, literature, and film. Populist images, belittled and denounced regularly in the press, remained appealing to many.

5. HEROES
FOR HARD TIMES

Notre époque est dure, violente, sans beauté.
[Our time is hard, violent, without beauty.]
—*Eugène Dabit*, Faubourgs de Paris *(1933)*

Tout va bien, tout va bien
Qu'on se la dise
Tout va bien.
Ne pensons plus à la crise.
Si nous savons la prendre avec gaîté,
Ce n'est plus qu'une cris' d'hilarité.

[Everything's fine, everything's fine
Let's say it
Everything's fine.
Let's no longer think of the crisis.
If we know how to take it with good humor,
It's no more than a laughing fit.]
"Tout va bien" (1933), lyrics by Jean Boyer

THE YEARS FROM THE CRASH of 1929 to Hitler's takeover in Germany in 1933 brought new threats to France and a special set of difficulties to French show business. The luxurious music halls began to falter, and foreign sound movies made successful forays into France, even before the nation's political and economic fortunes deteriorated. When the national economic decline became more widespread, the music halls and French cinema went into crisis. Most alarming were the travails of the movie industry, once a world leader and long a source of national pride. Several years before the Depression hit hard, the introduction of the talkies began to force French film producers and cinema owners to make huge investments in new equipment and pay steep royalties to the American and German companies that had developed sound technology. And French producers had to compete with such foreign giants as Paramount in the United States and Tobis in Germany, which were rapidly turning out French-language versions of their own films (or, after 1932, simply dubbing them). Since France's movie industry was weaker than its competitors to begin with, and since the market for French-language films was relatively small, the foreign threat seemed grave indeed. After 1933, production of French films fell off, receipts dipped, and a long-standing increase of spectators ended, while France's competitors enjoyed continuing audience growth. At the same time French cinema producers were battling with their own government over high taxes and censorship. Production companies incurred mounting deficits, and bankruptcy rates rose steeply. By 1936 and 1938, France's biggest movie companies met financial doom, although film production and receipts were showing some recovery. The bankruptcy of such giant old firms as Pathé and Gaumont sent new shock waves through a country already shaken by a general economic downturn and dismaying financial scandals.[1]

That series of problems forms the background to several questions that I address in this chapter, questions about how the French responded to the troubles and challenges of the Depression years. How did French moviemakers and the culture industry portray the nation's problems and the people's difficulties? What ways of responding, what stories and heroes did they highlight? And which ones had strong, broad appeal?

The initial French response to the Great Depression was to insist that the worldwide economic problems would not seriously afflict France. For the first two years after the crash, French economic and political leaders contended that their nation was, fortunately, different from the countries that had been hard hit. They assured themselves that unemployment would not be so widespread as in the more industrialized countries. The still large farming population would continue to be productive, and the colonies would come to the rescue of the motherland. Not all of this was simply wishful thinking, for the Depression was indeed late coming to France. It was not until 1931 that a business slowdown and unemployment began to assume alarming proportions. Even then, French leaders preferred to believe that their country's situation was different. In 1931 an opportune giant Colonial Exposition in Paris imparted to visitors a reassuring sense of the great varied resources of the empire.

Comforted by such views, most people tried to pursue their familiar pleasures as before the crash. Sumptuous music halls and costly theaters, however, encountered serious financial difficulties. Part of the reason was that the well-to-do French were shifting their patronage to less showy, more intimate places: cabarets and *boîtes à danse et à champagne*. But a larger part of the problem was due to the sharp decrease in the number of foreign tourists (from a high in 1929 of 1,910,000 to only 390,000 in 1935). The French masses, for their part, remained faithful patrons of the movie theaters, and there they came to know America's cultural re-

and tobacco." Phonograph records about such subjects, he explained, "represent all that we lack . . . all that is being taken away from the picturesque, nicely vulgar nature of the streets of Parisian faubourgs."[5] The unmistakably strong demand was more than the nostalgia for prewar ways of life discussed in the preceding chapter. The beleaguered nation was turning inward culturally. Audiences and reviewers alike showed new enthusiasm for songs and films about the French people—in French.

Nationalist concern and pride were all too often accompanied by rejection of the "other." As the economy declined, immigrant workers were laid off first and in large numbers (in industrialized departments, an estimated one-third of them).[6] At the same time "outsiders" came under attack for causing the movie industry's troubles. Writer Paul Morand developed such an indictment at length in a book entitled *France la doulce* (1934), which specifically targeted not the Americans, but the "pègre" of Jewish immigrants from Central Europe, especially from Nazi Germany.[7] "The riffraff" (*la racaille*), he charged, was dominating much of the movie industry and spoiling it. Views of this kind were shared widely enough to yield important political consequences in the years that followed. On the one hand, hostility toward a cabal of sinister "big guys" contributed to the political currents leading to the Popular Front; on the other, xenophobic nationalism and anti-Semitism went on to become themes of the Vichy regime.

Far from glitzy shows and political battles, crowds of Depression-era spectators follow the performances of old-fashioned fairground entertainers—at the Foire du trône 27 March 1937. Photo Rol, private collection.

"Monsieur France"

While old themes and nostalgia had their charms for many, so did some new types, representatives of specifically French ways of dealing with the new troubles. As the crisis sank in, new models of coping, new heroes, emerged—in film, in sports, and in songs and singers. One older model who took on new meaning was Maurice Chevalier. During the period of crises beginning with the Depression, Chevalier served as the most reassuring symbol of French success in an increasingly disturbing world. This phase of his career began in late 1928 when he went to the United States to make movies for Paramount Pictures. The star of the most chic music halls in Paris became a Hollywood leading man. The press greeted his Paramount contract with hosannas of national pride: finally, the Americans wanted a French star and were willing to pay a Frenchman astronomical sums. The commonplace view was also that Chevalier was going to the United States as a kind of ambassador of France, a representative Frenchman. After boxer Georges Carpentier and other sports champions "showed that we have muscles, you [Chevalier] will prove that in Paris we still know how to laugh . . . *à la Parisienne,*" proclaimed a writer for *Candide* at the time of the star's departure. Journalists expressed delight in the expectation that he would change the American image of the Frenchman from a cranky little man with a mustache to a tall, athletic, handsome, and affable fellow. So much attention and high hopes attended the performer's departure that a small backlash of letters and articles appeared criticizing all the publicity and praise accorded Chevalier.[8] His move to Hollywood had occurred at the very time when the "talkies" were taking over, and with his speaking and singing talents well-honed during years of music-hall performing, he shone on film, while most of the silent-film actors fell by the wayside.

Over the next few years Chevalier's American-made films came to French screens at the rate of two or three a year. As the general economy faltered, his publicity machine continuously reminded the French public that he was earning stupendous sums of *dollars* making movies in America. Not long after a time when the mighty greenback bought as many as thirty-five francs, the French learned that Chevalier was offered $25,000 a week for American music-hall appearances. "There's not a Frenchman worthy of the name who hasn't swelled with pride and who hasn't felt his wallet suddenly heavier in his pocket" in response to that news, a *Paris-Soir* writer declared. Early in 1930 an article entitled "avalanche of dollars" reported that "'our Maurice' will earn 600,000 dollars a year"—or 15.5 million francs.[9] An international superstar, Chevalier was France's player in the world game. He starred in American movies, spoke and sang English, sang *French* songs abroad, made big money right on the Americans' own turf, and regularly brought his money and smiles back to the homeland he obviously loved. He was not a man, but a legend, wrote one journalist in 1930: he was the child of the faubourg who "one day makes a shower of bills fall into his palace and into his pockets."[10] Thus French nationalism reacting to adversity at first worked to the benefit of Chevalier, celebrating him as the common Frenchman doing well in the face of foreigners deemed responsible for France's problems.

Certainly not all French performers competing with foreigners benefited from such a reaction; Chevalier's extraordinary talents did make a difference, and so did his persona on stage and screen. When a French jazz band led by Gregor appeared at the Empire in May 1930, critic Gustave Fréjaville reported disparagingly on its "noisy publicity campaign founded on a displaced nationalism" and judged it "a very mediocre imitation" of Jack Hylton's jazz.[11] Chevalier, a genuine débrouillard from the faubourgs, could never be disparaged as an imitation. During the early years of the Depression he served as a special French hero, exemplifying to his own people and to the world some of the most endearing French attributes. A reviewer of his first feature talkie (*La Chanson de Paris*) hailed him as "the charming amuser with the verve and banter that are so French, so popularly Parisian [*Parigot*] even."[12] While Charlie Chaplin comes across as the "universal man," a journalist explained in 1929, "Chevalier—he's the Parisian, the Frenchman. It's impossible to judge him as a foreigner. He is too close to our heart."[13] His most extraordinary achievement was to produce that feeling in his audiences regularly. With his unassuming, amiable manner, observers remarked again and again, he was able to make many people feel that he was like them and that he was like an old friend. A remarkably broad spectrum of society identified with him. He combined "English chic and the Parisian chic of the 'little guys' of the faubourg Montmartre," observed Paul Reboux in 1930. He was a streetwise wag but also "an exemplary spouse."[14] His humor was slightly off-color but never enough to offend the respectable bourgeois. He united the waggishness of the *mécano* with a cultivated grace, pleasing men and women of a range of social classes from the grande bourgeoisie down.[15] There was nothing specific about his personality or social character, explained one observer. "He is as close to the apprentice plumber as he is to the man of high society, to the pimp [*poisse*] as to the young store clerk."[16] He was socially an "average" man, whom the masses felt as though they knew intimately. Parisians called him "our Maurice."

Chevalier himself recognized that he was popular as the incarnation of a type, a representation of the common people of France and particularly of Paris. In an interview with *Paris-Soir* in 1930 Chevalier observed: "It's not me, me alone, that the world likes to see on the screen. It's the *Parigot*. It's the Parisian guy who's cunning [*dessalé*], tender, bitching [*rouspéteur*], heroic when necessary, a joker and [yet] sentimental, the type that, from Vincennes to Maillot and from La Chapelle to La Glacière, inspires the tunes that I sing and serves as my model."[17]

"Maurice Chevalier is the symbol of the French song," declared a journalist in an article entitled "Bravo! Chevalier" (June 1929).[18] An admiring article in *Pour Vous* (October 1929) acclaimed him as "symbol of the good French disposition [*humeur*]."[19] He was the "ambassador of French Gaiety," declared a photo caption in the daily *Le Matin* in 1930.[20] The periodical *Aux Ecoutes* (July 1930) called him "our national entertainer [*fantaisiste*]," who was even more popular in Paris after his departure for America than before.[21] A hostile critic, Georges Altman, in 1931 put it another way: Chevalier had become "Monsieur France," idolized by a public that some years earlier had embraced the boxer Georges Carpentier as "Monsieur France." The public's "cult of stars," a kind of "collective hysteria" encouraged by the press, had made the former *mécano* into "ambassador of the so well-known charm, grace, gaiety and wit of the Parisian boulevard" and "the symbol of the shrewd [*malin*] Frenchman."[22]

At the time of all this praise there was reason for French fans to feel that their idol now in Hollywood had abandoned them for American money. Chevalier's prologue to his first big American film was designed to counter that feeling. At the beginning of *La Chanson de Paris* he appears as himself in Hollywood and speaks in a seemingly impromptu way to French audiences, telling them about California, its sun and its moviemaking. "Finally, lowering his voice, he confides [to them] that he is very happy but that all the same he thinks often of Paris and of his compatriots— his voice trembles—and [he] misses the air of his country," recounted a reporter.[23] Sympathetic reviewers also helped keep the good feelings strong. All that counted with the public, wrote Maurice Huet in *Le Petit Parisien*, was that Chevalier was in America "making excellent publicity for us" with his charm and talent. "Ravished, the crowd listens and admires, at bottom proud to see that its illustrious star has been snatched up by the United States," declared a *Gringoire* reviewer.[24] Movie audiences commonly showed that they shared the most positive view of the star, who was so conspicuously a winner in the international arena. In a time famous for lionizing aviators as national heroes, the trailer for a film about pilots Costes and Bellonte— France's answers to Charles Lindbergh—appeared with a trailer for Chevalier's film

Maurice Chevalier as Hollywood star with Claudette Colbert in the movie *La Grande Mare* (The big pond) (1930). Playing a Frenchman named Pierre whose family has been impoverished by the war, he shows himself to be resourceful—and a romantic winner as well; he gains a fortune in America and a beautiful wife. Private collection.

Parade d'amour in a movie house on the boulevard Saint-Marcel. A journalist for *Oeil de Paris* reported two strikingly different audience reactions: "Some meager applause greeted the names of the two aviators, while the announcement of the film of Chevalier was marked by frenetic bravos."[25]

Criticism of *La Chanson de Paris* spared the star for the most part and instead attacked the American company that produced the film for the weak screenplay and the false, outdated sets chosen to represent Paris. After making such criticisms, J. C. Auriol summed up his review by calling the film a "*divertissement* whose principal attraction is the personality of Chevalier. . . . In the middle of this paltry story, he [Chevalier] already holds the spectators under his charm."[26] That kind of review praising the star regardless of the film became commonplace. Audiences seem to have made the same distinction.

After *La Chanson de Paris* Chevalier starred in a series of early Depression-era films that featured him as a man who ended up a successful figure of wealth and prestige. In *Parade d'amour* (The love parade) (1929) he played a count in a fictional kingdom who ended up not only marrying the queen, but becoming king and master over her. In his next film, *La Grande Mare* (The big pond), which came to Paris in July 1930, he appeared in the kind of role that made him much more clearly a representative of the French caught in the Depression. Chevalier played a "brave type de Parisien rigolo" who at the outset is not doing well. Though bearing an aristocratic name (with the particle "de"—a concession to American taste, one French reviewer explained), Pierre comes from a family that was ruined by the war. He is the "little Frenchman" without financial resources. But he is also a Gallic débrouillard, gifted with romantic charm and wit. After becoming romantically involved with a young American who is touring Europe, he follows her to the United States and becomes a successful inventor and businessman. In fact, he becomes Americanized to a fault, losing himself in overwork and overvaluing of money. Yet in the end he also succeeds as a romantic lover, drawing on innate French capacities that Americans are shown to lack. The movie had Hollywood's famous happy ending: the hero wins a fortune, marries the rich daughter of the factory owner, and finds happiness. The story pleased audiences if not critics, but, again, for many moviegoers what mattered above all was seeing Maurice Chevalier. In a regular stream of films throughout the 1930s Chevalier came through as a charming Parisian, a buoyant Frenchman, whom masses of spectators watched with admiration.

There were detractors, however. By going to America and making a stupendous salary he became the target of charges that he had abandoned his homeland and his people—and cared too much about dollars. Those criticisms began to swell into a noticeable chorus in 1930. A writer for the *Le Temps* that year judged Chevalier pretentious and vulgar: "a Ménilmontant that takes itself for the Champs-Elysées."[27] The reports of his fabulous earnings generated not only admiration, but also critical talk about how tight he was. Hecklers began going after him during performances, provoking angry responses from Chevalier. Journalists told the world about the skirmishes. In a Paris appearance in 1930, for example, a brazen young working guy—"un titi des populaires"—called out to the performer (whom the reporter described as "the most highly paid singer 'in the world' [the last phrase in English]): 'Hey Maurice . . . what do you pay?'" Chevalier responded with a hand gesture. The reporter describing the incident concluded by calling the star stingy.[28] In this same period Chevalier was receiving a great deal of favorable

Maurice Chevalier as a happy-go-lucky Parisian junk dealer charms Louise Level (played by Sylvia Beecher) in *La Chanson de Paris* (*Innocents of Paris*) (1929). Courtesy of Museum of Modern Art Film Stills.

publicity for his charitable donations to help sick and old entertainers, but the negative feelings about his wealth persisted and periodically made the news.

Chevalier had moved away from his audiences not just by going to America, but also by leaving the music hall for the movies. As Philippe Soupault pointed out, when Chevalier performed for the camera, he was unable to respond spontaneously to audiences; he could no longer shape his every note and nuance to their reactions. All in all, he was losing touch with the "little people," the source of his stage persona and the large, vaguely defined group that most warmly embraced him as their own.[29]

Invidious comparisons of Chevalier and Georgius began to appear. Chevalier was the kind of artistic and intellectual "fodder" served on ocean liners, while Georgius was "absolutely French," declared a reporter for *Le Quotidien* in September 1930. Send Georgius to America someday instead of Chevalier, he urged.[30] During the same month critic Gustave Fréjaville praised Georgius's performances at the Européen as "the best demonstration that one can oppose to those who go on spreading the baneful news of the Americanization of Paris and of the Parisian spirit." Chevalier was the "false popular" type, playing to the elite, asserted Fernand Léger (a café-concert fan) in 1934, while Georgius was "truly the perfect type of the 'gars du faubourg,' popular and thoroughbred. . . . Chevalier is decorative, Georgius is true." Léger added admiringly that Georgius still played the outlying halls filled with the modest people living nearby, and Georgius freely employed un-varnished expressions that his audience knew and also used—phrases that would have shocked Chevalier's audiences. At music halls like the Européen, Georgius did ten encores, notes Léger. "It's delirium; his audience works him to death; he leaves his skin in those places, but gloriously."[31]

Some critics not only found fault with the performer, but also denounced the society and media that made him a star. The more France's troubles increased, the more questionable appeared the amount of attention that the press and public gave Chevalier. In August 1930 when the star returned to Paris for a visit, a writer for *Aux Ecoutes* marveled at how "a whole people is engrossed by the thought that Maurice Chevalier has arrived, how it sees only that and speaks only of that." By giving him all that attention, the anonymous writer continued sarcastically, the peo-ple do not look at other subjects "infinitely less proper as objects of concern," such as the French evacuation of the Rhine and "the German danger . . . the threat on the Polish borders . . . the high cost of living, cornered wheat, expensive bread, ris-ing meat prices, vegetables out of sight, the raising of American tariffs, the collapse of stocks, the business slump, the rigors of taxes."[32] Another way of denigrating Chevalier's popularity was to subject it to a penetrating social analysis, as journal-ist J.-M. Aimot did. The "mécano gavroche" that the performer represented had not existed in Parisian life for years, observed Aimot, but it remained a "classic type," an easily understood "personnage de convention" that people still enjoyed

Maurice Chevalier as a tailor who passes for a baron happily wins the love of Princess Jeanette (Jeanette MacDonald) in *Love Me Tonight* (1932). Courtesy of MoMA Film Stills.

seeing onstage and in film. "The crowd . . . likes reality only [when it is] disguised, dressed in well-known clothing and without any novelty coming in to disturb the arrangement," Aimot argued. The "bon bourgeois," for his part, enjoys seeing "this image, without danger and without mystery, of the good Parisian worker." It is in that way, Aimot concluded, that one should study the popularity of Chevalier, "this unprecedented example of collective stultification [abêtissement]."[33] An even more biting critic, Georges Altman, damned Chevalier by identifying him as the symbol of Hollywood's "optimistic beatitude," "the Paramount ideology, whose Breasts are Platitude and Silliness [niaiserie]."[34]

During the 1930s still more detractors and difficulties emerged for "Monsieur France," yet the barbs never quite drowned out the applause. His photograph was on mantels and in stores everywhere, observed a reporter in 1932. "Maurice Chevalier represents the triumph of the average Frenchman," Le Soir proclaimed in the same year; "He is the prototype and the example of the gentleman who 'without special knowledge' knows how to achieve fortune and glory." Also in 1932, a Marianne reporter maintained, "He is currently the greatest world star of the screen and music hall," but "he has remained simple" and he "incarnates joie de vivre [and] good humor." Chevalier no longer enjoyed the ascendancy that he had known a few years earlier, yet for a multitude of fans he remained the smiling, lovable, cheerful, "regular guy" who had succeeded without changing his character.[35]

The Parisian Trickster

In a more purely comic vein, moviegoers took delight in following the farcical triumphs of an ordinary-looking fellow named Georges Milton. In the late fall of 1930 he gained fame as an extraordinarily successful wangler called Bouboule in the film Le Roi des resquilleurs (King of the wanglers). For many months the film drew huge audiences and high praise from the critics. Reportedly spectators laughed almost continuously from beginning to end, and at times their laughter drowned out the dialogue. Critics were cheered that at last France had produced a good comedy. During the "American invasion" of great comedies—a new Laurel and Hardy every two months— the French public had lost the habit of seeing French comic films, but Milton's first film brought them "a very French good humor," remarked Maurice Mairgance in L'Ami du peuple du soir.[36]

Milton as Bouboule was a model of resourcefulness, triumphing repeatedly over difficulties. In his film of 1930 he was a Parisian "little guy" who was a master

In 1930 the comedian Georges Milton demonstrated how the impecunious "little guy" can wangle to success after success in the extraordinarily popular movie *Le Roi des resquilleurs* (King of the wanglers). The song "J'ai ma combine" (I have my system), which he blithely sings in the movie, became a hit. Private collection.

of getting what he wanted and enjoying himself without paying. He was the street-smart faubourien who rises to success through a series of uncanny strokes of luck and wiliness. First he slips into a boxing match without a ticket by pretending to be a café waiter carrying a tray. While being chased around the ring by authorities, he drops the tray, which sounds like the official gong, and thereby saves the young French boxer who has just been knocked down. He gets into the Vélodrome d'hiver for the famous six-day bicycle race by posing as a worker carrying two spare wheels. In escaping the gate watchers he ends up on a stage as the band plays one of his favorite songs, which he joins in singing enthusiastically, winning over the crowd. Then he manages to take two charming young women to a grand café for champagne and gets away without paying—by putting the saucers and bill onto another table. In the final episode he gains entry to the France-England rugby match at the Colombes stadium by taking the part of a player from the provinces. He doesn't know how to play rugby, but in fleeing the field with the ball he unwittingly scores a goal. He ends up marrying Lulu, the highly desirable young woman who is not only attractive and prosperous, but also the sister of a bicycle racing champion.

After the victorious rugby match Milton sings the song "J'ai ma combine" (my system or my gimmick), in which he philosophizes about not letting oneself get bothered or upset: it's better to smile and "to know how to be happy all the time."

> Les soucis, merci, ça m'est égal!
> Les ennuis, tant pis, j' m'en fich' pas mal.
> J'ai ma combine.
> [Worries, thanks, I don't care!
> Troubles, too bad, I laugh them off.
> I have my system.][37]

Here again was the myth of the débrouillard that pleased both the dominant culture wanting stability and plebeians wanting relief from anxiety: don't worry, the ordinary "little guy" will come through. In fact, the French Everyman can. "The *resquilleur* belongs to all classes of society," a reviewer for *Le Journal* noted, "from high society to the *titi*."[38] The character Bouboule "represents liberty, nonconformism, and independence," explained Philippe Soupault. By all accounts the public response to that character was huge. For months, Soupault wrote in June 1931, "one hears on every street corner, in all the little stores, in the workshops people humming the chorus of the *Roi des resquilleurs*: 'J'ai ma combine' . . . Never before, in no other time and no other country, has a singer known such great popularity."[39]

Critics pointed out without disparagement that the film was constructed according to a formula that met well-known popular tastes and interests. Audiences fond of sports found themselves immersed in crowds of other fans at a boxing match, a bicycle race, and a rugby game, all in one film. Most judged the story just right for the times; it seemed more suited to the present than *Sous les Toits de Paris* was. For Bouboule succeeded by his ability in *sports* and not just by his singing. "Milton is more easily than Préjean the popular personage that both have incarnated," observed critic J.-M. Aimot. Milton seemed more naturally a Parisian "little guy," and Bouboule was more a current Parisian type, indeed "a new very Parisian type." Soupault also saw Bouboule as a "Parisian of Paris," indeed "the most representative of Parisians," but not a new type. "[Milton] represents one of the types preferred by the mass of people, the one that already in the Middle Ages was called 'the best son in the world' and that we call today the 'good boy.'" He was the irrepressible, mocking, slang-speaking, rebellious Parisian *titi* whom Victor Hugo called Gavroche (the name became a French word). "He is the beneficent optimist, the one who knows how to struggle with the difficulties of life while keeping the smile."[40] "The film develops the favorite image of popular sentiment," concluded François Vinneuil: "the needy and industrious [*besogneux*] '*petit gars*' who gets by honestly and owes his pleasures and his rise to fortune only to his craftiness [*astuce*]." Being crafty meant showing up the ineffectiveness of authorities and systems of control, as another critic pointed out.[41]

Bouboule's success included winning the woman of his desires, too, but the love story was not so central as it was in *Sous les Toits de Paris*. *Le Roi des resquilleurs* was basically a comedy. Its fast-paced buffoonery was a welcome antidote to the worries of the emergent Depression. People want to laugh, wrote a *Charivari* reviewer, and this film served them well.[42] It was such a hit that its producers went on to make sequels throughout the 1930s. In *La Bande à Bouboule* (1931), *Bouboule ıer, Roi nègre* (1933), and *Prince Bouboule* (1938), the hero falls into myriad difficulties and never fails to overcome them in comically unexpected ways. As Bouboule the First, for example, he finds himself pitted against a band of crooks smuggling diamonds from France to Senegal. Outwitting them, he not only foils their attempt to kill him but even ends up king of a Senegalese village.

Bouboule with his relatively harmless misdeeds afforded spectators an opportunity to see and laugh at a talented transgressor in action. He was the successful trickster, the cunning evader of rulers and the law. He appeared at a time of strong interest in such characters—shady types who coped resourcefully by breaking the law. In novels, magazines, and films they constituted an up-to-date pègre, one that was composed largely of foreigners and was less romantic than the prewar riffraff. Some were skillful thieves; some were what was known in English as "con artists," and a small number used violence. In the wake of such popular American movies as *Nuits de Chicago* (*Underworld*) and *Scarface*, French filmmakers put foreign-born criminals of Marseilles and Montmartre in the place of the Chicago gangsters of Hollywood movies. No clear heroes stood out, critic Frédéric Pottecher lamented in 1931. The lack of heroes, he observed, reflected "the modern turbulence," "intrigues," and violent reactions marking society of the times.[43] Georges Simenon's protagonist, Inspector Maigret, who made his film debut in 1932, was certainly unheroic, not a genius or a dashing figure, but an ordinary-looking "little guy" with plain and methodical ways, a salaried functionary just doing his job. Devoid of the comic antics of Bouboule, the lawbreakers of the early 1930s policiers were generally meant to be villains, although the murderer in Jean Renoir's *La Chienne* (1931) was presented in a sympathetic light, as were many others later in the decade. Casting them as foreigners was a way of reducing long-recognized audience sympathy for the outlaws, but they remained morally ambiguous for many spectators. French audiences, it seems, were not entirely sure that they would take the side of society or wanted to see the lawbreaker punished.

Demand for darker crime-and-police stories was also strong. A large reading and moviegoing public wanted to enter into stories that reflected the somber and dangerous times as Chevalier's and Bouboule's movies did not. Policiers evoked a universe full of danger, mystery and insecurity, struggle and killing. So did the popular newspapers and the mass-circulation illustrated weekly *Détective,* which first appeared in 1928.[44] During the 1930s it was not hard for many people to locate themselves in such a world and even to identify with the antisocial characters. "Each . . . feels himself not only a possible victim, but also a virtual criminal," harboring murderous impulses at least subconsciously, writer Paul Morand observed in 1934. "Everyone today can be suspected. The taste for death is in us."[45] Readers and moviegoers enjoyed the *frissons* produced by stories about crimes and mysteries, and yet it was commonly observed that they also often enjoyed seeing crimes and mysteries solved, the guilty one revealed. The public that often viewed criminals with ambivalence or sympathy also commonly accorded respect and admiration to a police inspector or detective who overcomes difficulty and danger and in the end shores up the established order.[46] Chevalier and Milton's adventures, then, served as an alternative not just to a difficult real world, but also to the dark, disturbing fictional worlds of the policiers. Cultural consumers wanted both kinds of stories and vicarious experience, and producers gave them a steady flow of offerings.

Sports Stars

For the many who enjoyed watching action and struggle that ended in clear victory for one side—without provoking moral uneasiness—there was still another kind of spectacle: athletic competitions. These provided another kind of hero for the times, the sports champion. "It's a truism to declare that our epoch lives under the sign of sport," noted journalist Marcel Berger in 1931. "Sport is everywhere today, installed in our ways of life, imposing itself on our attention, reigning over our diversions."[47] The press was doing more than ever before to focus public attention on the subject, and growing public interest supported that increased press coverage. The daily sports newspaper *L'Auto,* which had first organized the Tour de France back in 1903, saw its sales climb sharply from 495,000 copies a day in July 1923—the month of the race—to 730,000 in July 1933. Around 1930 political dailies began devoting an entire page to sports instead of the quarter page that had been the norm.

Another indication of rising interest was the steep rise of the number of football (soccer) clubs and players in the two decades after the Great War. The masses of working people came into the game, and the hitherto dominant middle classes lost interest. Between 1926 and 1931 the number of registered players doubled, rising from 75,000 to 145,000. Sports flourished above all as spectator entertainment. Before the war, soccer games with England and the French cup matches drew only 3,000–4,000 people; during the twenties such events regularly attracted well more than 20,000. In such great football cities as Paris, Marseilles, and Montpellier audiences were ten to fifteen times larger than before the war. From 1932 on, new openly professional football teams enjoyed an unprecedented following. New crowning competitions brought public interest to periodic peaks. The first professional championship of France was played in 1933. On the international level, the first World Cup was organized in 1930.[48] Through the press, movie newsreels, and

Professional soccer, like other sports, offered relief from the grim economic and political news. Here the nation's top players (the goalie wearing the emblematic worker's cap) play for the championship of France, April 1933. Cover of the sports weekly *Match.* Collection of the author.

The Tour de France was the most popular bicycle race, but numerous shorter races—like this 270-kilometer Paris-Troyes race in the spring of 1933—filled out the sporting year, providing more victors, local heroes at least. About 100 kilometers of this race was on an unpaved road—hence the annoying dust and numerous flat tires due to the gravel. The winner and runner-up were two men of the region, brothers Jean and Marcel Bidot. Cover of *Match*. Collection of the author.

radio broadcasts, these and other sporting attractions became an inescapable part of the life of the times.

Why this stronger interest in sports? Several observers have given some suggestive answers to that question. In 1931 entertainment reviewer Gustave Fréjaville linked the greater interest in sports to the public's diminished interest in theatrical spectacles. "People prefer the violent sensations that great sporting ordeals provide, which substitute real 'evasions' for the evasions of the imagination provided by spectacles."[49] Critic Bernard Champigneulle agreed: spectators preferred sporting events because there they experienced "stronger emotions" and gave free rein to "instinct." At motorcycle races, Champigneulle maintained, many spectators secretly harbored a desire to see "machines turn over and drivers crash on the ground." They enjoyed seeing their favorite athlete triumph and seeing the defeated crushed. They satisfied desires to see brute force dominate, but they also cheered "skill or caginess [*la ruse*]."[50] In an article subtitled "Why the Public Likes Sports Films" (1931), Pierre-Henry Proust emphasized a new generation's fascination with movement as well as its desire to share strong emotions at a football game or boxing match.[51] What mattered was action, emotional highs, and a decisive outcome.

"Sport films," Proust continued, "show us in action those who reap well-deserved laurels by their effort [*peine*] and their courage." Spectators participate in the winner's success; they experience the satisfaction of feeling that justice is done—that hard work and virtue are rewarded with victory and glory. The public of the stadiums and velodromes, like that of the cinemas, Proust observed, is "good-natured [*bon enfant*] and optimistic." Sporting competitions were "simple," like the mentality of that public, and the "heroes" who emerged were "close to . . . [the public's] own personality." Spectators also enjoyed the "picturesque" settings in which those heroes acted—"the open air" and sunshine, for example. And they enjoyed finding out what went on "behind the scenes of sportive glory" ("the attraction of forbidden fruit").[52] In sum, the favorite players' lives, struggles, and victories became another dimension of "real life" for a legion of fans. Sporting events offered the satisfactions of clear-cut clashes, eye-catching action, and worthy victors. During a time when the structures of community life seemed less and less supportive, athletic champions were idolized as winning individuals, gloriously

The grueling six-day bicycle race in the Paris Vélodrome d'hiver was one of the high times of the year for crowds of "little people" who cheered on their favorites and in the end celebrated the apotheosis of a champion. Cover of *Match*, 20 March 1934. Collection of the author.

Winner of the 1931 Tour de France, Antonin Magne, smiling, "modest and stalwart [*valeureux*]," races confidently through the Pau-Bordeaux stage of the 1934 Tour, which he ended up winning. Covers like this one (*Match*, 27 July 1934) and adulating commentary made "Tonin" and other sports figures familiar stars to a large public. Private collection.

"Tonin" Magne, shown during the 1938 Tour de France, was nearing the end of his racing days. In the last stage of this Tour he and André Leducq joined hands and exited from competitive cycling together. France Presse Voir. 17 July 1938. Private collection.

triumphing over difficulties. To the many beset with frustrations and disappointments in difficult times, sports heroes provided a vicarious sense of success.

Proust failed to point out that those heroes were most often "little guys" with whom people of modest circumstances could identify. The men who rose from obscurity to become star football players and bicycle racers were most often the sons of workers, the lower middle class, and peasants. In the Tour de France the early 1930s were years of triumph for a succession of Frenchmen of popular origins, after a decade in which foreigners won every year's race but one (1923). In 1930 and again in 1932 the winner was André Leducq, known as Dédé, who had grown up in the working-class suburbs of Saint-Ouen and Belleville. Like Maurice Chevalier, he was the fabled Parisian *titi*—the ironic, wisecracking good fellow. In 1931 and 1934 the victor was Antonin Magne, who was born in a village in Auvergne and raised in a Parisian *banlieue*. Unlike the Parisian titi, "Tonin" was not a great talker, but the press made him known to masses of fans as a devoted friend and team player, and he became the favorite of many. In 1933 the winner was Georges Speicher, another titi who resembled Chevalier even more than Leducq did. Like the entertainer, Speicher was from Ménilmontant and had the accent and the wit that went with the territory. He was handsome, dressed well, frequented ordinary dance halls, and was a charmer of women. The sporting press gave similar treatment to soccer stars, making them known to the public as exalted Everymen with familiar nicknames, modest backgrounds, and smiling ordinary faces. In short, these winners who rose out of plebeian obscurity became popular heroes, just as music-hall stars like Chevalier and Mistinguett had.[53]

And, like those singers, sports champions became representatives of France, particularly when they competed against foreigners and won. In the prewar and immediate postwar years that was the case for tennis ace Suzanne Lenglen and the light-heavyweight boxer Georges Carpentier (until he lost to Jack Dempsey in July 1921). Later in the 1920s French tennis players Jean-René Lacoste, Jean Borotra, Jacques Brugnon, and Henri Cochet—whom the press nicknamed the "four musketeers"—boosted national pride by winning the Davis Cup from 1927 to 1932. Around 1930 French fans also delighted in the numerous new world records set by distance runner Jules Ladoumègue and weightlifter Charles Rigoulot ("the strongest man in the world"), two world champions exceptionally popular with the press and public. "History has turned [a page]; war has passed," declared writer Lucien Dubech optimistically in a 1930 book on sports. Nations now fought on the playing fields, he observed: "today sport is an instrument of universal nationalism."[54] During the early thirties the opportunities for national triumphs on the playing fields increased, and the French won more frequently. For years French soccer teams had won only one international game out of three or four. During the 1920s they had regularly lost and lost badly to other Europeans. In 1930 France's soccer team won the first World Cup, and *footballeurs* in other international competitions improved the nation's record.[55] The Olympics, the World Cup, and the introduction of national teams into the Tour de France (1930) all provided occasions for French successes that were especially welcome during increasingly difficult economic times.

Several kinds of movies contributed to and responded to these growing interests. The novelesque documentary *Hardi les gars*—about racers of the Tour de France—was one good example of a sports story that captivated the masses, Pierre-Henry Proust observed, but *"Le Roi des resquilleurs* remains the model of the genre."[56] To film critic and novice director Marcel Carné, too, *Le Roi des resquilleurs* seemed "finally to have given honor in our studios to the sports film too often disdained to the profit of high-society melodramas and music-hall tableaus." The prominence of sports in the film was crucial to its "persistent, astonishing, even prodigious success." *Le Roi des resquilleurs* did more than feature a "type entirely of our time," "the cunning character that each of us has dreamed of being." It also showcased many of the traits that gave sports champions their magnetic hold over so many. Such stars as Pearl White and Douglas Fairbanks had already endeared athletic exploits to movie audiences, and numerous films had included scenes of sports or had been constructed around a sport (e.g., *Coureur,* starring Wallace Reid, Charlie Chaplin's *Charlot boxeur,* and *Soir de rafle,* starring Albert Préjean). "Youth, light, health, joie de vivre" were naturally attractions of such films. So were "movement and beauty of form." A "motif of optimism" also went with the genre. In sum, Carné maintained, *Le Roi des resquilleurs* could have been the sports film par excellence, offering all those pleasures and more—even "a means of analysis and of lyricism"—if its creators had not chosen to make it a "broad popular farce."[57]

More regularly and frequently than feature films, movie newsreels catered to the public appetite for sports, providing a seemingly endless series of politically uncontroversial stories that were welcome distractions from the troubles of the time. Like entertainment producers, the newsreel makers took a play-it-safe attitude even more than usual in that time of life-and-death business struggles. *Actualités* in the 1930s offered little reporting on Hitler and the Nazis but instead gave close attention to royal visits, the comings and goings of entertainers, all manner of ceremonial acts showcasing political leaders, and the high points of sporting events.[58] Scenes from the Grand Prix de Longchamp horse race, the Tour de France, long-distance airplane tests and competitions (*raids*), and the Rallye de Monte Carlo automobile race were noncontroversial national rituals, marking the seasons and the continuance of normality, like the grape harvest of Montmartre, the review of the Horse Guards by the king of England, and the Automobile Salons shown year after year. While those anodyne images filled the screen, the newscaster's voice typically rattled on in a chipper matter-of-fact tone that made the news a part of the entertainment for which audiences had paid their admission.

A New Generation

Another cheering spectacle in the early 1930s was the emergence of a number of new performers, strikingly young and buoyant, unscathed by war and economic turmoil. Representatives of a new generation, they introduced a fresh style of songs and quickly rose to stardom. Mireille, the duo Pills and Tabet, and Charles and Johnny were leading examples. Their fresh demeanor and lighthearted songs were an antidote to pessimism bred by the Depression and worries about France's long-term problems of a low birth rate and an aging population. They also provided relief from painful memories stirred by war movies. While the older populist performers and street singers recalled the people and the life of yesterday, the new young singers sang of the present and future with a new light and natural style. Their tunes were set to rhythms that were mostly American. Above all, the syncopation of jazz set them apart. Their lyrics were both modern and wholly French. The settings evoked were far from the cosmopolitan and urban scenes so central to the 1920s. The new singers told stories set in the country, and they sang of vacation journeys in the sunny provinces (a subject examined in chapter 6). Some of youth's leading representatives had an Anglo-American, collegian air: Ray Ventura and his band dubbed themselves Ray Ventura et ses Collégiens. The singer who called himself Pills was born René Ducos; he chose his stage name for its Anglo-American sound. Mireille was in 1930 a twenty-four-year-old singer, actor, and composer who had just spent several years in the United States performing and picking up the latest music. Her first hit, "Couchés dans le Foin" ("Lying in the Hay") was written for an American musical in the late twenties.

One of the places in Paris where those youthful images reigned was the ABC, a new music hall that opened in 1934 at 11, boulevard Poissonnière. As it had

Ray Ventura and his Collégiens, the new style jazz band of the 1930s, were youthful, modish singers of sketches. (15 Sept. 1936). Henri Roger, photographer. Private collection.

only a small stage, it could not present grand attractions of the circus as the Empire and Alhambra did. Instead it featured sketches, short operettas, and especially *tours de chant* by new *young* singers. It was there that a new generation of singers enthralled listeners and received the acclamations of their devoted fans. Mireille, Pills and Tabet, Charles (Trenet), and Johnny (Hess) all enjoyed consecrating triumphs in that venue. "What is striking in the new revue 'X-Y-Z' . . . at the Music-Hall de l'ABC . . . is its youthful look," observed a critic in October 1934. It was particularly striking, he explained, since "our gerontocracy has lost the habit of hearing the voice of youth."[59]

The youthful singers also gained an audience through the radio, whose number of listeners and hours of programming greatly increased during this generational shift. The "prodigious takeoff" of radio, as a journalist in 1935 put it, contributed to changes in the style of singing and the kinds of songs sung by the new singers.[60] Vulgarities and risqué songs traditional to the old cafés-concerts were dropped from performances heard on the air. And a big voice was no longer necessary. Indeed, the new medium permitted a performer to sing softly and to make all the words intelligible, establishing a sense of intimacy with listeners not possible in large halls. The new style of singing, seemingly directing lyrics to each listener personally, was particularly suited to romance, and the crooner was born. In France, Jean Sablon and Jean Lumière led the way and were especially beloved by largely feminine daytime audiences in homes. Most older singers—particularly older male singers—did not fare well on the radio.[61]

In 1934 music critic André Coeuroy described the shift of public favor away from older stars by naming the winners and losers: "In decline [are] Lucienne Boyer, Jack Smith, [the American duet] Layton and Johnston, Chevalier, Mistinguett, Josephine Baker, Dranem. On the rise [are] the Comedian Harmonists, the Mills Brothers, Marie Dubas, Lys Gauty."[62] Later that year the up-and-coming list would have included a dark, handsome young man from Corsica, Tino Rossi, who made a sensational debut as a romantic singer in a fall revue at the Casino de Paris.

The reason for Chevalier's decline was not just that he was becoming strikingly older in his singing style and appearance; it was also that he was the subject of growing doubts and criticisms. His troubles increased significantly during the years 1933–34, and the highly publicized image of happiness and success cracked. In 1933 Chevalier and his wife divorced. The next year it was reported that his salary had fallen to a quarter of what it had been at its height.[63] Chevalier left Paramount after a disagreement. He went over to MGM to make *The Merry Widow* (1934), but soon he fell out with that company, too, and moved back to France. He continued to be a big star, to be sure, particularly as a music-hall performer, and he continued

Tino Rossi with three hits of 1934, the year of his breakthrough to stardom. Private collection.

Jean Gabin (ca. 1933) was a rising movie actor already noted for playing a "man of the people," a new kind of Parisian worker character. Courtesy of BFI Stills, Posters, and Designs.

to find and record songs that became hits, but through the rest of the 1930s he met with a increasing number of new rivals and detractors. The man widely hailed as a representative of France experienced mounting troubles at the very time that the nation did. The old easy messages of cheerful coping met with new skepticism. And the increasing strains in daily life brought out doubts about the man who played both the traditional charmed faubourien and the successful cosmopolitan.

Maurice Chevalier and Georgius, two faces representing the French people from the previous decade, both encountered plenty of new competition in the thirties. In the movies in 1933 and 1934 a young actor named Jean Gabin was attracting extraordinary attention as a compelling, tough kind of bantering faubourien, more at home with current Parigot slang than Chevalier, more a rough-hewn natural working guy, yet a tender-hearted comrade underneath, given to deep friendship and love. From his film debut in 1930 to 1934 he appeared in more than a dozen movies. As early as January 1933 Marcel Carné could write that Gabin "has created on screen a character all his own—that of the 'chic type,' the jovial and unpretentious 'buddy' whom one can be sure to count on in case of need." The crowd,

Carné added, felt immediately drawn to him. "We understand him at a glance—sly and bantering, rebellious, ironic like every born Parisian."[64]

From late 1934 on, national attention also extended to Tino Rossi, who quickly became the new romantic idol of the era. His voice was a ringing clear tenor, smooth and sweet like his gestures and movements; the rhythms of his songs were Latin, and the lyrics amorous and unequivocal. He was the pure rapturous lover, in comparison with Chevalier's older persona that was partly comic and at times ribald and routinely rough-voiced. While Chevalier's career had peaked, Gabin and Tino Rossi were only beginning; both were stars for years to come. The publicized "show-biz" lives of these stars as well as their lyrics and screenplays represented an encouraging variety of ways of responding to adversities in that time of mounting trouble.

6. THE WISH
TO BE ELSEWHERE

HE WAS FED UP with his cramped existence in a cheap hotel with his streetwalking lover. He was tired of hiding out and being hunted down by ex-partners in crime. "I've had it, understand?" he exclaims to his lover—"I'm suffocating." Exasperated and desperate, the mysterious man who calls himself Edmond goes on to tell her that he needs to "change atmospheres." In that one phrase in the film *Hôtel du Nord* (1938), screenwriter Henri Jeanson gave classic expression to a common theme of songs and movies throughout the 1930s: the desire to get away and to experience life in a different place. Song after song celebrated the joys of a trip to the country and the charms of the provinces, while the movies focused more than ever on locales far from Paris and on characters wanting to go "elsewhere."[1] A major current of films from *A Nous la liberté* (1931) and *Marius* (1931) to *Le Quai des brumes* (1938) and *Hôtel du Nord* featured characters who wanted a change of air or scenery, who wanted to move on and to begin a new life, or who simply wanted to leave. They usually wanted to get out of Paris and sometimes even to get out of France. Moving on seemed to be a way of escaping frustrations, disappointments, and troubles.

It is not difficult to understand why producers and audiences took interest in those escapist themes during the decade of the Depression, growing Nazi power in Europe, and nightmares of war. But the notion of escapism by itself seems reductionist and simply negative. Another way of understanding stories and feelings of wanting to be "elsewhere" is to view them as expressions of the social imagination—collective dreams about attractive places and experiences away from the ordinary. The following account treats such dreams as part of an evolving tradition of utopian yearnings and visions of fulfillment. And it takes note of efforts to realize the utopian in everyday life—efforts that included some of the most characteristic cultural practices and political projects of the 1930s and 1940s.

Early in the thirties, Mireille's song "Couchés dans le Foin" became a hit. Its success, seen in retrospect, signaled a major cultural shift. Set off by a jazzy rhythm and a catchy melody built on minor-key modulations, it was an upbeat song about the joys of young lovers in the country. The narrator was, as usual, a city dweller, but the story that he playfully tells was as fresh as the rhythm. Breaking with song tradition, he does not recount going with his sweetheart on the traditional Sunday outing to a pastoral spot near Paris, to Nogent or Robinson. Instead, he tells of going deep into the countryside and of meeting a farmer's daughter. He admits to having a "holy horror" of cows, but he finds the young country girl charming and enjoys "other games" with her.[2]

The chorus sketches their idyll in the hay "with the sun as witness" and a little bird singing in the background. Their hair full of straw, they vow mutual love, embrace, and flutter about together ("On s'embrasse et l'on se trémousse"). "Ah life is sweet, sweet / Sacked out in the hay with the sun as witness" (Ah que la vie est douce, douce / Couchés dans le foin avec le soleil comme témoin).

Such happy naturalness is then contrasted with the artificial settings of luxury that city women typically had to have for their romantic moments. The narrator declares himself free of such needs. When one is young and vigorous, he says, "all those *décors* are superfluous. . . . I don't make love in a cage any more," he proclaims. "Keep your lighting for yourself." "Quand on est vigoureux, quand on aime et qu'on a mon âge [implied: he is young] / Tous ces décors sont superflus / Les canapés je n'en veux plus / Je ne fais plus l'amour en cage / Gardez, gardez vos éclairages." The song, written in 1928, soared to popularity in a rendition recorded in 1931 by the young duo Pills and Tabet. The year of the recording, eight million people flocked to see the Exposition Coloniale internationale in Paris, where they made a quick tour of the French Empire, from Africa to Indochina. During the same

A romantic idyll of a modern couple from the 1920s in a lush forest—a scene like those of Mireille's songs. Jean-Emile Laboureur, *The Brook in the Woods* (*Le Ruisseau sous bois*) (1927). Courtesy of the Fogg Art Museum, Harvard University. Engraving, gift of H. W. Bell.

period masses of French moviegoers relished the tropical "atmosphere" and romances of "primitives" that the new feature films *Kriss* and *Tabou* provided with their settings of Bali and the Polynesian islands.[3] The popularity of "Couchés dans le Foin" and the vogue of exotica marked a rise of public interest in new places far from the modern city. An older fascination with rural France and exotic lands returned with vigor. It had emerged strongly during the nineteenth century with Romanticism and then had waned, most markedly after the Great War. As such interests in "elsewhere" waxed during the late 1920s and 1930s, new representations of "the people" showed up in fresh settings. The new types became prominent nationally not only in film and song, but also in real life.

Youth in the Country

The vision of young urban people out in the countryside was far different from what promoters of tourism had imagined back in wartime and for several years afterward. Tourism planners had looked forward to a wave of mature, moneyed travelers from Britain and the United States coming to France to visit the blood-soaked battlefields whose names had haunted anxious minds for years. Another kind of expected tourist was the urban French man and woman driving their new automobile out to enjoy the countryside, leaving behind the jazz-paced cosmopolis. Well-to-do automobilists were seen as hungering for the beauty of nature and the traditions lingering in the provinces. Some of those traditions centered on the famous good food of France. To whet tourist appetites after the war, numerous new organizations created gastronomic fairs, exhibits, and competitions, building on groundwork laid by the *Guide Michelin*.[4] By their spending along the way, the tourists were supposed to boost the economy throughout the land.

One of the chief promoters of this vision was the Touring Club de France, which dated from 1890. Originally its program had centered on bicycle tours and cycling. During the years 1900–10 it added camping, but not as a main activity. After the war it concentrated on "automobilism" as the growth sector of tourism. The club successfully lobbied the state to open roads in the Alps and then widely publicized the scenic beauties to be discovered there. The future looked golden: tourism leaders anticipated an ever greater number of people acquiring cars and going out to explore the provinces. In a special issue on automobilism and tourism in 1923, the glossy *L'Illustration* cheerily looked ahead to a time of "the automobile for everyone," as was already the case in the United States.[5] Although the day of a car for everyone was still decades away, the number of automobiles in France was increasing rapidly—from 100,000 in 1913 to 750,000 in 1925 and then to more than a million in 1927. By 1933 the number was 1,760,000.[6] The regrettable result of this increase was that the streets of Paris, physically a nineteenth-century city, were congested with ever growing twentieth-century traffic. "France suffers from congestion of the head," wrote a *Figaro illustré* journalist in 1931, referring to both the crowded streets and the large population of the capital—four and a half million people out of the nation's total of forty million.[7] The boosters of automobile tourism had more than their publicity campaigns working for them.

An array of other interest groups joined in promoting travel to the provinces: gastronomic, spa, and mountain and seashore resort interests; the young skiing industry; hotel and restaurant owners; and regional and local tourist offices. In 1914, just before the war, they had begun to coordinate their efforts, and after a few years of interruption they resumed their work. In making their case, tourism boosters put the emphasis not just on the potential economic gains for the entire country, but also on moral benefits. "To bring the city dweller back to open air, this uprooted person often intoxicated by the vitiated atmosphere and the sophisms of a totally debilitating milieu, to put him back in immediate contact with this soil, the love of which remains so profoundly anchored to the heart of the peasant, is a work

of public health and social pacification," maintained a typical promoter. To facili-
tate the French people's access to their "cultural and natural patrimony" was to
"inculcate in them the notion and the love of the fatherland more surely than by
school texts."[8]

During the 1920s unprecedented attention was given to activities in the
country that youth could enjoy—especially hiking, camping, and skiing. Promoters of those activities urged young people to leave the routines of bourgeois life and
the crowded faubourgs for fun in the countryside. In 1923 the first regular magazine devoted to outdoors life appeared under the title *Camping*. It became the most
important publication serving those interests throughout the interwar period.[9] The
next year the Touring Club de France tapped into these growing interests with its
own new periodical, *Le Campeur*. These publications presented camping as part of
a life of adventure in nature that included hiking and cycling. The same interest
groups also worked to improve hiking trails and camping facilities, making the
wilds more attractive to a greater number of people. Among their accomplishments

Camping in the early 1930s. Young people arrive by automobile and tandem, pitch their tents, and
gather around a campfire in a stereotypic scene illustrating a new commercial camping song, "La
Marche des campeurs." Private collection.

was the construction of a new trail to the spectacular Verdon canyon ("the Colorado of Provence," it was called) with new huts and chalets built along the way.

Attractive images of outdoor life were directed initially toward the middle classes and received greatest responses from them. During the 1920s advocates for working-class people also took interest: labor and socialist leaders developed projects for extending vacation possibilities to the workers. Adding new urgency to such efforts was an awareness that increasing numbers of factory workers were suffering from the continued ten-hour day compounded by management's increasing demands on them—the tightened work discipline known in France (as in America) as Taylorization.[10] Some of the rank and file began to claim what they could on their own. During the early 1930s workers who did not yet enjoy a full weekend of leisure or paid vacation managed to get away from the constraining city and took brief camping trips after the week's work. "In summer when the weather is good I leave Saturday evenings with a folded up tent and a cover that I carry on my back," a worker in a Saint-Denis metallurgical factory explained. "I go set myself up in some woods beside some water, and I spend all Sunday fishing."[11] It was a recreation that their social superiors had reason to encourage, though the subalterns' abuse of any new leisure continued to be a worry. "Packed in like sardines in a can," a *Figaro illustré* writer warned in 1931, workers might make a revolution, as they had done repeatedly during the previous century.[12]

Young people were the first to go camping and hiking in a newly organized form: a youth hostel movement took off in France in 1930. Adopting an idea that had been realized in Germany since the early years of the twentieth century, pacifist and social-Catholicism leader Marc Sangnier introduced the *auberges de jeunesse* in France. At first he found little support, but he persevered, and on 24 August 1930 the first youth hostel in France opened. Some days later he founded the first hostel association in France: La Ligue française pour les Auberges de Jeunesse. In 1933 opponents of Catholic influence—center-to-Left leaders—founded a rival association, Le Centre laïque des Auberges de Jeunesse. Altogether the number of youth involved in the hostel movement did not go beyond some hundreds in the early thirties, but it grew steadily through the decade and expanded even faster when the Popular Front government subsidized the hostels during 1936–37. By 1939 nearly 900 hostels were functioning in France, frequented by 60,000 young people.[13]

This movement of youth was hailed by its supporters as a guarantor of France's future, a boost to national strength through the health and vigor of its rising generations. "On all the beaches of France," *L'Illustration* reported in August

Clochemerle (1934) and in movies as well. Bernard-Deschamps's *Le Rosier de Madame Husson* (1932), based on a story by Maupassant, makes great fun of small-town people—pompous volunteer firemen and gossipy, flirtatious wives trying to carry on the local custom of electing a virtuous maiden as rose queen or *rosière;* they cannot find a worthy young woman, so they settle on a simple silly young man played by Fernandel and try to put him through the ceremony (he flees and loses his innocence in a bar and brothel elsewhere). In *Tout va très bien, Madame la Marquise* (1936), Yonnik of Brittany bumbles his way around Paris before giving up and returning home. In *Le Schpountz* (1938), a Parisian movie crew makes a fool of a naïve Southerner (played by Fernandel). During the thirties these comic conventions met with strong new competition from respectful, even admiring song-and-film depictions of provincials in their daily lives.

The South—the Midi—became a particularly popular alternative to Paris modernity. Commercial songs conceived in Paris evoked the Midi with the ritualistic mention of certain familiar references: the main boulevard (the Canebière) and the Old Port of Marseilles, the "pont d'Avignon," the mistral, pastis, *petits cabanons* (country cabins), and the Southern *assent* (accent). During the twenties singers from Marseilles like Alibert and Andrée Turcy established themselves in Paris as generic Southerners, singing songs about their region with a pronounced accent and strongly rolled r's. Alibert became not only a star singer, but also a leading lyricist of Southern songs and Provençal operettas as well. These operettas generally premiered in Paris and became hits there before going to provincial centers, and Marseilles in particular. The apogee of Alibert's production came in the thir-

Fernandel (*at right*) as the naïve provincial movie fan—the "schpountz" in the movie of the same name (1938)—talking with his uncle (Charpin), the amiable, rotund Southern grocer. Private collection.

ties with such successful songs as "Au Pays du soleil" (1932), "Adieu Venise provençale" (1934), and "Les Pescadous—ouh, ouh" (1935). Many of the melodies were written by Marseilles-born Vincent Scotto, composer of thousands of songs, including some of the greatest hits of the century and the most often performed Marseillais operetta, *Un de la Canebière* (1935), a light love story about mate-seeking fishermen and local working women flirting and playing jokes on each other. Running through all these works was praise for the glories of Provence. Thus Alibert proclaimed Marseilles to be the center of earthly delights, chanting the fetish phrases "Cane Cane Canebière" (a song from the operetta) with the same kind of enthusiasm that Mistinguett showed in singing of Paris. By the thirties the Canebière had actually become (as journalist Blaise Cendrars described it) "an improbable pandemonium of cars, taxis, buses, tramways, carts, hand trucks, motor bikes, bicycles all devilishly entangled"—the whole scene a din of rumbling engines, horns, whistles, loudspeakers, and vendors' shouts.[19] Yet song and the show-business imagination nostalgically clung to a fabled quaint Canebière that was the warm heart of the South's most colorful city—the essential center of Marseilles chic and sociability.

Parisians found the Southern accent charming and amusing, and they were enchanted by the imagined presence of an ever blazing sun in blue skies. The sun was associated with an ease of life and good humor considered characteristic of the Provençal people and life in the South. Few other provincial settings evoked such attractive qualities. Mountain and farm landscapes were the settings of dark and tragic stories like Julien Duvivier's film *Poil de carotte* (1926, remade with sound in 1932), the tale of a despondent, abused boy nicknamed Carrot Top, his particularly cruel stepmother, and other family members living in bitter alienation. Director Henri Fescourt's *La Glu* (1926), set in Brittany, told the story of a solid Breton fisherman who is seduced by a vacationing Parisian woman, a femme fatale; his obsession with her ends only when she is brutally murdered by his mother. Brittany— poor, rocky, often rainy—conveyed "an impression of poignant melancholy that hangs on and disturbs you," observed Fescourt. And regions like the Pas-de-Calais were "flat or sad," director Marcel L'Herbier pointed out; they were simply not as photogenic as the South. "The Midi and principally Marseilles are always popular with the public," L'Herbier concluded.[20]

The mystique of the South extended well beyond Marseilles. At the ABC music hall in Paris on the first of June 1934, Tino Rossi made his sensational debut and quickly became a romantic superstar with the hit "O Corse, île d'amour."

The cover of "J'ai rêvé d'une fleur" (from the operetta *Au Pays du soleil*), displaying the essentials of the "land of the sun": the bright sun, Marseilles' cathedral and old port, and the jovial people of the Midi. Private collection.

Dressed in a pseudo-folkloric costume with a guitar around his neck (he was the first French singer to perform on stage with a guitar), he evoked dreams of romance in a Mediterranean paradise. Rossi's good looks, golden voice, and romantic songs made him the idol of millions of women, who screamed admiringly and mobbed him wherever he appeared (some even passed out). He went on to make hit after hit celebrating love in warm, romantic places—in Mediterranean France, Corsica, Naples, and Hawaii. Movies followed: *Au Son des guitares* (1936), *Naples au baiser de feu* (1937), and *Le Soleil a toujours raison* (1937), to mention only a few. What counted was his singing in every film. Meanwhile the sales of his records reached heights never before known in France. The majority of his most successful romantic songs were the work of Vincent Scotto, creator of the melodies of "O Corse, île d'amour," "Vieni, Vieni a cantame," "Marinella," "Bella ragazzina," "Loin des guitares," and many other hits.[21]

"French cinema is finally placed under the Mediterranean sign," an observer concluded in 1933 as he reviewed Marcel Pagnol's film projects.[22] Well before Tino Rossi's movies, the South of France had gained new importance in the movies with a series of films written by—and many of them directed by—Marseilles native Pagnol: *Marius* (1931), *Fanny* (1932), *Jofroi* (1933), *Angèle* (1934), *César* (1936), and *La Femme du boulanger* (1938). Breaking with the movie industry centralized in the capital, he built his studio in Marseilles and filmed on location in the Midi. A number of other major directors chose the South for some of their films during the same period: André Hugon's *Maurin des Maures* (1932) was about an amiable Provençal poacher and his love life, *Romarin* (1936) focused on an amiable Mediterranean fisherman, and René Pujol brought to the screen *Un de la Canebière* (1938).[23]

Pagnol's trilogy *Marius, Fanny,* and *César* had the greatest impact, powerfully stirring emotions and establishing the sympathetic Southern characters as fa-

In the role of a Corsican fisherman, Tino Rossi, a heartthrob of the thirties, plays the accordion and sings in *Au Son des guitares* (1936). Courtesy of BFI Stills, Posters, and Designs.

Lovers Marius (Pierre Fresnay) and Fanny (Orane Demazis) face their differences in *Marius* (1931).
Private collection.

The movie *Marius* (1931) engaged audiences all over France in the lives of the "little people" of the
port of Marseilles. Poster (1932) by Henry Florit. Phot. Bibl. Nat. de Fr.-Paris.

miliars to a national public. The story of young Marius's hunger for adventure at sea, the love between Marius and Fanny, and her realistic acceptance of life with the older Panisse played out conflicting desires that resonated with a large public during the troubled thirties. It was a story of the conflict between the desire to cap young love with familiar domesticity and the yearning to go away and try the unknown. Until the final film, five years after the first, audiences were held in suspense watching the characters' efforts to reconcile personal desires and family concerns, as the lovers' life choices and the differences between parents and adult children gradually came to a final resolution. The quintessential Marseilles setting had an appeal of its own: the port and its boats, a nautical shop, public places for playing boules, animated cafés, the fish market, the nearby cathedral created a picturesque atmosphere contrasting with the all too familiar atmosphere of Paris. Yet underneath the localized exterior the people of the Midi were readily understandable to outsiders, in large part because they were so much like the often depicted *petit peuple* of Paris. They had big hearts, joie de vivre, independence of mind, and a pragmatic realism. In Pagnol's universe no one was truly a villain. Panisse, who married the pregnant Fanny in Marius's absence, was an older, unromantic bourgeois, but he was generous and loving. All the characters were simply human, full of foibles and manias, quick to anger but amenable to reason and resignation, wishing what was best, colliding only in their honest pursuit of it. The story bore all the picturesque marks of the Midi, yet it was also "essentially French," reviewers noted. They meant that it brought out a convincing range of human emotions and experience, humor and passion, anger and love, pettiness and wisdom, all embodied in old-fashioned familiar types. That Frenchness was particularly evident to moviegoers inundated with German and American "talkies with modern settings."[24]

Another view of life in the South focused on comic characters with exaggerated stereotypic traits long associated with the region. Music-hall comedians telling Marseilles tall tales (*galéjades*) with a strong Southern accent were old favorites in Paris. In plays and films, too, comic characters from Provence amused Parisians. Such Southern-born actors as Fernandel and Raimu with their authentic accents became national stars through a run of comic roles as Southerners during the thirties. The excitable and fast-talking Fernandel acted silly with a perfect naturalness, making the most of his large, horselike mouth and big round eyes. He was a virtuoso of quick, big facial changes—from jaw-dropping bug-eyed dumbfoundment or tightly furrowed consternation to a huge ear-to-ear grin. Throughout the thirties he played a succession of memorable film roles (along with many

The weekend Eden enjoyed by modest Parisians. A postcard view of the Marne River near Paris at Champigny. Private collection.

popular psychologist of the period called such feelings a new "cult of *la petite patrie*," which he endorsed as healthy, compared to the "hysterical" world travel so prominent during the 1920s.[30] In 1931 the nation reached a demographic milestone that brought new attention to the decline of rural life: for the first time more than half the French population was urban. Then the spread of unemployment in the cities slowed the rural exodus to a stop. In conservative circles hopes of a return to the land began to rise. Rural France, however, continued to experience long-term cultural changes that can be described as the decline of tradition, which was increasingly identified with the past, enduring and morally solid even though steadily diminishing. Local ways were fading away as radio broadcasts and Parisian songs and slang penetrated to backwater villages. Nostalgically viewed, the old France

A *déjeuner sur l'herbe* after a trip out of the big city by motorbike with sidecar. Private collection.

of the countryside—*la France profonde*—strengthened its appeal throughout the 1930s.

Nostalgia and an attachment to tradition also surfaced in the continuing success of songs celebrating Sunday excursions to riverside cafés along the Marne and the Seine near Paris. The old plebeian way to "get a change of air" still played a role in the popular imagination all through the thirties, even after longer trips and vacations became the norm. The themes of this folklore had long been consecrated. In new song after new song—"Le Doux Caboulet" (1931), "Ici l'On pêche" (1933), "Les Beaux Dimanches de printemps" (1934), "Quand On s'promène au bord de l'eau" (1936), to mention only a few—the essential elements remained the same: young couples made their modest voyage to Cythera on sunny spring Sundays, enjoyed flowers and songs and dancing in a riverside *guingette,* and experienced the best times of their love. In the movie *La Belle Equipe* (1936), the new superstar Jean Gabin, playing a lucky worker enjoying a perfect day along the Marne, sang all the conventions of the old tradition to an old-fashioned waltz melody: "When we go for a stroll beside the water / How beautiful everything is. . . . / What a renewing. . . . / Paris in the distance seems like a prison / Our hearts are full of songs."[31] This vision of a little Parisian's paradise offered the populist satisfactions of the old and familiar. It did not satisfy the dream of a more definitive flight from it all. For that, for a more exciting new life, one had to go farther afield.

The Allure of Distant Lands

More distant and exotic settings enjoyed great favor during the thirties, and the great expanses of the colonial empire in particular stirred the imagination of many in the hexagon. In 1931 the Exposition Coloniale internationale brought to Paris a large display of the variety and extent of the French empire, giving visitors the experience of exploring a Sudanese village, a Moroccan palace, a Laotian pagoda, and the Great Mosque from Djenné in Mali. More than thirty-three million entry tickets were sold—most to inhabitants of the confining capital.[32] The show in the Bois de Vincennes offered ordinary Parisians a chance to sample the empire's settings of faraway adventure and *grand air*. Beyond familiar boundaries and domestic life lay antidotes to feelings of being stifled and cramped.

Politically, the interest in a France beyond the hexagon sprang from a combination of nationalist, imperialist, and conservative convictions. The saga of Frenchmen pushing into the unknown and enlarging the empire had long fascinated the public and had cheered many on the Right, but few had ventured out to see for themselves or to colonize the larger France. "For too long," one empire booster observed in 1927, "the Frenchman has remained an individual who cared little for travel and not at all for settling abroad."[33] That observer and numerous others hoped that new films showing the colonies' great resources would change minds. Similar hopes were placed in the Exposition Coloniale. At the time restive peoples were already threatening to break up the empire, but the exposition showed neither their unrest nor their poverty. Instead it celebrated France's famed "civilizing mission" and the larger-world identity of each French citizen. As the Minister of Colonies put it, "each of us must feel ourselves a citizen of *la Grande France*."[34]

Throughout the 1930s a stream of both documentary and feature films brought views and vicarious experiences of that larger world to French audiences. In the late thirties one-third of French films were set outside France.[35] Featured most often were hot climes, especially the deserts of Africa and the Sahara above all—the "mysterious Sahara," as it was commonly called. The setting was already consecrated as romantic and dangerous by Rudolph Valentino's international success as *The Sheik* (1922) and by the sad love song "Sous le Soleil Marocain" (1925). As the Americans had their wild open West, the French had North Africa. "It's the French California," observed one reviewer; "its types, scenery, spaces, lights are perfect [for cinema]."[36] On galloping horses, troops of Legionnaires and Algerian Arabs—*spahis* and *goumiers*—met the enemy in wide, open spaces and fought valiantly for France.

Those movies drew homeland audiences into the exciting drama of a Frenchman or a small group engaging in decisive action for greater France far from the gray, closed-in capital and the nagging problems there. During the era of silent films, documentaries about little-known parts of the globe had become audience favorites, but the protagonists were rarely French. The American film *Nanook of the North* and Oscar Olsson's *Au Coeur de l'Afrique sauvage* had been huge box-office successes when they appeared in 1922. The following year a film about the last polar expedition of the British explorer Sir Ernest Shackleton captivated French audiences. Weekly newsreels showed awe-inspiring footage of men of other nationalities climbing Mount Everest. A French documentary about a winning French expedition—director Léon Poirier's *La Croisière noire* (1926)—made an exceptionally strong impression. The film followed daring drivers racing from Morocco to Madagascar, encountering a fascinating diversity of African peoples along the way. Among fictional films, the greatest success was Jacques Feyder's *L'Atlantide* (premiered in 1921 and re-released in 1928), based on a best-selling novel. It was a thousand-and-one-nights tale about a Frenchman in the Sahara falling under the spell of a local femme fatale and suffering terrible consequences. Reviewer Jean Tedesco, like his colleagues generally, hailed the film as "the greatest cinematographic success." Dismissing the plot, Tedesco noted that it was "African nature and the Moslem soul" that interested French spectators, "that's all." A series of films about the great North African desert followed, highlighting the romances of Frenchmen and Arab women.[37]

During the thirties documentaries and feature films more regularly showed Frenchmen as leading players in great adventures and epic struggles overseas. Some of those films sang the praises of empire builders: the documentary *La Pacification du Maroc* (1935) and Marcel L'Herbier's fictional film *Les Hommes nouveaux* (1935) paid tribute to the heroic Marshal Lyautey and his successors in North Africa; Léon Poirier's *L'Appel du silence* (1936) admiringly recreated the life and work of missionary Charles de Foucauld. *Le Grand Jeu* (1933), *La Bandera* (1935), and *Un de la Légion* (1936) were even more successful at the box office (indeed, they were among the decade's most popular films of fiction), and in all of them the legionnaire was the hero.

In Jacques Feyder's *Le Grand Jeu,* the hero was a brilliant lawyer who found glory and death in the Foreign Legion after fleeing a scandal in France. More often the protagonist was a "man of the people." Now, thanks to the new soundtracks conveying his accent and slang, that social identity directly and immediately registered with audiences. The "little guy" ventured out from a known small community in France and struggled against new challenges, courageously meeting the unknown. In the Foreign Legion he was able to begin a new life and assume a new identity. He made a fresh beginning not only as an individual, but also as a member of a close new social group—with other "little guys" among whom there was an easy rapport of shared backgrounds. Life in that new community meant freedom from old constraints, but it also meant discipline and submission to new authorities. The legionnaires were ready to sacrifice themselves for the flag and the good of the group. In *La Bandera* audiences saw such a scenario featuring some do-or-die Frenchmen in the Spanish foreign legion—with a dénouement that was courageously heroic but tragic. The next year the ballad "Le Fanion de la Légion" (1936) told a similar tale that ended with a more uplifting scene of martial glory: out of thirty French legionnaires holding a hillside bastion against a week-long attack by a horde of *salopards,* three bloody defenders remain unbowed when a column of reinforcements arrives. They have run out of wine, water, bread, and ammunition,

"Mon Légionnaire" was first Marie Dubas's song, then Edith Piaf's—visions of hot sand, sun, a night of passion, and a lost lover. Private collection.

and their battalion flag has been stolen, but the three hold out, defiant tattered victors who, with images of their flag drawn in blood on their blackened chests, proudly shout during roll call, "Present, the Legion!" That same year *Un de la Légion* (directed by Christian-Jaque) presented the story of a "little" legionnaire who is initially a comic figure. Fernandel plays the silly, apparently simple Southerner who is abducted into the Legion and is sent to the embattled desert South of Algeria. He finds good times in the company of a faithful new buddy who is a Parisian titi, and he takes to the challenging life of adventure and fighting, showing himself to be brave and resourceful.[38]

The legionnaire was often shown to be fortunate in love, too. A local Arab woman or a visiting fashionable Parisienne would find him irresistible. The hit song "Mon Légionnaire" (1936), sung first by Marie Dubas and then by a twenty-two-year-old newcomer named Edith Piaf, spells out how strong his appeal was in the imagination of the era. The woman sings that she doesn't know his name or anything about him, but happily she proclaims: "He loved me all night / My legion-naire!. . . He was slender. . . he was handsome / He smelled good like hot sand."[39] Other songs such as "L'Etranger" (1934) and "L'Escale" (1938) related passionate one-night affairs between an ordinary sailor and a young woman who can never forget him. He leaves on a ship the next day and comes to a tragic end at sea, but his kiss "burns" her forever. Like Marius, the male protagonist acts on the impulse to leave, and the woman remains at home, dreaming of the love so briefly known and mourning its loss.

During the late thirties, to get away (*partir*) became an even more prominent theme of literature and film. In 1937 *Pépé le Moko* (directed by Jean Duvivier with the screenplay by Henri Jeanson) took spectators into the mysterious Casbah of Algiers (in reality a skillfully constructed studio set), where Pépé, a "bad guy" from Paris (played by Jean Gabin), was in hiding.[40] Pépé has entrenched himself in the hillside maze of alleyways and whitewashed buildings of an exotic inner city. He moves easily through the narrow streets and courtyards and bazaars crowded with fez-topped men in long djellabas and bejeweled women. Smiling and debonair, a natural winner in his little community (like the mythic faubourien), Pépé takes whatever food and drink he wants from omnipresent vendors. As an outlaw leader in a fascinating refuge, he has made a good life: he has friends, minions, and a devoted Arab lover. Yet he yearns to get away. His haven feels like a prison, particularly when a visiting Parisian beauty catches his eye and makes him realize how much he misses Paris. He falls in love and longs to go back to Paris with her. But in the end Pépé is trapped by the police. When he realizes that he cannot get away and that she is leaving, he chooses death by his own hand. After playing to fantasies of an exotic, sunny place, *Pépé le Moko* then spoke to doubts about whether one could really escape. This grim movie appeared at a time when raging enmities within France and Fascist strength abroad gave abundant reason for pessimism.

The next spring, after Hitler's troops marched into Austria and the Fuhrer began making demands on Czechoslovakia, audiences flocked to a new film that beautifully dramatized the sense of being trapped and the yearning to leave for faraway places: the movie was *Le Quai des brumes,* directed by Marcel Carné. Set in the port city of Le Havre, a place of departures, Carné's version of a Pierre MacOrlan story presented one of the most despairing scenarios of the times. The protagonist, a hapless colonial army deserter named Jean, lands in a seedy bar near the port and there happens to meet a woman he can love, beautiful young Nelly. Briefly they dream of enjoying a better life together far from France, but he is

In the narrow but sun-drenched street of the Casbah, Pépé, drunk and fed up with his life there, tries to leave, and his Arab lover Inès tries to stop him in *Pépé le Moko* (1937). Courtesy of BFI Stills, Posters, and Designs.

hunted down by a brutal destiny. Like Pépé, he fails to get away. Just when fulfillment in love seems to be realized, he meets a violent death. Jean was just one of many failures or losers (*ratés*) in the cast of unfortunate characters, as Paul Achard noted. They try to get away "by suicide, desertion, debauchery, depravation, theft, crime," but not one of them succeeds in escaping their bad luck. Right-wing critics found the characters disgusting and worried about the picture of decadence that the film sent abroad. But the general public evidently identified with the leading characters, who were played by the exceptionally appealing actors Jean Gabin and Michèle Morgan. *Le Quai des brumes* was a box-office success.[41]

Even though a number of widely viewed movies showed life elsewhere not to be better, many stories set far from Paris gave reason for hope. The focus on village and colonial life showed alternatives to the increasingly rationalized and strife-ridden society of the big cities. While many stories of the provinces resembled the gentle populist version of life in Paris, the brave adventurers in the outlying empire were an attractive contrast to both types of parochial "little guys." They were clearly serving the country and the larger realm, and they were living close to nature. Their lives demonstrated efforts at liberation and renewal. Stories about them allowed audiences to identify with heroes who did well outside the safe familiar order. They provided reassuring representations of individuals who did not fit comfortably into a small, intimate order but enjoyed mystery and the openness and freedom of moving beyond such an order. Often those adventurers found romance as well, particularly in hot, sunny places that movies and songs stereotyped as the natural setting for love.

The interest in "changing atmospheres," in short, was much more than a romantic yearning to get away or escape from tiresome treadmills and frustrations. The fascination with "elsewhere" was often joined to a concern about the nation and its renewal. In 1936 and 1937 that search for renewal produced important political consequences: first, a Popular Front law of 1936 mandated paid vacations, which gave millions of workers the chance to enjoy several weeks outside the cities (see chapter 8). The next year the provinces were brought to Paris in the exhibits of the 1937 Exposition internationale. It was officially "L'Exposition internationale des arts et techniques appliqués à la vie moderne," and, like previous expositions, it displayed some impressive technological advances in radio and cinema, the world's largest movie screen of 600 square meters). But more than its predecessors, it highlighted the enduring old-fashioned France of the provinces. Rather than stressing the marvels of machinery, it celebrated crafts, the work of artisans. It was a response to "rationalized and Taylorized industry," as one journalist noted.[42] In contrast to the 1925 celebration of an international modern style, the 1937 exposition lavished attention on the folklore and other traditions—food, dress, crafts—of diverse regions.

One of the goals of the exposition was to stimulate the economy through more tourism, luring visitors to the capital into the hinterland. At the Pavilion of Cinema thousands of visitors each day saw the best films on the regions of France: *Le Rouergue* by J. C. Bernard, *Occitanie* by Raymond Millet, *La Bourgogne* by Jean Epstein, and movies on Lorraine and the Jura, Savoy, and the Pyrenees. They extended a repeated *invitation au voyage*.

At the exposition's Rural Center visitors saw an ideal country village, up-to-date technologically yet full of the traditional charms. It was the Third Republic's utopian rural community, devoid of poverty, clericalism, and benighted parochialism. Reporters described the bright side at length, but some could not help recalling the grim past that the model village left out: the hundreds of thousands of peasants who did not come back from the war, and the many thousands who left the farms after the war, unable to support themselves on the land. The most striking and dominant image of the countryside, however, was a favorable one. A return to rural France, the model village suggested, was a way to promote social harmony and a simpler good life.[43]

In all their variety, the stories about "elsewhere" allowed moviegoers to explore alternative sides of their collective identity, to contemplate the possibilities of French life in a warm environment away from the fabled capital, long the setting of most commercial songs and movies.[44] Of all the places explored by consumers of French mass culture, the part of the world offering them the greatest hope of an accessible and livable alternative was the French countryside, the provincial heartland. During the thirties an infatuation with that countryside took a remarkable diversity of forms. This deep cultural current would be tapped by both ends of the political spectrum, the Left championing close-to-nature vacations for all, and the Right calling for a return to rural life.

7. BONHOMIE
AND MILITANCY

Political Culture Before the Era of the Popular Front

WHEN FIERCE POLITICAL BATTLES broke out in France in 1934, a new representation of the people emerged to rival the long-familiar one of young working men
and women strolling by twos down the streets. The good-humored *mécano* and
midinette of the mid-1920s became the demonstrating militant of 1934–36. The new
images were of massed throngs marching together resolutely, brandishing political banners and shouting slogans and songs. The political side of that story took
form in the history books long ago. What follows is an account that focuses on a
fundamental cultural struggle.[1] When Left and Right fought for control of the
streets and campaigned for votes and control of the government, they also engaged
in a struggle over representations of the people. In speeches, demonstrations, festivities, songs, and films, each side strove to impose its image of the people, its version of the politically activist "little guys." At the same time both sides proposed
alternatives to the images found in commercial mass culture.

Early in the Third Republic, during the 1880s, masses of common people had manifested political commitment by joining in public celebrations of

Bastille Day. Although some people were simply enjoying a holiday and its amusements, many were also celebrating the republic's ideals of liberty, equality, and fraternity. Later, notably in the decade after the Great War, public enthusiasm for the Third Republic withered almost to the point of dying. After the victory celebration in 1919, as the postwar economic difficulties set in, the republic seemed to be lackluster and an ineffectual system of government that did little and satisfied few. The regime that identified itself with the common people could no longer rally the people to join in festive fraternity even once a year. The present seemed too grim to warrant widespread rejoicing, and the once exciting historic memories had faded. To most of the population the political example set by militant artisans and laborers was remote and dim. The union movement's memory of heroic strikers had also faded. Hundreds of thousands of workers immersed in that tradition had been killed in the war, and their place in the economy was taken by insecure newcomers—a million peasants fresh off the land and more than a million foreign workers who immigrated to France in the decade or so after the war. In the wake of government repression following the war, the unions were quiescent and dispirited.[2]

During the late 1920s the lull ended. The sight of French people massing for political causes became commonplace. The part of that political history that most concerns me here is the scene of "the people" demonstrating and commemorating with new fervor. Viewed as spectacle, those demonstrations and their messages can be understood in a context of other images and messages of the period, in particular those coming from popular entertainment.

In the forefront of the new mass movements were several large veterans' groups. As Antoine Prost has recounted in his excellent study, organized veterans renewed their old camaraderie and showed their strength especially on armistice day anniversaries, when they gathered to honor the victims of the Great War, to praise the poilu, and to denounce the horrors of war. The former combatants also pursued narrower political objectives. Their politics covered the spectrum, but support for rightist (nationalistic, authoritarian) positions was strongest. During the early 1930s these organizations were at the height of their strength. Decorated veterans of the Croix de Feu, troops of middle-aged men with mustaches and berets, paraded gravely with a panoply of French flags. A nonpolitical association when it was founded in 1927, the Croix de Feu became stridently hostile to establishment politics and the parliamentary system. After 1929 under the leadership of Colonel de la Rocque, it enlarged its ranks by recruiting and training nonveterans for aux-

The powerful war veterans' organization of the Right, the Croix de Feu, showed its strength in a military-style march down the Champs-Elysées 14 July 1935, the participants each brandishing the national flag. Phot. Bibl. Nat. de Fr.-Paris.

iliary combat squads, ready to do battle in the streets with Communists and other enemies.[3]

Other rightist nationalists and antiparliamentary authoritarians were joining military-style leagues fashioned after the example of fascists abroad. From the mid-twenties on, the blue-shirted beret-capped Jeunesses patriotes and the blue-shirted, gray-hatted "Union [*Faiseau*] of Fighters" showed their growing force in periodic rallies and demonstrations.[4] Uniformed members of these leagues marched in military formation with an air of controlled anger and grim determination. Their marches culminated at symbolic sites dear to rightist nationalists—the statue of Joan of Arc and the Arc de Triomphe. After Hitler came to power in 1933, two other leagues were formed in the most blatant imitation of fascists abroad: the Solidarité française and the blue-shirted Francistes—small but attention-grabbing organizations of men in uniform, ready to fight, taking their stand against parliamentary politics, Jews and immigrants, Communists and Socialists. The league members (all men) demonstrated as an elite corps of the French people, making an aggressive show of their nationalist identity.

The Left was much less visible, and its strength was less impressive. Heated rivalries kept it divided—Communist labor unions against non-Communist unions, the Socialist party and the Communist party bitterly opposed to each other since their split in 1920, the Radical party fiercely opposing both Marxist parties.

Staying close to the political center, France's Radicals—the largest nonsocialist party on the Left—championed liberty for the "little guy" in its rhetoric and legislative action, but the Radicals immersed themselves in parliamentary politics and showed no interest in stirring the masses into action. Nor did the Socialists. The Communist party, the smallest of the three, followed a hard-line Moscow and Comintern policy of class warfare against everyone but proletarians during the late twenties and early thirties. Its appeal in France then declined drastically, its electoral support faded, and its membership shrank to an all-time low in 1933.[5]

During the twenties these self-regarding parties and unions worked for future strength most effectively through youth organizations. Many French young people were eager for change in society. Anxious and energetic, they sought new forms of social organization that would give human dignity to more people.[6] As Robert Wohl has shown, many youth had developed self-consciousness as a generation, defining themselves in opposition to older, establishment people. From the late twenties on, they were increasingly cast in political molds through new organizations for leisure and social service activities. They were organized in scout troops, youth hostel associations, athletic teams and leagues, Catholic action movements, and the social action groups of political parties and unions. Particularly strong were the youth organizations of the Socialist party, the Communist party, and the huge union federation that was the Confédération générale du travail (CGT).[7]

For these groups of the Left to unite, it took a new awareness of common dangers threatening them and France. Anxiety about such dangers sharply increased from 1931 to 1933. Rising unemployment in 1932 made it harder to believe that the French would be spared the worst of the Depression, and the threat of a new aggressive Germany loomed larger. Journalists reported regularly about the menace of the Nazis, particularly after Hitler became chancellor in January 1933. In February 1934, for example, a special issue of *Le Crapouillot* was devoted to "Dangers to the World." In an article on "the Hitlerian menace," Paul Achard warned that Germany, Japan, and Italy—three strongly nationalistic countries with hopes of expansion—might join their armies together to pursue their aggressive ends. In the July issue Dr. Henri Dejust envisaged future air and chemical warfare and argued that protecting civilians would not be possible; to try to protect them was "to content oneself with a symptomatic and impotent therapeutic."[8] The reasons for alarm were clearly set forth, though they did not seriously disturb most people before 1934. The millions of Frenchmen who followed events through the weekly newsreels scarcely had reason to believe that fascism and war were imminent dangers. What they saw most in the movie news was footage of the comings and goings of celebrities in politics and show business, fashion, and sports. Then in early 1934, danger hit home. In February 1934 some bloody battles in the streets of Paris and the threat of a fascist coup brought a sense of crisis that few could ignore.

Struggle and Fête

On the night of 6 February 1934, the nation's political fears and dark hatreds joined in street battle in the heart of the capital. Right-wing veterans and leagues, outraged over the government's handling of a financial scandal, gathered in the Place de la Concorde late in the day with the intent of protesting and marching on the Chamber of Deputies. The scandal involved swindler Serge Stavisky, who represented all that the Right imagined and hated as the "other": he was foreign-born and Jewish. The leagues' offensives were more than a protest against Stavisky but less than a coordinated fascist conspiracy; they were aimed at changing the government whose high officials appeared to have protected the crook. Partisans of the Left—veterans associated with the Communists—came out for counteraction, and violent clashes ensued in the night. When the murky battle around the Place de la Concorde ended, 15 people were dead and 1,435 had been wounded. In response to the Right's assaults that night, the Communists and their trade union held a large daytime demonstration on 9 February to display their force. Their show of strength took place on the working-class side of town in a site symbolically identified with the Republic—the Place de la République. There were again massed militants, and more bloody fighting. Battles with the police that day resulted in six deaths and hundreds of people wounded. Next, the nation's biggest trade union, the CGT, called a general strike for Monday 12 February, and on that day unionists along with partisans of the Socialist and Communist parties filled the large Cours de Vincennes and the Place de la Nation with shoulder-to-shoulder marchers and identifying banners. Assuming the role of combatants, they shouted a cry adopted from the battle of Verdun: "the fascists will not prevail!" (Ils ne passeront pas!).[9]

The threats posed by the leagues had jolted French citizens of the center and Left into action—as antifascists above all. Altogether the street battles from 6 to 12 February left thirty-seven people dead and brought anger and fear to the boiling point. To the outraged Right it seemed that a corrupt government had deliberately assaulted decent, concerned citizens on 6 February. To the Left, the leagues seemed to threaten the very existence of liberal democracy, as Mussolini's Fascists had in Italy a little more than a decade before. Antidemocratic forces seemed to

Battle-weary demonstrators of the Right after the night of 6 February 1934. *Le Journal* photograph. Private collection.

be preparing for a coup, perhaps working in conjunction with Hitlerian forces. Adrenaline-charged foes of the "fascists," like the young teacher Claude Jamet in Bourges, scurried to answer the threat with antifascist manifestos and marches.[10]

Both sides took to the streets in more demonstrations and mass processions, producing a period of agitation not seen for decades. Over the next two years the French Right and Left vied with each other nearly daily in the no-man's-land of urban spaces, each side intent on impressing the public and the government with the strength and will of its demonstrators. By their size and regularity the demonstrations were unprecedented.[11] Demonstrations, counterdemonstrations, political meetings, and corteges—the spectacle of militant masses became a part of everyday life. The streets were now battlefields. They were also a stage for the self-dramatization of the people now in action as militants.

The Left's tens of thousands presented an image of the people fighting back—against war, against fascism, and against unemployment. Sometimes they fought literally, too, with right-wing groups and with the police, but the main struggle was in the arena of representations, in the display of a mobilized mass of partisans. That display of power was as crucial to galvanizing the participants with a sense of their own strength as it was to influencing public opinion. When the beleaguered government tried to impose new restrictions on demonstrations in the fall of 1934, Communist and Socialist leaders protested and spelled out what was at stake: "The working people [*le peuple des travailleurs*] have two effective arms at their disposal: the force of worker [*ouvrier*] organization and the display [*manifestation*] of their mass power."[12]

Armistice Day 1934 became one of many days of clashing political offensives in the streets. Right-wing political organizations and rightist veterans' groups showed their strength between the Place de la Concorde and the Arc de Triomphe, while the Left mustered its partisans in the working-class end of the city—on the Place de la République and the Place de la Nation.[13] Several months later, on the first anniversary of the February demonstrations, both sides held demonstrations commemorating the *journées* of the year before. On 6 February right-wing groups paid homage to the dead with assemblies in front of Notre Dame, at the Place Saint-Michel, and near the Place de la Concorde. The Left called on "republican and antifascist workers [*travailleurs*]" to assemble at the Place de la République and to place there a "red flower of remembrance." Between 50,000 and 100,000 people responded.

Longer-term historic memory provided occasions for other demonstrations of numbers and commitment. The unions and their political allies came out en masse on 1 May, the traditional day for labor to celebrate and to flex its muscle publicly. On 13 May the Right showed its organized strength on the holiday honoring Joan of Arc. The next week the Left massed to commemorate the execution of the last Communards near a wall in Père Lachaise cemetery. An unusually large number of activists of the Left went to the famous wall on 19 May to pay their respects and to rededicate their will to the struggle. The police estimated the crowd there at 50,000; the organizers estimated 200,000 to 300,000.[14]

After the shocks of February 1934, Bastille Day ceased being a quiet summer holiday and became a prime time for political battle. On 14 July 1935, one of the most emotionally charged Bastille Days of the twentieth century, throngs of the now politically active turned the holiday into a day of mass marches and ritual oath-taking. Up the Champs-Elysées to the Etoile marched more than 150,000 partisans of nationalist and right-wing organizations. On the other side of the city where working people predominated, the Left assembled in mid-afternoon at the Place de la Bastille. Communist, Socialist, and Radical leaders—Maurice Thorez, Léon Blum, and Edouard Daladier, respectively—and tens of thousands of their supporters took an oath to defend democratic liberties against the fascists. Then the demonstrators (500,000 according to their leaders, 50,000 according to the police) marched to the Place de la Nation in a cortege that went on for five or six hours. The streets were a slowly advancing sea of workers' caps, raised fists, banderoles, and banners. So the Left paraded its troops from the site of the people's revolutionary victory to the large square honoring the nation, a place dominated by a large alle-

Bastille Day, 14 July 1935. "The people" as militants unite in street marches manifesting their unity and readiness for struggle against "the Fascists," the "enemies of the people," according to the Comité national de Rassemblement populaire, which produced an illustrated booklet that contained these photomontages. Participants included Socialists, Communists, members of the Radical party (which was the least "radical"), and unionists. Private collection. All rights reserved.

gorical statue of the Republic. Similar marches and demonstrations of the Left took place in provincial towns throughout France. Although these actions were in part tactical offensives, the marchers presented them as defensive, like the poilus' struggle against the invaders. In the militants' view they were not only defending the republic against fascist forces, but they were also taking a stand against pay cuts, unemployment, and the government's budget cuts.

While the battle for the streets went on, another battle was joined for control of national symbols and the national memory. Through ritual and rhetoric the self-styled defenders of the republic and the nation pointedly identified their struggle with the cause of the revolutionaries of 1789 and 1790. The morning of 14 July 1935, partisans of the Left gathered at the Vélodrome Buffalo (in the Parisian suburb of Montrouge) for symbolic acts and speeches invoking the revolutionaries' heroic deeds. Delegations from the provinces and some forty-eight organizations—a throng that organizers numbered at 10,000—took an oath to remain united to "defend democracy in France" and to "disarm and dissolve the factious leagues." They further vowed "to give bread to the workers [*travailleurs*], work to youth, and to the world, a great humane peace." Youthful militants in particular stressed the need for jobs.

The Left's cultural offensive included reclaiming nationalist symbols that the Right had appropriated. Addressing the Vélodrome crowd that 14 July, Nobel Prize-winning physicist Jean Perrin lamented that the Rightists had taken over powerful symbols not really appropriate to their values: Joan of Arc—"this daughter of the *peuple*, abandoned by the king whom popular élan had just made victorious and burned by the priests who since have canonized her"; the tricolor, the flag of 1789; and "this heroic 'Marseillaise,' this ferocious and revolutionary song."[15] To rally the broadest possible following, the Left now had to reappropriate those focal points of the national memory. Communist party spokesman Jacques Duclos urged "fighters for liberty" under the tricolor to join with those who fought under the red flag. Accordingly, the crowd sang both the "Internationale" and "La Marseillaise." Many wore the red Phrygian cap that had been a favorite in 1789. In short, there was a "rebirth of revolutionary folklore," as one contemporary put it.[16] That folklore combined with new practices to create what historians call the culture of the Popular Front.

The immediate consequences were not encouraging. Forty-eight hours after the crowds had their big day, Premier Pierre Laval issued decrees prohibiting further demonstrations and reducing salaries in the public sector. The Popular

Front had lost a round, but during the nine months that followed it continued to gain organized strength and prominence. Demonstrators regularly fought battles with police until new decrees in October 1935 allowed gatherings and demonstrations (on condition that advance notice be given and the prefect's authorization be obtained). More orderly and peaceful demonstrations resumed.

Delegations from leftist youth groups took greater part in the demonstrations, marches, and rallies of 1935–36. So did more and more women and children. The crowd scenes in the street took on the appearance of family activities, exuding more often a spirit of celebration than of struggle. Again and again their marches and rallies showed those the Left called "the people" to be good-natured and fun-loving even while engaged in battle. They made a striking contrast to the sober, disciplined, militaristic all-male corteges of the Right.[17] Their image, created in the street and reproduced in newspaper and magazine photos, also contrasted with portrayals in song and film of "the people" as frivolous and amusing characters immersed in their private lives.

The marchers for the Left were no longer the anxious antifascist combatants of February 1934. Taking delight in their gathering strength, they mixed festivity with political action. Putting themselves on parade as "the people," Popular Front demonstrators decked themselves out with red liberty caps and colorful insignia, slogan-filled banners and signs, tricolor flags and red flags. Arms intertwined in solidarity, they sang the "Internationale" and "La Marseillaise," and they raised their fists in a gesture of determination and solidarity. Some demonstrations included colorful parade floats full of political allegory. Loudspeakers boomed exhortations from the leaders, and bands added militant music to the festive excess. After the marches came banquets and dances with participants celebrating electoral victories and rallying for coming battles. Carnival rides and games—*fêtes foraines,* too—found their way into programs, as they did on traditional holidays.[18] Like the poilu on the front as imagined by the home front, the Popular Front combatants brought touches of a famed Gallic gaiety to the struggle.

While the leftist leaders marshaled demonstrations and powerful symbols for their cause, they also crafted a new verbal identity for their following. Striving to group as many people as possible in a unified movement, they cast their appeals in more socially inclusive terms than the old language of the left. Terms stressing class divisions—*ouvriers* and *classe ouvrière*—were too limiting. So in 1934 CGT spokesmen addressed their appeals instead to the "people," "workers" (*travailleurs*), and "popular forces." Leftist and union leaders also adopted the phrases *masses laborieuses* and *masses populaires*. These ambiguous group names not only spoke to a wide social range, but they also avoided reminders of a divided left. Only the Communists and their branch of the CGT continued to speak at times of "proletarian action" and the "classe ouvrière."[19] By July 1935 Socialist and Communist leaders alike were endorsing what was called a *Front populaire* to combat fascism. For its part the Right reached out for support by addressing its appeals to "the French," which in rightist discourse connoted an ethnic group excluding immigrants and Jews. At the same time rightist leaders called for a *Front national* to combat the Left. Against them were the despised others, readily categorized by an array of old epithets. The right-wing press scornfully referred to Popular Front demonstrators as "blind" hate-filled "mobs" dominated by the "riffraff," aliens (*métèques*), and treacherous Communists.[20]

The Left's discourse portrayed the "little people" as a multitude marshaled against foes who were identified (vaguely) as "the big ones" and "the two hundred families" (the number of controlling stockholders of the Bank of France). From the mid-1920s on, the Radicals in particular spoke frequently of a struggle of "the *petits* against the *gros*." From 1935 on, *L'Humanité* referred regularly to the struggles of "the French people against the two hundred families." Socialists joined in attacks on "the two hundred families" as the Popular Front began to take form. Also identified as enemies of the people were descendants of aristocratic counterrevolutionary émigrés, "trusts," "feudal powers" (*féodalités, féodaux*), "big arms dealers" (*marchands de canons*), "kings of commerce," and big capitalists (*les gros*). To many during that time such phrases called to mind a group not identified by name: Jews. As for the Radicals, the mention of the Rothschilds alone sufficed to identify and disparage a whole group. In this matter of anti-Semitism the Right was not to be outdone: it mounted an exceptionally ferocious campaign of attacks on Socialist leader Léon Blum as a Jew and on "international finance," another code word playing to anti-Semitism.[21]

The Left's verbal appeals were strategic efforts to create a new alliance of classes, redrawing the line that marked off the social identity of "the people" and recasting the way in which their past was remembered. Building a new movement entailed embracing old symbols and ideological motifs that had broad appeal: the Popular Front reclaimed not only the tricolor of 1789 and "La Marseillaise" but, unfortunately, also some anti-Semitism. At the same time it implanted the new social representations in everyday public space, regularly massing crowds in demonstrations, assembling diverse groups impressive in their numbers and unity. In the city streets, newspapers, and magazines, the spectacle of the "laboring masses" became manifest day after day. As workers and their allies the *petits bourgeois* gained ascendancy on the streets, they asserted their role in national life to be a preeminent one. In 1936 they moved to the front of the national stage and took the lead in the spring electoral campaign.

Mass-Culture Images of Workers

Meanwhile, at the movies, people saw little of that turmoil. Government authorities did not permit newsreel footage of the fighting on 6 February 1934 to be shown, and later newsreel coverage of the Left's demonstrations was kept to a minimum.[22] During the years leading up to the Popular Front victory of 1936, commercial films rarely showed workers uniting, making demands, and displaying solidarity in the face of the economic and political power holders. Images of demonstrating workers were taboo, and most films did not show workers at all, particularly industrial workers and their workplaces. During the heyday of the Popular Front the films set in Paris (almost two-thirds of French production) showed either picturesque old quarters like Ménilmontant or chic quartiers of luxurious townhouses and restaurants.[23]

Several important exceptions made a small countercurrent. One that preceded the Popular Front by several years was René Clair's *A Nous la liberté* (1931), a satire on the emptiness of lives in the industrial workplace. For the boss and the lowly worker alike, the factory was like a prison. Finally, the wealthy man and the worker escape and find friendship and happiness in freedom—as tramps. Although *A Nous la liberté* expressed yearnings for liberty and indicted dehumanizing work, it did not oppose the boss to the worker as the Popular Front mentality did. And it did not depict workers engaged in political or union action of the kind that was central to Popular Front culture. Nevertheless, it was too critical and disturbing for amusement-seeking audiences in the early 1930s and was not a box-office success.[24] Several years later, however, it inspired Charlie Chaplin's *Modern Times* (*Les Temps modernes*) of 1935, which was commercially successful in France. By then audiences were more receptive to the critical spirit (critical of dehumanized work, though Chaplin's film was no more political than Clair's was), and in addition it featured the well-established popular favorite, "Charlot."

Other exceptions were two Jean Renoir movies of 1934 and 1935. *Toni*, made during the summer of 1934 and released in February 1935, was unusual in putting the spotlight not just on workers, but on immigrant workers. The hero is

Toni, a man of Italian origin, who has come to the South of France with immigrants of other lands to work in a quarry. The "other" is a brutal French foreman named Albert. The foreman seduces Josepha, whom Toni loves, and marries her. Toni marries Maria, his landlady. Neither marriage is happy, and two years later Josepha kills Albert. Toni takes the blame and then attempts to escape, but he ends up being shot on the railroad tracks that bring a train full of new immigrants to the area. Worker camaraderie, portrayed by real-life workers, contrasted with a villainous boss, foreshadowing scenes of Popular Front militancy. Toni and his co-workers, however, do not have a notion of a union or a sense of political consciousness.[25]

Renoir's *Le Crime de Monsieur Lange*, made in late 1935, also portrayed a worker sympathetically, in this case an employee of a small publishing company, Amédée Lange, who is a gentle dreamer and a story writer. When he creates a series of adventures about his fictional hero, Arizona Jim, his work meets with commercial success, but his unscrupulous boss, Batala, cheats him out of his due, just as Batala fleeces the company's creditors. Lange finds love with a savvy, cheerful working woman named Valentine who owns a laundry, which opens onto the same courtyard as Batala's business and Lange's modest apartment. The character Valentine was a break with cinema convention in several respects: she runs her own business, is clear-sighted and strong, and boldly takes the lead in denouncing Batala after he preys on and impregnates a pretty young woman who works in the laundry. At the same time Valentine is traditional in her central concern for love and her nurturing support of Lange, and she is the one who sings a bluesy number about how sad life is. Despite the success of Lange's work, the company runs aground. Batala lets debts pile up and one day flees and is reportedly killed in a train wreck. The workers, resourceful and industrious, save the business by organizing it as a cooperative, which prospers. Then one day Batala returns and tries to take back control. Ridiculing the cooperative as a big mess (*la pagaille*), he declares the need for authority. The formerly trusting Lange confronts a taunting Batala (dressed in a priest's clothing) back in the office and ends up killing him. Then he speeds away with Valentine in a car driven by the big-hearted son of a major creditor. In a café on the Franco-Belgian border, a group of "little people" learns of the murder and the story behind it; in the end they decide to let the fleeing couple go.

At first glance the work as a whole seems to reflect a climate of politicized passion and class conflict. The scenario, written by Jacques Prévert, pits the good, hard-working "little guys" against a villainous bourgeois. The workers' cooperative reminded some conservative spectators of a Bolshevik Soviet when the film

Amédée Lange (René Lefèvre) and Valentine (Florelle), both wronged by his boss, Batala, go on with their lives, work, and love in *Le Crime de Monsieur Lange* (1935). Courtesy of MoMA Film Stills.

was first screened in early 1936. Yet reviewers, even those on the Right, did not find the film to be subversive. Rather it seemed to most to be a populist work, depicting a complete microcosm of "little people" in a courtyard. The people have their flaws; individually they are anything but heroic, yet they struggle on.

Most remarkably, *Le Crime de Monsieur Lange* even showed them joining together in courageous solidarity to deal with a crisis, and it ended with the people sanctioning violent action against an oppressor. Renoir wrote that his intention was to show that every human being who had achieved something had "the right to defend it against a robber, even when this robber supports his action on legal principles."[26] When the film reached the theaters of France, the air was filled with demands for "bread" and work, denunciations of fascist enemies, and talk about the people's right to defend themselves against their exploiters. During the early months of 1936 Premier Laval and his successor Albert Sarraut were pursuing a deflationary policy; working people suffered pay cuts, and unemployment spread. Increasing political tensions manifested themselves dramatically in February when a right-winger brutally assaulted Socialist leader Léon Blum, leaving him with multiple head injuries. *Le Crime de Monsieur Lange* had its première in those explosive times, just three months before the Popular Front won the elections. The film was still playing during the weeks of hard-hitting electoral campaigns.

For the most part the mass media introduced political motifs into their productions only in minor and cautious ways—well after public life had become intensely politicized. Films, traditionally apolitical, expressed what was already commonplace when they showed anything overtly political. During 1936 the most popular movies, according to *La Cinématographie française,* were (in order): *César* by Marcel Pagnol (completing the trilogy begun with *Marius* and *Fanny*); *L'Appel du silence* by Léon Poirier (about the missionary Charles de Foucauld in Algeria and Morocco, a film favorite of conservatives); Pierre Colombier's *Le Roi* (a satirical story of a rich Socialist deputy who is twice cuckolded and overlooks it for political gains); Anatol Litvak's *Mayerling* (the tragic love story of the fin-de-siècle Habsburgs); Marcel L'Herbier's *Veille d'armes* (about a ship captain who deals with a mutiny and a family imbroglio); *Les Temps modernes* starring Charlie Chaplin; and Pierre Caron's *Marinella,* starring Tino Rossi (the story of a singing house painter who becomes a star). Next came Jean Renoir's *Les Bas-Fonds (The Lower Depths),* based on Maxim Gorky's play set in Czarist Russia, with Jean Gabin as a jaunty, true-hearted thief ultimately making his way out of a dark flophouse. Tenth was Fernandel's half-comic, half-military epic *Un de la Légion.*[27]

Populist works during the era of the Popular Front rarely ventured into po-

The scoundrel boss, Batala (Jules Berry), cocky as ever, describes his plans to resume control of the publishing firm, and he mockingly suggests that Lange (René Lefèvre) kill him. Courtesy of MoMA Film Stills.

litical territory. The movie *Ménilmontant* (1936) by René Guissart presented only a few more critical edges than did earlier populist films by, for example, René Clair. In one of the poorest quarters in Paris, three toy vendors return a lost ring to a rich woman and receive a reward. With the reward money they construct a park for children. The tale ends by showing big merchants profiteering and politicians claiming credit for good works they did not do, while the humble benefactors of the people are denied access to the ceremony dedicating the playground. What struck most reviewers was not so much the critical touches as the sentimental populism. Ferdinand Lot, who found the film too optimistic, summed up sarcastically: "Never were the good people of Paris so perfectly good." Another reviewer declared the moral of the film to be: those who have nothing should "sign an armistice with those who have everything, provided that the latter show a certain kindness to them." The scenes of the rich woman helping the poor, he observed, contrasted jarringly with recent events in the offices of the Premier, where management delegations always insisted as a condition of negotiations that they never be in direct contact with the workers.[28]

The old rags-to-riches myth—the essential fable of nonpolitical, individualist happiness—occupied an important place on the cultural scene in the year of the Popular Front's victory. Indeed, the myth's classic purveyors—Maurice Chevalier and Mistinguett—took lead roles in new updated versions. Director Maurice Tourneur's film *Avec le Sourire* (1936) gave Chevalier fans another fable of a smiling débrouillard rising to heights of success. Chevalier as the penniless Victor first steals the position of doorman at the Palace music hall, then maneuvers his way to become a program seller, and ends up becoming director of the music hall and then of the Opéra. Now a rich man, he marries a beautiful dancer. His former boss, an honest man, falls to the depths of poverty until finally Victor, learning of the unfortunate man's plight, saves him. One unamused critic summed up the message this way: "The scenario appears destined to illustrate this morality of our noble epoch: anyone can by any means become anything anytime, provided that he is dishonest and devoid of scruples." A reviewer who understood audiences' enjoyment wrote: "We have known the *Roi des resquilleurs*; now here is the emperor of *débrouillards*." Even this enthusiastic reviewer, however, did not like the scene in which the young opportunist gained a lucrative job as doorman by causing the holder of that job to be fired. (Victor anonymously telephoned the doorman a report about his wife's daily rendez-vous with a lover, prompting the cuckolded man to leave work abruptly.) But most of the movie, "considered as a series of sketches,"

Maurice Chevalier in *Avec le Sourire*—this time the movie—during the Popular Front era (1936). Cover of magazine *Le Film complet du mardi*. Private collection.

was amusing. Audiences evidently agreed, identifying less with the unfortunates than with the wily and beaming charmer appropriately named Victor.[29]

Avec le Sourire and similar scenarios played on a continuing tension in French society between admiration for the successful rulebreaker and respect for the honest but poor individual. Actor and author Sacha Guitry contributed to the ongoing debate with the film *Le Roman d'un tricheur* (1936—translated as *The Story of a Cheat* for American audiences), in which a man gains riches by gambling and cheating and then loses it all after deciding to lead an honest life. An even more pessimistic tale of the common man's rise and fall was Julien Duvivier's *L'Homme du jour* (1936), starring Maurice Chevalier. After saving the life of a famous actress, an unsophisticated electrician (Chevalier) enjoys a brief yet exhilarating time of fame ("the man of the day"), mixing with theater stars and the wealthy, but soon a series of mishaps takes its toll. He drops back to his obscure humble life but not to a good-hearted populist community: on returning to his boarding house, he finds his fellow lodgers unbearably small-minded and even malicious (one of them steals Alfred's money), and he gets into a fight with them. Meanwhile his girlfriend, Suzanne, has moved into music-hall limelight with the dream of stardom, encouraged and manipulated by a roguish older man with designs on her. In the end her bubble bursts, and Alfred and Suzanne get back together in their proper places (Alfred's own conclusion) as electrician and typist and as simple music-hall spectators. What they see onstage in the last scene is Maurice Chevalier, playing himself, singing enthusiastically of Paris.[30] All these variant tales passed over the possibility of collective action and highlighted the role of chance and individual wiliness.

A female version of the rise-to-glory myth came in the movie *Rigolboche* (1936), directed by Christian-Jaque and starring Chevalier's old partner Mistinguett. She begins as a dance hostess (*entraineuse*) in a seedy bar in Dakar, Senegal. When, on a rowboat one day, she apparently drowns an aggressive young man, she panics and flees for France. In Paris she finds work in a nightclub, where eventually she encounters difficulties with the law—for the murder in Africa, she believes. Then she learns that the victim is still alive and had not brought any charges. Her love, a handsome count, consoles her by making her the director and star of her own music hall. Love and luck pay off, but so does an attitude that Mistinguett makes explicit in a song: "Pour être heureux . . . chantez!" (To be happy . . . sing!). The pep cry of the Great War propagandists echoed throughout the thirties.

Songs proclaiming inanities flourished with the waxing of worries and hardship in the tumultuous year 1936. While the nation struggled economically and fought out its deep domestic divisions, fears of a new war mounted, especially after Hitler defiantly moved German troops into the hitherto demilitarized Rhineland in March. The ever prolific Georgius provided comic relief with a batch of new nonsense songs. One that quickly became a hit was a silly sketch entitled "Au Lycée Papillon," which re-creates a day in school when pupil after pupil rises to be questioned by a visiting inspector. All the best students who pride themselves on knowing the answers give hopelessly garbled responses. Finally, one student who admits to knowing nothing and in turn demonstrates it declares that he wants to become a cabinet minister so as to be important. The inspector says "bravo," but gives him a zero anyway. Each examination ends with the chorus of uncomprehending students proclaiming happily: "We're not imbeciles / We even have education / At the Lycée Papa . . . / At the Lycée Papil . . . / At the Lycée Papillon." This song did more than lampoon French education as earnest but futile effort; it invited listeners to laugh at their shared values and formative experience, and it gave them a chance to mock the many who could not understand their own stupidity. More than 100,000 copies of the sheet music and 12,000 records sold in less than three months. More than 200,000 copies of the song sold in 1937. The movie that followed was a musical enactment of the song with Georgius himself as the inspector.[31] As the irrepressible don't-give-a-damn, laugh-it-up Parisian, he was at his best during those stressful times. Amid the high tide of social hatreds and Popular Front idealism, the comic singer found audiences particularly eager for the deflating humor of satirical songs. His fullest shotgun blast came in "Quand les Andouilles voleront" (1936), whose verses ridiculed a broad range of social types—a nobleman's son, a peasant from the back country, a snobbish widow, a young aviator (all verses safely avoiding the types so passionately targeted by Left and Right). Each is promised that when *andouilles* fly (the word meant both sausages and imbeciles), "you will be the leader of the squadron."

One hit of 1936 more directly addressed anxieties by proposing the comforting thought that things could be worse. "It's better than catching scarlet fever" reasoned a song by Misraki and Hornez ("Ça vaux mieux que d'attraper la scarlatine"). The misfortune that people fret about isn't really so important, the song contends. Worry is needless.[32] The old smile-away-your-troubles theme was back— now in an ironic form and with an overall humorous effect. The invitation to laugh in order not to cry found a receptive audience; in effect it also urged listeners to take the nonpolitical or conservative stance of resignation and acceptance of the status quo.

Many other songs filling the air in 1936 played to the heart—to personal fantasies and feelings, including the desire to cry. Heartthrob tenor Tino Rossi's hit "Marinella" evoked the happy feelings of new love, and crooner Jean Sablon's "Vous qui passez sans me voir" expressed the sweet feelings of a romance that is just a dreamed possibility. Other love songs elicited sadness and tears, emotional release from hearing a lover's joy and then disappointment. The most popular songs at that time led listeners to a headlong emotional plunge by recounting a fleeting love affair and subsequent heartbreak. Lys Gauty's "Le Chaland qui passe" evoked in sad insistent strains a night at a riverside bal musette and a barge moving quietly toward some "uncertain destiny"; like two barges pushed along by the current, a pair of uneasy lovers embrace the uncertainties of a night's love with a determination not to think of what the morrow might bring. In early 1936 twenty-one-year-old Edith Piaf sang a similar but more developed tale entitled "L'Etranger," about a downcast and love-hungry wanderer who loves a *fille* one night and leaves her.

"La Môme Piaf"—meaning "kid Sparrow"—leaving behind a hard childhood and years as a street singer, rose to fame during the era of the Popular Front, singing nonpolitical songs about the poor and the heartbroken. Ca. 1937. Phot. Bibl. Nat. de Fr.-Paris.

She would have gone anywhere with him, she sings, but he didn't ask her to, and all she has is the memory—and the terrible news that the body of a young sailor was pulled from the sea near the port. Melodrama was also still the staple of Damia's career. In early 1936 she made popular an international hit called "Sombre Dimanche," a dirge which was so depressing that it reportedly caused a number of suicides. The Sunday in question was a day when a woman's lover failed to show up for a rendez-vous; grieving and in shock, and depressed about a long, empty day ahead, she sings a low, slow plaint that makes it clear that even before reaching the empty room she had known that the love affair was over and that there was nothing to do but mourn.

Most songs, like "Sombre Dimanche," still directed attention to private sorrows and romantic love during a period of sweeping political struggles and collective confrontations, but the reason was not simply that the powerful favored that channeling of emotions to the personal realm. "Those who suffer cannot com-

plain," noted Simone Weil of her fellow factory workers in 1935. She described elo-
quently how they suffered from crushing fatigue, monotony, fear, and humiliation,
and she often referred to the workers' condition as slavery. But workers showed no
sympathy for each other, she noted after describing several "melancholic" women
in her shop. Those who complained "would not be understood by others, would be
perhaps mocked by those who do not suffer, would be considered as tiresome bores
by those who, suffering, have quite enough of their own suffering. Everywhere the
same hardness as on the part of the bosses, with some rare exceptions."[33] The sad
stories served up by songs and films vented at least some of the hurt: they allowed
the many who suffered to give free rein to feelings of sadness, without encountering others' hardness.

The Flowering of Militant Culture

While commercial songs of these kinds flowed continuously to mass audiences, politically engaged people were busy developing a fuller culture of militant songs,
plays, and films. From 1932 on the talented playwrights and musicians of the left-
wing cultural action association Groupe Octobre tried to produce more theater for
workers, but it was slow to exploit the potential of movies for their cause. The Communists paid more attention to film than other parties did, but they remained content with private screenings of works that the censors would not pass, notably Soviet films. During the early thirties the French Left made only a handful of films,
none of which reached a mass audience.[34]

Songwriters for the Left were more productive and reached far more people than did filmmakers. The effective seedbeds for their works were such periodicals as *La Muse rouge*, political choral groups, and the youth organizations of the
Communists and Socialists. Unlike most political songs, some new ones by the Left
found an audience that included many besides militants. "Au-devant de la Vie" (Toward life), whose lyrics were by a revolutionary named Jeanne Perret with a melody
by Dmitry Shostakovich, was a favorite hiking and camping song of young people
from 1933 on. As the Popular Front emerged, it took on more political meaning, the
literal words about leaving the factory and hiking together in the country expressing hope for liberation and new joyful community. "La Chanson des loisirs" even
more directly conveyed the desire for greater fulfillment and more leisure. Actor
and singer Jean Villard's angrier ideological song "Dollar" (1932) pictured thousands of ruined farmers, shopkeepers, and workers leaving Europe to go to the land
of the dollar, only to be ground down there by an out-of-control system based on

worship of money, specifically the almighty American currency. Denunciations of the rich, of exploitation, of war, and of the sacrifice of people for profits were the staples of the militant song during the Depression years. The cry of the unemployed for "work and bread" rang out in "Le Chant des chômeurs," published by the Association des écrivains et artistes révolutionnaires (AEAR). Another song from the AEAR, "Y a trop de tout"(there's too much of everything) had the bourgeois remarking that there were too many machines, products, and workers, but never too many soldiers. Subsequent verses express the worker's thinking: since there's too much, let's work fewer hours and raise wages—and "no need for war."[35]

One song that became a standard hymn of the Popular Front summed up the movement's hopes: "Le Pain, la paix, la liberté," joining words resonant of 1789—those for bread and liberty—to the postwar demand for peace. One verse urges the "sovereign people on the bastilles" to shout that they want the sun that will shine tomorrow to shine for "bread, peace, and liberty." The song goes on to denounce unemployment and inequality along with those who are responsible for shortages of necessities. Why don't the out-of-work have bread and wine, when French grain rots in the barns and the grape harvest has been deliberately destroyed?[36] The sun will shine tomorrow, but meanwhile there is much that is wrong. In varying proportions both anger and hope reverberated in song, as they did in the Popular Front's collective actions.

The Left also made good use of film as an instrument of mass politics in 1936. Its first major film and the most notable was *La Vie est à nous,* commissioned by the French Communist party as part of its campaign for the spring elections. Financed largely by collections at party meetings, the movie was made by a team of directors, most prominent of whom was Jean Renoir. Weaving together documentary footage and dramatized scenes, *La Vie est à nous* depicted masses of ordinary unemployed people lined up at soup kitchens. It also showed how the Communist party defended a factory worker and a peasant against injustice and provided social support to marginal and excluded individuals: an out-of-work young Frenchman finds friendly comrades in party meetings, and an immigrant car-washer named Mohammed receives friendship and help. Against them are ranged the powerful two hundred families, shown in photo-album pictures. Excerpts from party leaders' speeches attacking the two hundred make the message explicit, and so does a spoken chorus: "France does not [now] belong to the French; it belongs to the two hundred families." That oppressive elite made an appearance as rich aristocratic young men shooting at a worker's cap on the grounds of a château. The enemies of the people also appeared as marching leagues of dark-shirted right-wingers wearing berets. In a brief appearance Hitler is ridiculed, shown making a speech with the barking of a dog substituted for his voice. *La Vie est à nous* as a whole urged working people to take political action—and support the Communist party—in the large struggle against menacing fascist movements abroad and at home. From beginning to end, it argued that common people, without great leaders, could change the course of history. Fearful of right-wing disorders, the government banned the film, but it was seen in private gatherings of the Left.[37]

Out in the streets "the people" of the Popular Front had gained possession of what had been no-man's-land. In late April and early May 1936, they went on to gain control of the Chamber of Deputies and the government by winning two rounds of elections. Next came a phase of entrenchment—and, surprisingly, further struggle. After the Popular Front's victories at the polls, hundreds of thousands of workers went on strike. By early June almost two million had joined in the strikes, demonstrating even more fighting spirit and force than the street marchers had. These were not just the traditional militant unionists and politicized workers; the massive revolt included a multitude of hitherto nonunionized workers in the textile, metals, and food industries and the service sector. Many of the strikers not only refused to work, but also occupied about nine thousand workplaces—from the Breguet aeronautics factory in Le Havre and Paris department stores to the Latécoère aeronautics factory in Toulouse.[38] Taking over work sites, a new tactic in the

In the final moments of *La Vie est à nous* (1936), crowds of men show their solidarity by defiantly raising their fists as they mobilize against abuses of power by the privileged class. MoMA Film Stills.

Department store strikers in June 1936 mock authority and celebrate their victories. Phot. Bibl. Nat. de Fr.-Paris.

labor struggle, afforded a new experience of worker control and freedom in what had been a place of constraint and submission. The work sites now became both home turf, like the faubourg, and front lines on the battlefield. Workers and their families now became frontline communities within the factory walls. A gathered group of "us" holding off "them," they were on the defensive as much as the offensive, like the poilus in the trenches.

Abattoir workers, too, engaged in sit-down strikes and amused themselves, even in the cold meat lockers of La Villette, June 1936. Phot. Bibl. Nat. de Fr.-Paris.

The comic Milton, who showed how to be a winning trickster in his hit film of 1930, *Le Roi des resquilleurs,* clowns with and sings to the strikers of June 1936. Phot. Bibl. Nat. de Fr.-Paris.

As a community, the strikers experienced an exceptionally extended period of conjoined festivity and struggle.[39] Inside the factories and department stores the embattled workers, good débrouillards, quickly found amusements. They played cards and soccer, and young workers lifted weights. Some strikers learned new sports. Boxing champions came by to teach their techniques, and other *sportifs* initiated workers in the new pastimes of ping-pong, basketball, and footraces.[40] In place of silence or machine noises, conversations and songs filled the air: phonograph records and radios played on, and strikers sang, danced, and chatted. In a few well-publicized places, such stars as Mistinguett, Georges Milton, and Marianne Oswald sang for the workers. The strikers also put on their own performances, as the poilus had done at the front. In a workplace near the Pont du Carrousel, about one hundred strikers improvised sketches. They kept in touch with outside events by listening to news on a radio lent by a neighborhood merchant.[41] Day after day newspapers favorable to the Popular Front disseminated enthusiastic reports about the high spirits and the cooperative, fraternal acts of the strikers inside and their families and friends outside. Like the fabled poilus, they seemed to reconcile struggle and joviality with a grace long identified as a distinctly French trait.

A favorite song of the workers during the spring of 1936 suggests more complicated feelings and expectations. An ironic song introduced the year before, "Tout va très bien, madame la marquise" on the face of it mocked the upper classes.[42] In each verse the marquise's hirelings assure her that everything is fine, but they quickly add a disturbing new bit of news in a growing series of catastrophes: the death of her gray mare is linked to a fire in the stables, which is later linked to a fire in the château. Finally, the servant explains it all: the fire originated when the marquis committed suicide and fell, overturning some candles. "But, except for that," the servant always concludes, "madame la marquise, everything's fine, everything's fine" (tout va très bien, tout va très bien). As sung by workers, the song seems also to be a tension-relieving joke about themselves and their struggle, viewed in light of their long stalwart service to the powerful and old habits of cheerful coping. Evoking a chain of calamities, the singers mocked the clichéd response of bravado, and they hinted at doubts about the chances of improving their lot in life. While the workers struggled hopefully, they sang out ironically.

8. STRUGGLE
AND VACATION

AFTER THE ELECTORAL STRUGGLES and the sit-down strikes, the Popular Front forces claimed the fruits of victory. First the government and unions extracted sizable wage increases from employers. Then, after most of the strikers had gone back to work, the Blum government gave working people a forty-hour week *and* an epoch-making new benefit: a vacation with pay, an annual time of liberation henceforth. As of 20 June 1936, by law every worker had the right to a minimum of fifteen days of paid leave for anyone employed continuously for more than a year. For the many who had fought in the election campaign and had joined in the strikes, that new right was an unanticipated bonus. It turned out to be the Popular Front reform that the masses most enthusiastically embraced in their lives and dreams.

After the victories of May and June came time to celebrate in July and August. Like a furloughed poilu leaving combat for the pleasures of Paris, supporters of the Popular Front threw themselves into high times of enjoyment. Yet the prospect of further struggles cast a shadow on the celebrations. Again and again through the rest of the decade, the specter of new battles insistently intruded on dreams of holiday release. At the same time those divergent possibilities, struggle and festivity, recurred in songs, films, and news reports, competing for the attention of the nation all through those roller-coaster years before the Second World War.

The celebrations of the summer of 1936 began with the national holiday, 14 July, which that year became a victory party for the Popular Front. It was a triumphant "festival of liberty," with the old battle cry "liberté" now taking on new dimensions as leisure. The crowds in the streets were even larger than the year before and their spirits higher. Yet the news gave them plenty to worry about. The rightist leagues had been dissolved by the Blum government in June, but their leaders quickly reorganized them as new political parties and continued their virulent campaigns against the Popular Front.[1] Foreign fascists were worrisome, too, particularly after Hitler sent troops to reoccupy the Rhineland in March. On 14 July at the customary military parade in Paris, concern about the Nazis was manifest: tens of thousands of working people came out and joined in doing what the less plebeian rightists had done alone for years: they cheered the army.

In the afternoon another history-making crowd took the Parisian stage: the largest ever throngs of chanting and singing supporters of the Popular Front marched along two thoroughfares to the Place de la Nation for a "great victory rally."[2] Similarly massive marches took place in provincial cities, encountering only minor counterdemonstrations. At Popular Front rallies everywhere, orators exalted "the people" and flatteringly identified them with the revolutionaries of 1789. After the rallies the Left's illustrated press sent out the same messages, spreading the images of the now victorious, united "people"—wide-angle images of masses with fists raised and an array of flags and banners. The evening of the fourteenth, crowds continued the celebration at open-air dances with accordion music, drawing especially large numbers in the "red" banlieues of Paris. Others attended programs of songs and historic dramas that echoed the praise of the militant people.

In Paris the most notable of the plays was Romain Rolland's rousing *Le 14 Juillet*, presented by the Association of Revolutionary Writers and Artists' mass cultural organization at the Alhambra music hall. For three hours, actors representing ordinary people carried out the heroic deeds of liberation and achieved a new fraternity. The show ended triumphantly with actors and spectators singing "La Marseillaise" and "L'Internationale." It was a moving tribute to both distant heroes and their current counterparts. The audience consisted mostly of students and the well educated, but the show reached others via live broadcast on Radio Paris, and additional performances took place over the next three weeks.[3] Still, for all the talk about a unified "people," the leaders of the Popular Front had difficulty producing inclusive cultural events for the "laboring masses." They did much better with festive gatherings in the streets.

The good times resumed in August when workers began taking their first paid vacations under the new law, leaving behind their workplaces and neighborhoods. What can be called the legend of the worker-vacationer emerged as newspaper and magazine photographs and newsreels propagated the essential images of the summer of 1936: workers gleefully peddling their tandem bicycles to the country or packing into special trains for the big trip away from the congested city and the workaday grind. The legend was essentially a story of liberation. In the press of the Left, going on vacation was portrayed as a release from prison, a historic breakthrough reminiscent of the freeing of prisoners from the Bastille. In their joyful flight from work and the dreary city, workers experienced a dream come true. According to this version of history, in August 1936 for the first time the masses were able to leave the confines of home and work and to enjoy open space and free time. Parisian workers in particular experienced the novel joy of leaving the big city for a trip to the seashore or a journey deep into the country. For the first time in their lives they saw the ocean, breathed clean country air, visited old family homes in the provinces, and embraced relatives not seen in years. During the summer of 1936 workers finally won for themselves what the bourgeois and youth had acquired decades earlier.

Much about that legend, however, has to be judged inaccurate in light of the historical record. The "conquest of vacations" was the culmination of an old struggle, and it was by no means as sudden or as complete as it appeared in journalists' accounts of 1936. Recent studies indicate that, in fact, by 1936 the majority of French workers had already gained the right to a vacation.[4] Middle-class employees by and large had gained some annual vacation before the First World War. Charitable programs giving poor city children a summer vacation in the country also dated from that era. Some reformers then began advocating vacations for all, arguing that children should not be separated too long from their families. In the years just after the war, French workers in a "great number" of Parisian factories and shops had gained one to three weeks' paid summer vacation, Valdour observed in 1924. The new benefit not only helped them maintain good spirits (*bonne humeur*), he noted, but also resulted in workers' coming back "with a provision of physical health and energy from which everyone profits."[5] The opportunity for a vacation was not just a deserved right, this conservative worker and journalist argued, but also a compensation for hard work and a condition for greater productivity.

During the 1920s French proponents of vacations for everyone pointed to

Summer days on the Normandy beaches, crowded with plebeians during the era of the Popular Front. Postcard scenes Collection of the author.

Vacations for everyone—spent swimming in the ocean and camping—were making news, but many youth of the industrial suburbs of Paris still played and swam in the Seine. 1 August 1938. SAFARA. Private collection.

Bicycles built for two were the vehicles of choice for couples of modest means going to the country for weekends or vacations. On "Tandems Day," 13–14 May 1938, couples showed off their bicycles and matching outfits on the Champs-Elysées. Phot. Bibl. Nat. de Fr.-Paris.

gains made in neighboring countries. By 1930 many nations of Europe had established laws granting an annual vacation to all workers—with Fascist Italy's program the most generous and far-reaching of all. France was clearly behind in this area of social legislation, but it took a big step forward in 1930 with the creation of a key planning and advocacy group—the Comité national des loisirs. This committee was made up of representatives of the Fédération nationale des coopératives de consommation and the president of the International Labor Organization, Albert Thomas, formerly a Socialist political leader. During the early 1930s Thomas's organization also forged ahead with new cooperatives that actually facilitated travel for workers. Its Société coopérative nationale des voyages et d'excursions began to organize moderately priced, "instructive" vacations. And its Société coopérative nationale d'hôtels et de stations de vacances began building a network of hotels for vacationers of modest means.[6] Thus, from the late 1920s on, the groundwork for the summer of 1936 was being laid by nongovernmental organizations.

The essential themes of the vacation story appeared first in songs long before the summer of 1936. For several years thousands of youth in auberges de jeunesse had sung of a happy freedom as they hiked in the country and gathered around evening campfires. Their song "Au-devant de la Vie" expressed the joy of leaving the city, singing and walking along with friends, and finding renewal in nature. The

Publications of the Left, as well as commercial song and film, celebrated the happy faces of French young people hiking together in the country. Cover of *Regards*, 8 July 1937. Private collection.

words, reminiscent of some old military songs, are those of a young man addressing his "blonde" (girlfriend) as the two saunter into the fresh air of the morning: "My blonde, do you hear in the city / The whistling of mills and trains? / Let's go toward the breeze, / Let's go toward the morning." The chorus evokes the delight of friends marching together toward happiness in a country that is also moving ahead in the right direction:

> Get up, my blonde, let's sing to the wind
> Up, friends!
> It's going toward the rising sun
> Our country.

> Joy awakens you, my blonde
> Let's go join in this choir
> Let's march toward glory and the world,
> Let's march toward happiness.

The third verse suggests more clearly an activist political solidarity: "And we will salute the brigade / And we will smile at friends." Then the singers urge everyone to join in close community:

> Let's share, comrades,
> our plans, our works, our cares.
>
> In their triumphal joyfulness
> The young bound forth singing,
> Soon a new youth
> Will come to the front of our ranks.
>
> (chorus)
> Let's go toward life,
> Let's go toward love.[7]

In song and in practice, leftist youth led the way, striding cheerfully into bucolic settings associated with liberation and a happier future.

Even though the extension of vacations to the masses was not so sudden as the legend had it, 1936 nonetheless was a record year: the number of first-time vacationers was double that of the year before, according to Marc Boyer.[8] The images of young people taking off on bicycles in 1936 inspired others to do likewise the following year. In August 1937 middle-aged Frenchmen—forty-year-olds and older—took to the roads as "cyclotourists" in greater numbers than ever before, observed *Le Petit Dauphinois* of Grenoble.[9] Popular response to the August break was clearly enthusiastic.

The vacation legislation was just one of many new initiatives taken by the Popular Front government, aided by private associations, to enhance the leisure and cultural opportunities of working people. Under the Popular Front, France was bubbling over with cultural projects: popular theater productions, plans for new popular libraries and mobile libraries (the *bibliobus*), efforts to democratize such elite sports as flying and skiing, and the creation of a national museum of folklore, the Musée des Arts et Traditions populaires. Although their impact during the late thirties was limited, these were seminal accomplishments.[10] Yet none of the Popular Front leisure programs made the impression on everyday life and memory that annual paid vacations did.

Contrary to stereotypes of the young hikers and of songs like "Au-devant de la Vie," most vacationers left behind the solidarity of neighborhood and workplace when they strode off "toward life." For older vacationers, camaraderie in the countryside turned out to be not so important as it was for the youth of the auberges. Many, even young people, went their own separate ways, cycling, swimming, or cultivating their gardens. "Tandem biking and camping, notably, are killing athletic programs [athlétisme]," a reporter noted during the second summer of the new order. Instead of competing in teams, "people [engaged in sports] for themselves, each by himself, on the water, on the roads, in the mountains, in the sea."[11] Workers now enjoying what had been middle-class privileges took their new leisure in the individualistic way of the bourgeois.

The vacations were over by the end of August for most people, and so was the euphoria of spring and early summer. Indeed, even during that month of holidays, distressing events intruded. The Spanish Civil War, raging since mid-July, divided and demoralized the French Popular Front. Those of the Left who wanted to help their fellow republicans across the Pyrenees bitterly dissented when Blum's government decided to stay out of the conflict. In the fall they looked on with anguish as the fascists began to overpower the Spanish Popular Front. They also anguished over France's persistent economic troubles—rising prices, increasing unemployment, and a national budget crisis. In September, the Blum government devalued the franc. The political struggles continued, but the festive spirit was gone. In February 1937 Blum announced a "pause" in the reforms to calm domestic strife. On 16 March a right-wing meeting in a Clichy movie theater was met by a counterdemonstration of Socialists and Communists, and the police intervened. Shots were fired; five counterdemonstrators were killed, and several hundred were wounded. Outraged unionists formed a giant cortege following the coffins of the victims. There was talk of civil war.[12] The time of merry street marches and holidays was over.

The celebration that broke out in 1936 continued, however, in the songs of the effervescent young Charles Trenet. Maintaining those high spirits was possible only by turning away from all thought of political action and struggle. Trenet's "Y'a d'la joie" and "Je chante" (both 1937) expressed the happiness of those who did just that, looking beyond the depressing political and economic scenes to the joys of nature. Old master-of-the-smile Maurice Chevalier first made a hit of "Y'a d'la joie," giving it a smashing debut in the revue Paris en joie at the Casino de Paris early in 1937. Chevalier released a recording of it in October, and by the spring of 1938 its sales hit new highs.[13] Trenet also recorded the song and often performed it live, singing it with more nuances of mood and more dramatic deftness than Chevalier did. "There Is Joy" became a hit during a period plagued by persistent economic

Charles Trenet, an exuberant youthful singer, starred in the film *Je chante* (1938). Poster. Phot. Bibl. Nat. de Fr.-Paris.

malaise, political hatreds, and the distant rumble of marching Nazis: "Y'a d'la joie, bonjour bonjour les hirondelles [swallows] / Y'a d'la joie, dans le ciel par-dessus le toit / Y'a d'la joie et du soleil dans les ruelles / Y'a d'la joie, partout y a d'la joie." "There's joy in the sky above the roof," and "there's joy and sunshine in the narrow streets," the song proclaims, concluding, "Everywhere there's joy."

It was not just nature that brought joy. It was also love—love of a twenty-year-old (who speaks through the song) in the springtime—not for one particular young woman, but for all. "All day my heart beats, turns upside down, and falters / It's love that comes with I-don't-know-what. / It's love, bonjour bonjour girls / There's joy, everywhere there's joy."[14] The middle of the song makes it clear that the words are about a dream, from which the happy singer awakens to find the sky gray; he must get up and drag himself through humdrum routine. But he declares that the dream has been good, "for it has allowed me to make a song—a song of spring, of love, a song of a twenty-year-old, song of forever." Dream and illusion offer the only sources of hope and joy.

"Je chante" made the same point even more forcefully. "I sing / I sing evening and morning / I sing on my way / I sing," chirps the vagabond singer. He sings for his bread, sleeps on the grass, and feels happy that he "has everything" and "has nothing." The tone could hardly be more upbeat. But halfway through the lyrics the singer recounts falling down, half-dead with hunger. The gendarmes take him off to jail, and there he finds a string and a way out: he hangs himself. As a phantom he again sings gaily on the road; he no longer knows hunger, and he is "happy and finally free."[15] Did anyone pay attention to the singer's downfall and suicide? Contemporary references to the song suggest that listeners tended to hear and hold onto only the cheerful lines and the perky music. The well-established image of singing one's way to happiness prevailed over the depressing events.

In 1938 Trenet also gave a troubled, pessimistic France the bouncy love song "Boum"—a riot of joyous solipsism. The singer projects his feelings of a love born just yesterday into the entire world:

> Boom
> When our heart goes Boom
> Everything with it says Boom
> And it's love that awakens
>
> Boom
> The entire world goes Boom
> The whole universe goes Boom
> Because my heart goes Boom Boom
> Boom
> I hear only Boom Boom.[16]

His recording of the song, which won the Grand Prix du Disque in 1938, became a standard and was frequently played on phonographs and on the radio.

Trenet became a star of the first magnitude in 1938 after performing his songs onstage at the ABC music hall in late March, only weeks after Hitler's annexation of Austria. A tall blond twenty-five-year-old, he jumped on the piano and played and rhymed and sang with a swinging free spirit and energy that ravished his young listeners. The audience's enthusiasm was so great that the management asked him to stay on as the star of a new program beginning 15 April. Trenet's exuberant imagination and unrestrained performance style struck observers as naïve and crazy (*fou*); his lyrics were surreal in places. He was called "the singing crazy man" (*le fou chantant*). As a singer and songwriter he incarnated youth, energy, and a fresh poetic vision of the world in darkening times.

During this period Trenet also made films celebrating freedom and travel through the countryside. In *La Route enchantée* (1938) he played a joyous singing vagabond, the romantic street singer now on the open road, performing "Boum" and other songs of his own. He falls in love with a woman who lives in a ruined château, and he takes her to Paris where she becomes an operetta star. In 1938 he also starred in *Je chante,* in which he played a singing troubadour whose songs had a magical power.[17] Building on the old belief in the magic of singing, Trenet's musicals served up modern fairy-tales and dream images of happy romance.

Georgius worked some of the same veins during the late thirties but to a comic effect. "I would like to sing as one sings a dream," he acknowledged in an interview in 1939. He meant that he wanted to evoke images held together "by a single bond: the unreal." Such songs, he believed, would have a "new charm," and they would be "a means of evasion that the public would use to enter into the domain of the marvelous."[18] Surrealists appreciated his manic power of imagination, but it is not clear that the public was ready to accompany him into "the domain of the marvelous."[19]

The public relished Georgius's more down-to-earth looniness. A prolific songwriter, he followed his "Au Lycée Papillon" (1936) with other comic hits. In 1937 he came up with "Y'a de la mise en bouteille au château," which tells about men putting "corks" in "bottles" and women bearing the results nine months later. In 1938 he wrote and sang "Ça . . . c'est d'la bagnole" and "Sur la Route de Penzac." In the song about the *bagnole* (car) the "little guy" sings proudly of buying a used automobile so that he can impress his girlfriend Mimi and take her on rides. Because he had little money, the car that he could afford had problems: it was noisy, and the wheel lugs required continuous tightening. When one wheel fell off, he explains contentedly, he still had three others, and many people didn't have that many. The song about the road to Penzac (in Brittany) plays with funny-sounding Breton names ("Gouz gouz la irac") and satirizes commercial versions of Breton songs. It tells the tale of the marriage night of Maryvonne, which ends with a sudden cry coming from an enlaced couple in the brush, prompting grandfather to predict the appearance of a new little Breton the next year. Georgius's performances gave audiences a "transfusion of Rabelais," one reviewer remarked. With Georgius, "everything becomes a carnival."[20]

Other songs from the year of the *Anschluss* and the Munich crisis directly argued not to worry. "What are people waiting for to be happy?" asked the singers of a number with that title ("Qu'est-ce qu'on attend pour être heureux?") in 1938. What are they waiting for . . . when there are violets, grapes, and butterflies out there. "The sky is blue . . . and there's hope in everyone's eyes." Why wait to have a great time (*fair' la fête*)?—we are a couple, and love is there waiting for us. Another song of the period urged quite simply, "Amusez-Vous"—have fun—an injunction for which there was always a receptive audience. "Have fun, don't give a damn about anything"; life is short. "Amusez-vous / Foutez-vous d'tout / La vie, entre nous, est si brève / Amusez-vous comme des fous."[21]

In the grim times of 1938 young French men and women amused themselves with the rollicking new rhythm of swing (imported from America) and the wacky clownish fashion of dressing known as "Zazou" (pants that were too short and a jacket that was too big, clashing stripes). The new hit "Je suis swing" exclaimed the old live-it-up message in a fresh stream of bouncy monosyllables: "Oh je suis swing, je suis swing / Da crou da dou da dou je m'amuse comme un fou."[22] "I have fun like a crazy man," cried singing star Johnny Hess to the cheers of a legion of fans.

The old daydreams of love in exotic warm places also flourished in the atmosphere of raging political animosities and anxiety from the Popular Front to the Second World War. Writing in October 1936, critic Pierre Varenne made a point of congratulating Tino Rossi especially for still singing of love "in our epoch devoted to hatred." At that time, right-wing leaders were spewing their ferocious hatred of Popular Front leaders, and Blum in particular, with flagrant anti-Semitism. The tender Tino Rossi, wrote Varenne, did not demand anyone's execution—"he is only languor, sweetness, suavity."[23] In the year of crisis 1938, Tino Rossi's song "Marinella" was still popular, and he continued to offer romance on records and in movies with huge success. His big film that year was *Naples au baiser du feu,* a musical comedy. His fan mail—73,000 letters a year, most from women—was setting records. "My wife and I are transported by your songs, which make us forget all the little miseries of life," wrote one admirer whose wife never missed one of Rossi's concerts and whose new son was named

Tino Rossi as a singer in a Neapolitan trattoria has a beautiful fiancée, but then another beauty (Viviane Romance) comes into his life in the movie *Naples au baiser de feu* (1937). Courtesy of MoMA Film Stills.

Tino.[24] Meanwhile, the tender voice of Italian-born Rina Ketty made a hit of a song about romance in enchanting Andalusia. The lyrics of "Sombreros et mantilles" (1938) evoked "love, under an ever more beautiful sky" and conjured up all the traditional icons of Spain—sombreros and guitar serenades, fandangos and boleros, dark-eyed Carmens and Figaros—without any troubling references to that country's political travails.

There was still a demand for sad songs about love, too. Continuing a well-established tradition, the darker side of romance was left to female singers. Berthe Sylva, Fréhel, and Damia had specialized in pathos for years. A short, slight singer called "la Môme Piaf" (Kid Piaf) was just beginning to achieve fame. After singing in the streets of Paris for years and working in some lesser nightspots, she made her début on a major music-hall stage (the ABC) at the age of twenty-one in March 1937, a time when Blum's first Popular Front government was approaching its fall. The young Piaf and the aging Fréhel sang of the defeated, those for whom the struggle was over, people without hope, melancholy streetwalkers and the *misérables* of the faubourgs. They sang regularly of brief, passionate encounters and heartbreaks, tales set traditionally in the faubourgs and now more often set in port towns frequented by sailors and legionnaires. "Without a day after / Without anything that lasts / A man comes by / And

For a photograph used on a magazine cover in 1939, Edith Piaf, wearing a fur coat that bespeaks her success, returns to the streets where she grew up and first sang. Phot. Bibl. Nat. de Fr.-Paris.

then goes away / Without a day after," went one of Fréhel's dirgelike refrains of 1938. That same year the singer, shapeless and worn down by alcohol and drugs, intoned romantic nostalgia in a new hit "La Java bleue," telling of nights of close dancing and falling in love at a bal musette. "But these oaths full of love," Fréhel acknowledges in closing, "people know that they won't keep them forever." Pressing her dance partner against her, she feels momentary joy, but it is tempered with sad resignation. The times were right for dreaming, but not for believing that the dreams came true.[25]

Split Screens

Historian Louis Chevalier recalls that in Montmartre where he was living, the specter of war was strangely absent from people's consciousness and from much of the press during the late thirties. His friend Céline, obsessed with war, was an egregious exception. A re-reading of the newspaper accounts does not bear out Chevalier's observation. He is on surer ground when he adds the clarifying remark: "Looking through the press of those years 1937, 1938, and 1939 and comparing people's narratives, one has the strange impression that this perspective [of war worries] and the affairs of pleasure constituted two isolated domains, two chapters of existence, alien and almost indifferent to each other."[26] I would say that a gap separated most popular culture—but not all—from international problems.

Going on vacation and dreaming about it, getting away from the worries, and immersing oneself in private life and enjoyments were common ways of coping with the trials and worries of the late thirties. At home more and more people diverted themselves by listening to the radio. The number of radios in France increased rapidly, from 3,200,000 in 1936 to 4,700,000 at the end of 1939.[27] Through words and music—songs, comedy, serials, and news—the radio evoked already fa-

Edith Piaf in a publicity photo (ca. 1939), dramatizing sadness and heartbreak in the tradition of Fréhel and Damia. Phot. Bibl. Nat. de Fr.-Paris.

close-knit community. The popular Jean Gabin played Jean, a house painter. *La Belle Equipe*, Bénigno Cacérès has written, introduced to French cinema "a new hero: the worker." Jean Gabin first gave France a bigger-than-life movie image of the modest guy in a cap who was so widely disdained and so unprivileged. "Jean Gabin did not play the worker. He was the worker, similar to those millions who had just gone on strike in May and June 1936. The workers felt themselves represented for the first time in French cinema. Jean Gabin alone personified the working class."[35] He was tough, courageous, and quick to anger, but he was also tender with his sweetheart and amiable with his buddies, who looked to him with the awe due to a natural superior.

Along with his four friends, Jean wins 100,000 francs in the lottery. The jubilant comrades decide to use the money to build a café, a riverside *guinguette*, out along the Marne. Happily they work together and finally realize their collective dream, creating a place that is both their own business based on cooperative labor and a pleasure spot for the larger community. The café opens on Easter, a glorious sunny spring day. The rest of the story is how the men's community and its work are destroyed. Jacques, secretly in love with Mario's fiancée, leaves for Canada. Raymond is killed in an accident as he raises the flag on the roof of the just-finished café building. The Spanish refugee Mario is expelled from France. Jean kills his buddy Charles over a woman, and at the end a policeman takes him off to prison. The guinguette falls into the hands of an unsavory businessman.

The five men who worked together to build their own paradisiacal café-restaurant in *La Belle Equipe* (1936) enjoy an all-too-brief golden time—springtime—of friendship and love. (Jean Gabin is at left.) Courtesy of BFI Stills, Posters, and Designs.

This resonant tale of the times paralleled the Left's emotional swing from the high of the spring to a growing sense of defeat only months later. The workers' hopeful cooperative efforts were shown to end badly just when the Popular Front was running aground. When the film appeared in September, discouragement was growing over the fascist onslaught against the Spanish Popular Front and over the continuing economic stagnation with widespread unemployment in France. Enemies of Blum's government intensified their attacks. In November a shocking event revealed how stressful the Popular Front's struggles were. After right-wing newspapers maligned Minister of the Interior Roger Salengro for having deserted the army in 1915, the tired and disheartened leader committed suicide.

Earlier in the fall of 1936 *La Belle Equipe* had struck its first audiences as too pessimistic. In response to those reactions, the producers decided that the ending had to be changed. In the revised version, Jean and Charles stick together, giving up the woman who divided them.[36] Still, a workers' utopia had failed; a community of "little guys" had met defeat. The solidarity and efforts of the friends were undone by mysterious and hostile fate, working in large part through the men's relationships with women and the rivalries that followed.

The reviews of the film seem to tell us most about opinions held within the middle classes. Most did not judge the movie so unfavorably as those early audiences that disliked the first ending. The reviewer for *Le Figaro* concluded that the film would "please everyone": it showed workers in a fruitful camaraderie but it also showed them choosing the French tricolor, not a red internationalist flag, to raise over their new place. To the extreme Right, however, the story seemed too much the "collectivist" line of the Popular Front. The reviews bespeak social as well as political prejudices. Clearly some reviewers approached the story with populist sympathy and others with distrust. The workers' slang struck some critics as artificial and overdone; to others it was authentic. These may be merely limited hints about divergent audience reactions, but they underscore the general point: the solidarity apparent in the spring was no longer there in the autumn.

That depressing tale was just one of a series that continued through the end of the thirties. In 1935 Julien Duvivier had made *La Bandera*, in which all the good legionnaires are killed, including the hero, a luckless "little guy" from Paris played by Jean Gabin. Immediately after *La Belle Equipe* came Duvivier's *Pépé le Moko* in early 1937, a film whose place in the vogue of exotic places was noted in chapter 6. Here it merits mention again to emphasize the hero's downward course to fatal despair. In *Pépé le Moko*, as in *La Bandera*, the "little guy" coped for a time by flee-

In *Gueule d'amour* (1937), the dashing colonial cavalryman from the provinces (Jean Gabin) falls for the mysterious beauty from Paris (Mireille Balin). Courtesy of MoMA Film Stills.

ing his old battles in France, but he finds neither satisfaction in love nor a consoling community. The likable "bad guy" Pépé—Jean Gabin again—was a hunted man who in the end loses hope of joining the beautiful visiting Parisian woman and returning to Paris. The last scene shows him handcuffed behind a large gate, watching his love sail away; before anyone realizes what he is doing, he pulls out a knife from inside his jacket, pushes it into his stomach, and collapses to the ground.

Later in 1937, director Jean Grémillon's *Gueule d'amour* added another story of a doomed hero to the gloomy series, this time giving a nightmarish twist to the romantic fantasy about the love life of the handsome man in uniform. A dashing cavalry lieutenant in exotic French Algerian outfits, Lucien Bourrache (Gabin), like the mythic poilu, was a lighthearted, respected comrade with the men and an "ace" with women—hence the nickname *gueule d'amour* (love mug). Garrisoned in the South of France (in Orange), he leads a charmed life until he falls in love with Madeleine, a beautiful rich Parisian (Mireille Balin). After a romantic evening in Cannes, she disappears mysteriously. Disappointed and unable to forget her, Lucien is no longer the happy-go-lucky commoner hero. His voice and every movement betray his loss of zest for life. He quits the military, finds a job in a printer's shop in Paris, and finds his enigmatic Madeleine again, but again love turns out to be disappointing. She chooses to keep her rich older lover and rejects Lucien. He begins a new life running a bistro and gas station back in the South (he wears a worker's cap and washes dishes himself). He renews ties with an old buddy from the regiment, René, but he is still disconsolate. Madeleine arrives one day and tries to begin again with him, but he can no longer believe her. He sees that she still lacks any understanding of his feelings, and he is aghast at hearing her on the telephone brutally break off her recently formed relationship with René. Finally, in a surge of uncontrollable anger, Lucien strangles her. Afterward he flees the country, but he is a broken man, escaping only because René makes the decision and puts him on a train with a ticket and money.

In all these scenarios the Gabin character was the jaunty, wily common-man hero who enjoyed the admiration and camaraderie of a supportive male community. At the same time he and his buddies are outsiders in relation to the society at large. His love for a woman is the complicating and even fatal piece of the drama.[37] For a time he manages to hold it all together, but this complicated synthesis—involving an alternation between struggle and respite, work and relaxation with the men and love with the woman—eventually breaks down. The hero tries to get out of the struggle and end the tension, but the woman he loves eludes him, and his life unravels. The society outside his close circle ends up defeating him.

In mid-1937, as that Gabin "myth" was becoming familiar to millions and as Blum's Popular Front government was going into its death throes, Jean Renoir brought out his film about the Great War, provocatively entitled *La Grande Illusion*. It was not another in the series of Gabin tragedies, but a somber reminder of staggering disappointments and sorrows. Renoir, a war veteran and a militant leftist, used Gabin and other actors to enact a story that reworked popular myths of the war, of the poilu, and of the faubourien. For months after its première in early June 1937 the public flocked to see it and made it one of the biggest box-office successes of the year.

The story shows Frenchmen as prisoners of war, removed from the battlefield but continuing their characteristic ways of relating to others and responding to adversity. One central character that Renoir took over from Great War tradition is the man of the people, a likable unpretentious faubourien named Maréchal, a Parisian mechanic who connects easily with all types around him. In the military he is a pilot and a lieutenant. Maréchal, played by Jean Gabin, has a feisty courage and concern for others that other representatives of the people—a teacher, an engineer, and an actor—seem to lack. A natural leader in all anti-German acts, he is

the one who announces the news that the French have retaken the fort of Douaumont, news that touches off the group's emotional singing of "La Marseillaise."
Maréchal and his fellow prisoners are socially diverse, but they all are united in their
love for France.

Working with such well-established representations, Renoir broke with
convention in a number of ways. As he developed the character of the actor (played
by Julien Carette), he subverted the type of the amusing Parigot so celebrated in
wartime popular culture, showing him to be irritating and ineffectual. Renoir also
contradicted movie stereotypes of the period by featuring a Jewish soldier from a
rich banking family as a man of character. Generous and courageous, Rosenthal
(Marcel Dalio) is the faithful partner of Maréchal in the most difficult situations.
Thrown together as prisoners of war, these men from varied backgrounds form a
small community and forge friendships. Resourceful and unbroken in spirit, they
work together in attempts to escape. Yet they also remain aware of their class differences. The German and French aristocratic officers come together in mutual respect
and understanding, knowing that they are both separated socially from their men.
They also recognize that theirs is a dying breed and that the future belongs to men
like Maréchal and Rosenthal. Despite their social differences, the French prisoners
cooperate well enough for Maréchal and Rosenthal to escape. During their difficult
flight they stay together as friends, even though at one point Maréchal admits to not
being able to "stomach Jews."

The film then goes into a cliché-shattering depiction of the romantic side
of the poilu. The Parisian mechanic takes refuge with a farm woman named Elsa
and her young daughter. Elsa is a blonde, warm young woman graciously receiving the weary, lonely soldier—the poilu's dream "godmother." Yet in Renoir's version there is one big difference: Elsa is German. The woman's husband has been
killed at Verdun, but she is not embittered or hostile toward the French. Elsa and
Maréchal slip easily into a love relationship—paralleling the friendship between the
two officers of the enemy nations—despite national and language differences. But
both lovers know that their idyllic interlude (like a vacation) has to end soon as the
realities of the war once more intrude. As the mechanic and Rosenthal flee Germany, German border guards spot them from afar but let them continue and live on
into an undefined future.

The story was rich and complex: parts seemed nationalistic in spirit, some
pacifist, and some socialist. For those different reasons viewers on the Right and
Left applauded the film.[38] To many it conveyed the sense that the war was a tragic

folly, and it showed the combatants to be victims of illusions that the war would be fought according to civilized rules and would end with a clear-cut victory. *La Grande Illusion*, nonetheless, was not as pessimistic as the other major Gabin films of the time. It offered hope for all manner of reconciliations, and it showed the French "little guy" to be resourceful, amiable, cooperative, deeply attached to liberty and France, but not hateful toward the Germans.

Through 1938 and 1939, right up to the outbreak of a new war, pessimism predominated in a stream of major films that drew big audiences. *Le Quai des brumes* (1938) slammed down on hopes of getting away and starting over; it also moved the Gabin myth beyond the earlier bad-guy versions. This time the Gabin character was a man whose only crime was to desert the colonial army. Like the small stray dog he befriends, he is alone, lacking the close male community that surrounded the earlier heroes Gabin played. He doesn't fit in with the group of sordid types he encounters in the Le Havre dive. He is as out of place as the beautiful young Nelly (Michèle Morgan). Nelly and Jean have one happy evening at a fun fair and a night of love in a hotel, but Jean is by then a hunted man whose doom would be sealed with any one of several missteps or strokes of bad luck. He ends up being gunned down in the street by a young hoodlum whom he had earlier humiliated. This film became a box-office success and won critical acclaim for a number of reasons—the love story and yearning for "elsewhere," the gritty drama, the stars Gabin and Morgan, the beautifully photographed atmosphere of the port city and its seamy sections. The film, like most mass audience successes, brought together a complex of familiar hopes and played them out against tensions and fears. Then it showed an ending that struck down wishful fantasies. The decent characters with whom audiences identified most came out unfulfilled. The hopes of love and a new life were crushed. "Never perhaps have we seen a darker, more bitter, more atrociously despairing film," or one with "more ugliness, more discouragement, more sadness," concluded reviewer Suzanne Chantal. In the gloom of 1938, remarkably, the public was highly receptive to a story that was commonly greeted as the most pessimistic of the era, the darkest of the films noirs.[39]

At the same time, however, it is clear that French audiences never took to a steady diet of somber films. The millions who relished the zaniness of Georgius brought box-office success to a succession of comedies and light romances. In 1937 one such crowd-pleaser was *Ignace,* about a simple optimist—a good-natured bumpkin named Ignace Bloitaclou—doing his obligatory (peacetime) military service and coming through the shoals of work and love life winningly. It starred Fer-

Superstars Jean Gabin and Michèle Morgan as doomed lovers in *Le Quai des brumes* (1938). Poster, Phot. Bibl. Nat. de Fr.-Paris.

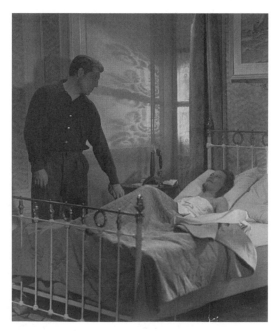

The lovers part after a night together, their last night together, in *Le Quai des brumes*. Courtesy of BFI Stills, Posters, and Designs.

Flight to a new life and fresh love come to a cruel, abrupt end: Jean is gunned down in the street in *Le Quai des brumes*. Courtesy of BFI Stills, Posters, and Designs.

nandel, who was now an established star and a national icon of silly but wily cheerfulness. In 1937 cinema professionals chose Fernandel as the most popular actor of the year, and the next year he came in second. One of his specialties was playing the old role of comic soldier in new military farces, almost all of them set safely back in the "good old days" before 1914. Amid omens of approaching war, audiences in 1937 still enjoyed seeing army life depicted in comic sketches featuring foot-soldiers as not-so-bright but débrouillard "little guys" and officers as bumptious but ineffectual heavies. It is worth noting that the year of *La Grande Illusion* was also the year of two Fernandel comic-soldier movies—*Ignace* and *Les Dégourdis de la 11ème* (the cunning ones—or débrouillards—of the eleventh regiment). *Ignace* was even voted number two on *La Cinématographie française*'s list of movies of the year.[40]

In 1938, *Le Quai des brumes* was second in popularity to a light, cheering American film: Walt Disney's animated *Blanche-Neige* (*Snow White*).[41] The ever popular crime and detective stories brought a kind of cheer as well. As one critic observed, they showed that after "many vicissitudes, complications, and catastrophes," good finally triumphs over evil, and in the end "a strict logic" emerges from the "craziest unlikelihood." René Bizet remarked in May 1939, "This optimistic conception of life comforts the crowds."[42] The striking novelty of the late thirties was that film directors and the public also found such a large place for stories of tragedy and defeat.

The series of depressing tales continued with director Marcel Carné's *Hôtel du Nord*, which made its debut in December 1938.[43] Like the earlier populist films, it did not show the modern industrial parts of Paris or unemployed masses, but rather a close-knit community of "little people" and small shops along the canal Saint-Martin. The film opens with the sound of an accordion playing a popular waltz to which is added the voices of children at play; the first views are of lovers descending a high arched bridge over the canal. The center of the people's shared life is the bar and restaurant of the Hôtel du Nord, where truck drivers, construction workers, a lock-keeper, a baker, and the neighborhood cop socialize, together with the proprietors and tenants of the hotel. The humble couple who own and run the hotel are the warm and generous mother and father presiding over the neighborhood "family." Only a small and occasional hint of the period's difficulties intrudes—an orphan from war-torn Spain and the mention of a strike. The "good little people" live their days and seasons together in timeless fashion, sharing drinks in the café and relaxing together in the green parks along the canal and on the bridge over it. Together they also celebrate such special times as a girl's first communion with a banquet and the fourteenth of July with dancing in the street and fireworks.

Fernandel as the simple provincial conscript in *Ignace* (1937). Courtesy of MoMA Film Stills.

During the biggest celebration of the year—14 July—the warm rites of the archetypical *faubourg* community went on day and night with dancing in the small street, but the troubled lovers Renée (Annabella) and Pierre (Jean-Pierre Aumont) in *Hôtel du Nord* (1938) could not find happiness there. Courtesy of BFI Stills, Posters, and Designs.

But the life of the people in community does not satisfy the central characters of the story. Two of those characters are young lovers caught up in despair: Pierre, who has worked as an artist, and Renée, who used to work in a bakery, has no family, and is wholly devoted to Pierre. The lovers do not have jobs or income and do not fit into the community of working people; and they want to escape their difficulties together. Tired of the struggle and the frustration, they agree on a double suicide. Their attempt fails, and they are separated. Pierre, who has wounded his lover with a gunshot, is put in prison. After recovering from her wounds, Renée is given a job in the Hôtel du Nord, but the work and family atmosphere do not fulfill her need for romance. After some time she chooses evasion by running away with a pimp known as Edmond, who has his own desperate reasons for fleeing. He is tired of his confined life in the hotel with a hooker named Raymonde (Arletty), and he is depressed, knowing that former buddies are hunting him down.

The new twist to the old theme of escaping the familiar faubourg is the con-

In *Le Jour se lève* (1939), François (Jean Gabin) sleeps with Clara (Arletty) in her room on Sundays, but she knows that he loves the younger, apparently more innocent woman, Françoise (Jacqueline Laurent). Courtesy of BFI Stills, Posters, and Designs.

François and Françoise share their dreams and love in *Le Jour se lève*. Courtesy of BFI Stills, Posters, and Designs.

in love with a lovely young woman, Françoise, whose impoverished childhood as an orphan was like his own. Happily they share the little Parisian's modest dream of biking to the country at Easter time to pick lilacs. Then François finds out about Françoise's unsavory fatherly friend and seducer (Jules Berry)—a petty showman, fast-talking and duplicitous, who dresses and acts like a bourgeois. One day the showman provokes François into a rage and the worker, bitterly disappointed in love, kills him. Cornered in his room high above the somber street, François waits out a lonely night, playing out the last act of a life that seemed doomed to failure from the time his parents abandoned him as a child. The crowd gathered below is curious and sympathetic, but they can do nothing for him and are held back by brigades of policemen. Finally, as the police move in at daybreak, François ends his own life. Here in the stark gray-and-black of a modern working-class suburb was the hapless, good "little guy" as tragic hero, a man who led his difficult life stoically, grasped at one last chance of happiness through love with a beautiful young woman, and suffered disappointment and then defeat in a desolate isolation.

   Le Jour se lève was not successful at the box office.[48] Was the picture too gloomy for audiences during that depressing time? Reviewers, particularly those

A curious and concerned crowd watches and waits anxiously as the police gather force and prepare to storm François's apartment in *Le Jour se lève*. Courtesy of BFI Stills, Posters, and Designs.

The terrible night, the shooting, and the standoff end: François dead on the floor of his small room in *Le Jour se lève*. Courtesy of BFI Stills, Posters, and Designs.

of the Right, thought so and complained of being surfeited by films about criminals and degenerates. They lamented the frequent depictions of the French people as petty and silly. And they worried aloud about the impression made by those films abroad. Ordinary moviegoers, however, did not show signs of being overwhelmed, nor did they show concern about what foreigners thought of France. The box-office receipts indicate rather that they had found some satisfaction in most of the depressing stories of the period—at least up to 1939.

If one takes a Gramscian view of these Gabin movies of the late thirties, one would say that powerful groups exercising hegemony in France were sending a message to the workers and other supporters of the Popular Front. The message was that the "little people" and their efforts for change were, like the screen hero, destined to go down in defeat. Alternatively, one can argue that the films reflected fears and presentiments of what lay ahead for France as Nazi Germany grew stronger and more aggressive. Historian Jean-Pierre Jeancolas has maintained that in the Gabin films France tried "to exorcise the menaces by a sacrifice." The French sacrificed Jean Gabin—indeed, repeatedly killed him, Jeancolas asserts.[49] I would put it differently: in Gabin's characters moviegoers found tensions and frustration and desperate hope reminiscent of what they knew in their own lives. They also experienced a vicarious resolution of those tensions, seeing their worst fears acted out before their eyes. As film scholar André Braun-Larrieu wrote in 1938, spectators felt pleasure in the "psychic tension" and "strong emotions" aroused by such films and still more pleasure in "deliverance and liberation."[50] In the Gabin scenarios, deliverance came through defeat and death. Through the dark films of the period, French audiences watched that ending repeatedly and were fascinated by it, as though trying it out as a possibility for their own lives. Identifying with the hero and his downfall, audiences were left where "realist" songs had long left them—with a sense of nothing more to lose, release from anxiety and struggle, and quiet mourning.

Those diverse readings are not mutually exclusive. There is little reason to believe that any one interpretation prevailed. During the 1930s observers on the Right went so far as to assert that the depressing movies were demoralizing the public and weakening France. What their indictments overlooked is that the movies showed not only transgressions and marginal people, but also the terrible consequences of being isolated and of giving up the fight. Such scenarios may well have served as cautionary tales that mitigated viewers' tendencies to be passive and defeatist. In these questions of collective psychology, there is no conclusive evidence.

Only weeks after the première of *Le Jour se lève,* a second powerfully disturbing film appeared: Jean Renoir's *La Règle du jeu* (*Rules of the Game*) opened in Paris at the Colisée Cinéma on 7 July. Set in the present, it showed the middle and upper classes to be as false and destructive, as repugnant in their egotism as the most irresponsible nobles in the twilight of the ancien régime. At the end of the film the audience booed and howled. Renoir's picture of elite character and behavior was too unsettling at that tense time, particularly for the audience of well-off people gathered in that first-class movie theater. The common people in the story also failed to measure up to the challenges facing the nation. The "man of the people," Marceau, thanks the marquis for raising him up by making him a servant. Abandoning the struggle for liberty, the people (Renoir suggests) fell for the lure of security in a state of servitude.[51]

Renoir's *La Règle du jeu* capped the series of pitiless portraits of the French people at a time when the clouds of war were gathering. Granted, those portraits shared the screens with more optimistic films. In the months before the war, for example, moviegoers who did not want to see a heavy drama flocked to the latest Fernandel film, *Les Cinq Sous de Lavarède,* which showed the good-natured simple "little guy" as a virtuoso débrouillard, and a comically lucky one, too. In order to inherit a fortune, he must travel all around the world in just a few months with a paltry five sous in his pocket. Taking up the challenge, he uses varied disguises and ruses, cannily finds a way from one check point to another, and miraculously escapes danger at the last second time after time.[52] Moviegoers always had a choice of fare in the mass-culture marketplace, and no one genre or theme ever drove out the others. It is nonetheless noteworthy that the proportional importance of themes and genres changed from the early to the late thirties. Toward the end of the decade French audiences saw few representations of the people or elites successfully meeting difficult challenges, especially in the present. What they saw was an unprecedented number of movies showing friendship and love failing—and ordinary people's struggles ending in defeat and death.

If the movies did not provide enough relief through much of 1939, people could look forward to vacation, getting away from it all in August. Despite the unraveling of the Popular Front and rumors of war, vacations went on as scheduled. Despite the threat of Nazi aggression against Poland, most of France's leaders took time off as usual in August 1939. The president of the cabinet, Edouard Daladier, who was also minister of defense, spent his vacation on a friend's yacht in the Mediterranean off the Côte d'Azur. Finance Minister Paul Reynaud went to Corsica on a friend's yacht and then to Le Touquet on the English Channel and Arcachon on the Atlantic coast. President Albert Lebrun vacationed in his Lorraine home in the village of Mercy-le-Haut. Minister of Justice Paul Marchandeau spent twelve days at Evian. Minister of Foreign Affairs Georges Bonnet, however, rested only briefly at Saint-Georges de Didonne, and Minister of Colonies Georges Mandel—who had long argued for resisting Nazi moves—spent only three days at Deauville. Only British Prime Minister Winston Churchill's travel that August

War was imminent, but August 1939 was vacation time for most, perhaps a last camping trip. SAFARA. Private collection.

showed graver concerns: at the prompting of General Maurice Gamelin, he conspicuously visited France's great concrete shield, the Maginot Line.[53]

For weeks talk of a coming war had dogged the working people of France, too, but they—like their leaders—were not willing to curtail their now usual summer respite from routine constraints. To some, vacation during a critical time was especially attractive. "Danger makes the charm of vacation taste better than before," observed a journalist in early 1939.[54] Yet it was only a vacation, not a total flight from reality. The French people eagerly took one more opportunity to enjoy the only clear gain from the struggles of 1936 before submitting again to the exigencies of war and sacrifice. In 1939 public opinion generally was readier to accept war than it had been in 1936 and in the year of the Munich crisis.[55] A large majority was ready to have French soldiers "die for Danzig" if need be—but after vacation.

9. CULTURAL STRATEGIES
IN A NEW WAR

A "Funny" War: Poilus and Madelon Again

A LITTLE MORE THAN TWO decades after the "war to end all wars," the French declared war on Germany and moved anew into a cultural no-man's-land. They had prepared for that new conflict by building the massive Maginot Line, and Parisians had equipped themselves with gas masks, but were they mentally prepared for war? They had a ready supply of rallying cries and myths left over from the ordeal of the Great War, but would the old ones work again? It was far from certain that images of cheerful and resourceful "little" patriots would do anything for morale this time. No one knew if they were still credible—or if they would simply remind the public of the propagandist hyperbole and the disillusionments of 1914–18.

That earlier ordeal had begun with a German invasion of French soil, and the response required of the French was evident, but this time nothing about the war was clear. The German army did not invade France after attacking Poland on 1 September 1939, and the French made no serious effort to mount an offensive. Reconnaissance groups crossed some kilometers into Germany and then made a strategic withdrawal. No important engagement occurred on the Western Front.

The movie theater promised escape, and the radio offered plenty of upbeat distraction about the unflappable French, but this crowd of Parisians seemed anxious as they listened for the latest radio news about the war. 20 September 1939. Phot. Bibl. Nat. de Fr.-Paris.

The French army stood guard week after week, month after month. From early October 1939 to 10 May 1940 it waited. The fervent fighting songs that had resounded in the other war did not seem appropriate this time. In fall of 1939 the song that the French heard everywhere was a quiet romantic piece about lovers who have to wait through an indefinite period of separation. A woman tenderly promises to wait for her lover's return "night and day . . . forever." "J'attendrai, le jour et la nuit, / J'attendrai toujours—J'attendrai ton retour." Georges Sadoul described it in October 1940 as a "very sad love song that the radio has popularized, and that everyone has hummed with an obsessive melancholy in the streets and in the barracks since the first weeks [of the war]."[1] "J'attendrai," already a couple of years old, tapped sadness that was both widespread and deep. There was the sadness of loved ones parting and facing the terrible dangers of war. And there was the longer-term sadness of a nation haunted by memories of the last war, still grieving and weary of crisis and disappointment. The soft refrains of "J'attendrai" also expressed one of the most fundamental and widespread desires emerging after the mobilization: the desire to hear the promise of faithful love. The unspoken hope behind the promise was hope that this time the waiting—and the war—would be brief.[2]

Although the early months of the new war were far different from those of 1914, some memories of the earlier experience came into the limelight: select pleasant ones. Toward the end of September *Le Petit Parisien* announced that Maurice Chevalier was going to introduce a new war song about a daughter of the poilus' beloved Madelon. The lyrics of "Victoire la fille à Madelon" happily bring the Great War story up to the present. The new heroine named Victory, now twenty years old, is the daughter of Madelon and a corporal (the officer who in vain proposed marriage in the 1914 lyrics). Victory was somewhere between Belfort and Thionville, one verse tells us. The soldiers call for her and sing "la victoire." The last lines deliver a happy double-entendre ending: "To all our victorious soldiers / Victory has promised her heart." Cheery as always, Chevalier was reported to be confident that the new song "will be quickly adopted by all the 'poilus' of 1939."[3] Invoked like beneficent spirits, the imaginary figures of the Great War were back for the new war. At times the troops' own frontline newspapers also used the legendary name *poilus* for the new soldiers. Often without using that label, the Parisian newspapers and radio simply reported that the soldiers on the front were living up to tradition and hopes as joking, singing, wine-drinking warriors like the men of 1914–18.[4] Identifying the soldiers of 1939 with the poilus suggested their toughness, joviality, patriotism, and more: now it also evoked the memory of victory over the Germans. No one publicly brought up the painful memories of carnage and dissension.

And no one this time publicly questioned whether it was all right to be lighthearted in wartime. During the First World War it had been many months before

In the tense *drôle de guerre* through the winter of 1939–40, a front soldier appears to reincarnate the mythic poilu of 1914–18, as, pipe in hand, he smiles and drinks his pinard. Musée d'histoire contemporaine—BDIC (Universités de Paris).

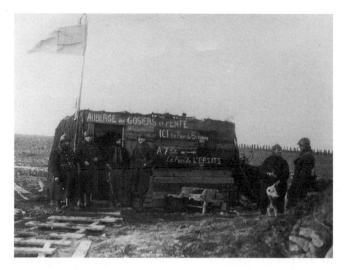

The muddy terrain on the front was desolate during the cold winter of late 1939, but smiling frontline soldiers appeared to live up to traditions of Gallic gaiety. They have identified their shack as "L'Auberge des Gosiers en Pente" (the Inn of the Sloping Gullets—that is, always thirsty) and their country as "Le Pays du Sourire" (the land of the smile), just seven kilometers from "the land of the *Ersatz*." Musée d'histoire contemporaine—BDIC (Universités de Paris).

military authorities recognized the problem of boredom on the front and provided entertainment. During the fall of 1939 the problem was quickly addressed. The Théâtre aux Armées swung into action within the first six weeks. In mid-October the popular weekly *Match* reported that the Théâtre aux Armées had recently performed one of its first shows for the front troops in a small northern village: the entertainment included a play about Madelon. The heroine of 1914–18, played by a soldier in a 1939-style evening dress, concedes that she is a little old now, but suggests hopefully that the latter-day poilus will perhaps say: "She pleased my papa, so she will please me." The audience shouted its approval and applauded with delight.[5] The soldiers of the new war accepted the wartime identity of their fathers and assumed the role of Madelon's admirers. The troops also warmly greeted a charming male figure from the Great War, a former poilu who was now one of the first entertainers to perform in the war zone: Maurice Chevalier. With Josephine Baker and young "half-star" Nita Raya (then his companion), he made a singing tour of the front lines, performing for the troops at Metz and Thionville and for other units nearby.[6] All such entertainment was, of course, intended to foster good morale, so that jovial, coping latter-day poilus might emerge from the untested young army.

From the mutinies of the First World War authorities had learned how important furloughs were to morale, and this time they were not slow to grant leaves to frontline soldiers. At first the policy was that a leave of ten days was to be granted after four months of active duty, but during the late fall that prerequisite period of service was reduced—for fathers first. By late November the first furloughed men from the front were arriving in Paris at the Gare de l'Est and Gare du Nord.[7] Many visited their adopted godmothers or *marraines,* just as their fathers had. By a decree of 21 November the government took further action against boredom and anxiety on the front: it created a department of "reading, arts and leisure for the armies."[8] For their part the men quickly found their own diversions. Through the long, hard winter of 1939–40 on and behind the Maginot Line they played cards (especially belote) for hours on end, drank warm wine (the men still called it pinard), listened to the radio, read frontline newspapers that quickly multiplied, and whiled away time in the canteen.[9] With their magical pinard and their Maginot Line the new poilus seemed ready to meet any challenge the war might bring, if one believed the press and new topical songs.

On the front the radio was the most important new feature of day-to-day leisure, but much of what was broadcast was not new. Radio listeners regularly heard Maurice Chevalier singing songs in French and English. One of his new offerings in the late fall was "Mimile," an upbeat tale about the classic little Parisian—a *gars de Ménilmontant*—who becomes a soldier and serves France well and awaits a medal. Another characteristic Chevalier contribution was an updated version of his hit "Ça fait d'excellents Français"—now "Ça fait d'excellents soldats"—singing the praises of the reservists.[10] The song cheerfully acclaims the willingness of Frenchmen of all social stations and political persuasions to join together as patriotic soldiers, forming a new *union sacrée.* The colonel who was in finance, the commandant who was in industry, the captain who was in insurance, the lieutenant who was in the grocery business, the sergeant who was a pastry baker, and the corporal who was "in ignorance"—"all those make excellent Frenchmen." The colonel who was in the Action française, the sergeant who was a devoted Socialist, and the corporal who "registers on all the lists"—"all those make excellent Frenchmen." One chorus asks how those aging hearty fellows (*gaillards*) can appear so fit, just like twenty-year-olds: "Whence comes this miracle?" The answer harks back to the myth of the poilu: "But from pinard and tobacco!"[11] Waiting, however, was all that the excellent Frenchmen did for months. "J'attendrai" (I will wait for you), a favorite of the men in the Maginot Line, continued to play on the radio hauntingly through the long winter of the "phony war" (*la drôle de guerre*).

Although (heavily censored) press reports also painted the optimistic picture of the morale of the "excellent Frenchmen" on the front during the winter of 1939–40, other evidence gives reason for skepticism.[12] Chevalier's refrains about social harmony and unanimous patriotic devotion were, unfortunately, wishful thinking and patriotic cheerleading. Soldiers commonly felt contempt toward officers and bitterly rejected songs that smacked of propaganda. The men refused to sing the hit of the earlier war, "Quand Madelon," which authorities had tried for months to revive. Some soldiers—provocatively, defiantly—sang "L'Internationale" to Premier Daladier when he visited the front lines in the Saar. When an off-duty soldier tried to play "La Marseillaise" and "Quand Madelon" to his comrades on the front, reported Georges Sadoul, they hooted insults at him. The men knew what they liked: ribald songs, long-time favorites of the barracks. The only time that Sadoul heard "La Madelon" was when a fellow soldier sang it with new, vulgar words. The famous last line "Madelon! Madelon! Madelon!" was replaced with "Du croupion! du croupion! du croupion!" (some ass! some ass! some ass!).[13]

After invoking Great War symbols and talismans for months, morale managers in the press and the government pointed up some happy contrasts between the two conflicts. In a speech on 22 December to the Chamber of Deputies, Daladier reported with satisfaction on how few lives had been lost—fewer than 2,000—compared to the 450,000 killed by December 1914. A strange war, a phony war it was turning out to be. Some people wishfully thought that it might never become a real war. Official communications maintained that time was on the side of the democracies. The French were becoming better prepared and better organized, and a blockade would put pressure on Germany, and Hitler the bluffer might be overthrown or ask for quarter.[14]

The press kept up a cheerful tone, reporting only encouraging news. A popular song (imported from Britain) of the late fall went so far as to assert, "We're going to hang out our washing on the Siegfried Line." In the French lyrics by Paul Misraki, "un petit Tommy" (British soldier) sings the song, and "all the joyous *p'tits poilus*" learn the chorus: "Everything's great [*Tout va pour le mieux*]; we're going to hang out our washing on the Siegfried Line." It is not clear that soldiers on the front actually sang it, but there is no doubt that civilians heard it frequently in Paris.[15] The blustery show of confidence continued throughout the long dreary winter; so did the waiting, the anxiety, and the worries. In the spring of 1940 Daladier attended to the morale problem by providing ten thousand soccer balls for the troops.[16] French soldiers made advances toward the Siegfried Line in soccer games, but that was all. Even with the better weather of spring, the men still filled most of their waking hours listening to the radio, chatting, drinking, card playing, and attending music-hall performances. The strange war did not produce many new stories about Frenchman furiously doing battle, but reports about the men's leisure activities—games, wine drinking, and singing—provided reassurance that at least the famous Gallic gaiety in wartime lived on.

"Paris Will Always Be Paris"

Life in the capital also quickly resumed its familiar routines in the fall of 1939. The massive bombardments that Parisians expected did not come. Nor did chemical attacks. People carried their gas masks around like umbrellas or hung them on a belt, but other evidence of the war was scant. Without deprivations to remind them of the war, civilians often tried to forget the perils to the east by distracting themselves with amusements. The movie theaters of Paris were continually full, packed with British soldiers as well as Parisians.

What they saw were films that had passed stringent national censors, who eliminated anything less than upbeat from public view. In October Renoir's *La Règle du jeu* was banned: censors judged it demoralizing. Also censored were *La Grande Illusion, La Bête humaine, Hôtel du Nord,* and many others deemed "depressing, morbid, and immoral."[17] Light films, old and new, filled the screens. The audiences for those movies had suffered through weeks of tension, worry, and danger. Enervation and depression were common.[18] Under those conditions a strong demand for entertainment persisted. In fact, the business of distractions enjoyed a boom throughout the war, and the German occupation as well.

The nation's leading entertainers, having little interest in politics and war, simply continued their careers as before, modeling and communicating their versions of French normality. After their tour of the front lines, Maurice Chevalier, Josephine Baker, and Nita Raya shared star billing at the Casino de Paris in early December. The new revue, entitled *Paris-London,* was "dedicated to Franco-British friendship." Chevalier's first song proclaimed jauntily that "Paris will always be Paris." Even though the city's streetlights were now darkened nightly, and its statues were swathed in protective earthworks, and the Champs-Elysées was turned topsy-turvy, "Paris will always be Paris / The most beautiful city in the world. / The more its lighting is reduced / The more people see shining its courage / Its good humor and its wit / Paris will always be Paris!" Soldiers on leave, he continued, would find there some of the capital's charm. Even though women's dresses were more sober and feminine beauty was less showy, the capital was still full of "pretty women," and its elegance became only more precious.[19] That kind of entertainment helped encourage the many who wanted to believe that the war was going be a brief and minor disruption, just a time of defensive maneuvers, at least for France. The Casino de Paris was never less than full throughout the winter and early spring. Despite bombing alerts and blackouts, the music-hall season was almost a normal one, Chevalier recalled in his memoirs.[20]

Through the long months of the "phony war," the entertainer who performed the most in benefits and concerts for the armies was the ever smiling optimist, Maurice Chevalier. In May 1940, on the eve of the German invasion of Belgium, he sang once more "Ça fait d'excellents Français," this time in a gala at the Bobino to benefit the French Red Cross. "*Oui,* all these brave men have left with style / To do as yesteryear all that their fathers did for their sons." Chevalier was followed by Marie Dubas, who summoned more memories of yesteryear by singing that old favorite, "Quand Madelon."[21]

The next day, finally, a shooting war broke out, unlike any known to the poilus and their Madelon. On 10 May Germany launched its Blitzkrieg, its "lightning war" of Panzers and Stukas that crashed their way into France, penetrating even part of the touted Maginot Line. This time war touched off no grandiloquent speeches from France's leaders, no exalted talk about heroic sacrifice. This time political and military leaders and the press took the poilu tack of shunning the high rhetoric. The reassuring clichés of popular culture resounded without much competition: don't worry—*tout ça s'arrangera.* Somehow the French would be débrouillard—as before.[22]

Counterattack on Popular Culture and "Anti-France"

Over the next month, as the French army and its defenses collapsed under the force of the German invasion, French public opinion seethed with shock, humiliation, confusion, and anger at being misled. The Nazi Blitzkrieg had defeated France's armies in just four weeks. Premier Paul Reynaud, who had succeeded Daladier in March, resigned on 16 June, and the old "victor of Verdun," Marshal Philippe Pétain, took over and sought a quick armistice to "save" France and the army. The majority of the French people seem to have readily accepted the peace deal, which produced a new armistice signed in the same railroad car used for the 1918 armistice ceremony.[23] The Germans allowed two-fifths of France (the center and South) to be under a nominally sovereign French government, while they put the rest—the

North and the Atlantic coast—directly under the control of occupying German forces. Now Pétain and his supporters established a new government at Vichy, the famous spa town about 350 kilometers south of Paris, and there they made laws that applied to all of France, though the German authorities held veto power.

Pétain had quickly decided to avoid the prolonged carnage experienced in the earlier war. He and the many who followed him made that decision not out of a simple pacifism nor a despairing suicide-wish or defeatism. The attitude that prevailed was primarily one of resignation, acceptance of what seemingly had to be accepted. The French during the Second World War passed quickly into what had been a middle phase of the First World War: a time of partial numbness and a sad, grim resolve to go on living a life that was imposed on them without bothering to try to understand it all. It was a time for the poignant contemplation of the misfortune and tragedy that life can entail, a contemplation of how unjust and cruel fate can be—an attitude long cultivated by realist songs.

After the armistice, the stunned French had to adapt to a disturbingly unfamiliar world. The old republican identity stories were officially discarded and replaced by new antirepublican versions of French history. In redefining France, the new government at Vichy appropriated some well-established currents of culture and attacked other popular trends. It met with opposition on these matters well before the political Resistance took shape. In popular songs and films and political discourse, several different constructions of "the average Frenchman" clashed throughout the dark times of the Second World War.

The new authorities began by offering their explanations for the defeat. No longer able to attack the Germans, Vichy spokesmen gave themselves over to attacking the now defunct republic and the popular culture that they considered pernicious. With crusading zeal they censored movies and publications, banned dancing, and condemned everything that they believed to be responsible for France's weaknesses. In their analysis it was the egoist pursuit of pleasure and corrupting "cosmopolitan" (meaning non-French) influences that had brought down France and the Third Republic. Those conclusions built on years of jeremiads from conservatives and church spokesmen, decrying the influence of popular literature, radio, and movies on the people, an influence they considered ruinous. On Radio-Paris in early 1939, for example, the Jesuit Father Alphonse de Parvillez gave a "religious talk" on "the assault of [those] invisible forces" which propagated "obscenities" and "sentimental stories destined to teach girls that love is the only thing that matters." He concluded by proclaiming the urgent need for moral reform (re-

dressement) with the church as a guide.[24] Adopting the rhetoric of moral renewal, right-wing leaders at Vichy extolled the old virtues of work, family, and *la patrie*. While attacking everything that seemed to have led to the defeat, France's new leaders set out to reverse the decadence and regenerate the nation.

To right-wing critics of the cinema, the vogue of realist populism and pessimistic fatalism of the preceding years had been particularly demoralizing and corrupting. Stories about the lowest order of Frenchmen and some not-so-low going ineluctably to terrible ends communicated a sense of what former *Action française* critic Lucien Rebatet called a "degrading determinism."[25] Rebatet's explanation for the deplorable state of film and theater was simple: Jews and "cosmopolitans" were in control. In accord with Vichy ideology, his attacks were aimed at the masters of the entertainment industry not as *les gros* or capitalists, but as Jews.[26] Rebatet's venomous book *Les Tribus du cinéma et du théâtre* (1941) was an all-out indictment, charging Jews with bringing bad taste, immorality, corruption, and financial ruin to theater and cinema in France. He scorned director after director— Jean Epstein, Pierre Braunberger, Henri Diamant-Berger, Bernard Natan, Raymond Bernard—as he spelled out their faults, of which the primary ones were their being Jewish and being of recent "importation." France underwent "the great invasion" after 1918, he asserted. "The dregs of the ghetto" descended on Paris: "the worst riffraff, crooks [*filous*] of the lowest kind." "The Jews take everywhere the vices of their race," he declared early in the book. Even Marcel Carné, whom Rebatet recognized as "Aryan," "was impregnated with all the Jewish influences."

> He has been the most accomplished representative in France of
> that Marxist aesthetic which is everywhere one of the fruits of
> the proliferation of Jews and which spontaneously engenders de-
> terioration and decline—political, financial, and spiritual. . . .
> This aesthetic is at once querulous and brutal. It takes its subjects
> in the mud and blood. It treats them with a systematic naturalism,
> which is accompanied by social symbols seething with revolt and
> hatred, shifty and also flabby, evoking the destructive labor of
> the so readily nihilist Jew. . . . The leprous and foggy suburbs
> which serve him as a setting exhale only sordid sentiments, spite-
> ful and bitter demands. . . . His heroes are mediocre assassins,
> candidates for suicide, pimps, whores, female procurers.[27]

Turning to the world of the music hall, Rebatet denounced the power of

Max Viterbo, owner of the Empire music hall, and "a Romanian Jew, Goldin," who owned the ABC and the Mogador. One of Goldin's alleged crimes was to promote in his establishment "a crowd of congeners, among others those two fruits of the ghetto, those two complete examples of Jewish affectation [*grimace*] and hysteria: the *pollacke* Marie Dubas, the Judeo-German ape [*guenon*] Marianne Oswald." Rebatet further accused Jewish impresarios of having "supported the white-slave traffic" and of having "contributed to all forms of clandestine prostitution of the dancer, chorus member or homosexual."[28]

Rebatet's conclusion was, predictably, that France must be rid of Jews. "The theater of France must be purged of Jews, from its high places down to the prompter's hole." Again and again he called for the ouster of "the Jew" from every job in the theater. He even called for the burning of all plays by Jewish playwrights, except for a half dozen or so to be placed "in a cupboard for future curious students" as a "literary zoology collection." All that was still not enough. "It will be necessary sooner or later to drive from our soil several hundreds of thousands of Jews," including—immediately—"the quasi-totality of Jews of the cinema world."[29]

From the fall of 1940 on, such thinking had engendered anti-Semitic legislation and persecution. Attacks on Jews multiplied in the press, in school textbooks, in short films, and on the radio. Jews were purged from the film industry, theater, radio, and press in both Vichy and occupied France. And censorship in both zones eliminated even semi-sympathetic depictions of Jews, "cosmopolitan" foreigners, and the riffraff (*pègre*) from film. Vichy deemed such measures necessary for France's regeneration. Within weeks of the armistice Pétain himself pronounced on French identity in terms of polar oppositions and exclusions: "There is no neutrality possible," he declared, "between the true and the false, between the good and the evil, between health and sickness, between order and disorder, between France and anti-France."[30] Everyone not with him was "anti-France."

Continuity and New Order

In framing a new order Vichy spokesmen made some conspicuous links with the past—in particular certain memories and myths of the First World War. In their efforts to foster unity, they invoked the memory of the "sacred union" of 1914, patriotic solidarity as the time-honored response to national emergency. They also made use of the public image of Pétain himself as a national symbol, ensuring the rightfulness of the new order. Pétain, the hero of Verdun and a patriarchal figure of indisputable patriotism, served as a legitimizing link with the past.[31] According to his propagandists, he was even a Messiah, a Christlike figure, redeeming his fallen country and bringing salvation.[32] Some supporters hailed him as simply the nation incarnate: "Pétain is France" and "France is Pétain," declared the Cardinal Gerlier, archbishop of Lyon, in 1940. "Pétain, c'est la France / La France, c'est Pétain," echoed the lines of a song of 1941, "Maréchal, nous voilà!" which was played on the radio daily.[33]

Official voices of the "national revolution" went on to redefine the national identity. According to them, the Frenchman par excellence, the incarnation of needed virtues, was not that darling of recent mass culture, the faubourien of troublesome Paris. And it was certainly not the industrial worker, so closely associated with the Left and social strife. Rather it was the peasant, the villager, the provincial, the country artisan, uncorrupted by foreign and Parisian ways.[34] It was the rural and small-town Frenchman, working hard in a traditional way of life, living in a close-knit family, abiding by old-fashioned morality and gender roles, respecting religion and authority, and loving la patrie.

Vichy propagandists sought to return France to a supposedly authentic French culture by promoting, even glorifying, local rural life, the terroir, especially during the first two years of the regime, while preparing for the new Europe. The new regime encouraged regional theater and folklore—local songs, dances, traditional festivals, and pilgrimages. Vichy also sponsored the production of movies about peasants and old-fashioned artisans. From 1940 to 1942 about sixty government-subsidized documentaries were made about "la France profonde"—a peaceful, fruitful rural France.[35] Work and the land were deemed the saving graces, the guarantors of an "eternal France." Rural artisans and peasants served as models of respect for authorities and for tradition and even a deeply ingrained attitude of resignation. The French people of the villages were the ones who counted and on whom one could count.

As the countryside was deemed healthier than the cities, it was not enough just to sing about it and to show it in films. Vichy authorities set up a program that took young men out of the cities and deep into the countryside—not for vacation, but for work, exercise, and "moral training" in camps called Chantiers de jeunesse. In contrast to the earlier auberge movement with its lure of freedom and adventure for young men and women, the new order required twenty-year-old men to labor in teams—felling trees, making charcoal, and building roads—roughing it in remote sites for months.[36]

In speeches, posters, and films, the Vichy government projected the ideal of a strong healthy youth that disciplined itself in exercise and excelled in sports out of a desire to serve la patrie. The discourse was matched by a substantial increase in state financial support for physical education programs and sports. Vichy leaders did not acknowledge that through these programs they were continuing the work of their old foes, the Popular Front. For their part, young people responded. In spite of undernourishment and some opposition from the church, young French men and women joined sporting organizations and practiced sports in growing numbers through the Vichy period. Particularly popular were skiing, mountain climbing, gliding, canoeing, bicycle touring, and hunting. Officials expressed pride in youth's positive response as evidence of support for the new regime. To historians today, that response appears to have been more a matter of patriotism and a need to counter boredom and depression.

If the Vichy model of youth was clear, so was the model of the "other," especially after 1942 when the Germans occupied the entire country. French authorities tightened their hold on sporting organizations, and the anti-Semitism of the Nazis and Vichy entered the domain of sports. The most famous French swimmer of the time, Alfred Nakache, a teacher in Toulouse (and Jewish), was arrested along with his wife and daughter at the end of 1943 and sent to Nazi concentration camps.[37] Even French sports heroes could become "anti-France."

There remained much about French life and culture that the moralists of the new order did not or could not change—and did not grasp. Though they iden-

The anti-Semitic imagery of "Assez" (Enough) on a wall in Dieppe solicits support for the expulsion of Jews. A poster by Venabert (1942). Courtesy of the Musée d'histoire contemporaine—BDIC (Universités de Paris).

tified mass culture as a cause of disaster, some of the messages of that culture had eased ordinary people's way through disaster, offering guidance and solace in the debacle of 1940. In orienting themselves day to day, people drew not only on the preachments of the new authorities, but also on the received repertory of responses to misfortune. For years movies had given defeat a mystique, showing the good Frenchman going down with dignity. And since the First World War, songs had expressed and legitimized an attitude of the *j'm'en foutiste*, the fatalist position, not giving a damn about even disastrous events.

Songs had also kept in public consciousness the idea that the good Frenchman goes on smiling and singing and enjoying the pleasures of Paris and the beauties of France, no matter how bad events are. This was a continuing echo of the Great War chants about Gallic gaiety naturally carrying the Frenchman through the worst of circumstances. Let's be French, and "let's keep on singing" (Chantons toujours). That was the title of a musical revue presented, appropriately, at the Théâtre des Optimistes in June 1940. It was also the de facto motto of the flourishing entertainment industry under the German occupation.

The pursuit of pleasures went on conspicuously in the capital even though Vichy spokesmen denounced them, praised work, and promoted the quiet provincial life. Restaurants, which had closed during the invasion, reopened in July with menus in German. Cafés quickly regained their crowds of customers. Movie houses and music halls played to consistently large audiences. In September the theaters resumed their normal activity of the new season.[38] In December 1940 the Hot Club de France organized a jazz festival in the Salle Pleyel, where large audiences applauded what the authorities routinely denounced as "degenerate, Jewish, and Negro music."[39] As a song of the previous year put it breezily, "Paris sera toujours Paris." The unbroken continuity proclaimed by the song was partly true. It was also a comforting denial of the German victory and occupation.

Moviemaking that the war had interrupted in the spring resumed in August 1940. The earliest film to be resumed and released was Marcel Pagnol's *La Fille du puisatier* (*The well-digger's daughter*), which referred to the war as a distant worry and above all as the cause of an unmarried father's absence. The stars were Pagnol's old favorites, Raimu and Fernandel, as good Southern workingmen, and the ending was a happy one. Another major film whose making spanned the war came out in late 1941: Grémillon's *Remorques,* starring the high-voltage stars Jean Gabin and Michèle Morgan as lovers. Many older movies of the 1930s (now condemned) were shown regularly on screens after the defeat, even though Vichy officially banned all

Maurice Chevalier during the "black years" of the Second World War continued to appear bigger than life as the debonair Frenchman meeting every trial with a smile and hope. The cover of *La Semaine* (3 July 1941), announced that he composed "Notre Espoir" on the Côte d'Azur (keeping his distance from German-occupied Paris). Private collection.

French films released before October 1937 and subsequent "demoralizing" ones (*Le Jour se lève*, for example). Films were screened only after the names of Jewish directors were removed from the credits, and scenes of Jewish actors or others now deemed "undesirables" were cut out by censors.

Many stars of the entertainment world—but far from all—helped to provide a reassuring continuity with the old days. Some decided early on not to risk trouble and not to lend their presence to the post-armistice regimes in the North or South of France. Fearful of the new anti-Semitic laws and actions, Ray Ventura took his orchestra to South America in late 1941.[40] Singer Marie Dubas departed for South America just before the outbreak of the war; she stayed there eighteen months and then returned to Europe to spend the latter part of the war in Switzerland. Maurice Chevalier, then living with Romanian-born (Jewish) singer Nita Raya, fled Paris for his second home, a villa near Cannes. A galaxy of film directors and actors went into exile, many of them moving to Hollywood for the duration of

The face of the new French order given star treatment: Pétain on the cover of *La Semaine* (25 September 1941, photo TAS) with the caption "The Marshal receives 2,000 letters each day." His photograph, sold by schoolchildren for a national charity, was also enshrined on mantels and walls of millions of homes in both the occupied and "free" zones. Private collection.

the war. Gone were directors René Clair, Julien Duvivier, Jacques Feyder, Jean Renoir, Pierre Chenal, Max Ophuls, and Robert Siodmak, among others; gone, too, were Jean Gabin and Michèle Morgan (by mid-1941), Françoise Rosay, Louis Jouvet, Dalio, Erich von Stroheim, and Jean-Pierre Aumont.

Because so many stars of film and the music hall left Paris, those who stayed or returned to perform there counted all the more as symbols of continuity and normality. Only weeks after the armistice, big-name entertainers began reappearing on Parisian stages. In July Charles Trenet sang at the Avenue, while Jacques Pills and Marguerite Gilbert sang at the ABC. Maurice Chevalier stayed at his Mediterranean villa more than a year, but in September 1941 he came back to his beloved Paname, principally to sing in a gala organized by *Paris-Soir* for the benefit of prisoners of war. His return to Paris was hailed in the press as a major event, a turn for the better in the Nazi-controlled capital. In addition to his cheering presence, he brought an upbeat new song that he had written himself: "Notre espoir." The exact content of "our hope" remained ambiguous, perhaps in part to circumvent the censor. In an interview with a reporter, however, he explained his position in the clearest terms: "Having come back to Paris, I blindly follow the Marshal, and I believe that everything that can bring about collaboration between the French and German peoples must be undertaken."[41] He later claimed that German officials had altered his words for their purposes. While in the capital he also sang on Nazi-controlled Radio-Paris, made recordings for it, and appeared in concerts sponsored by collaborators.[42]

Devotion to the old leader at Vichy was expressed in a more resounding way through the song entitled "Maréchal, nous voilà!" (1941), which Chevalier and tenor André Dassary made popular, each with his own recording. "An elated France salutes you, Marshal, / All your children who love you and venerate your years / have responded to your supreme appeal 'Present!'" In the chorus the singers call Pétain "the savior of France," "the hero of Verdun" who is saving France a second time. The singing people swear to serve and follow his steps, for he has "renewed hope: the fatherland will be reborn!" In the place of monstrous war and hatred, the people will "exalt work and maintain confidence in a new destiny," "for Pétain is France" and "France is Pétain!"[43]

Although Chevalier spoke of collaboration with the German victor, as a singer he proclaimed a patriotic preference for what was truly French. "The French song has a role to play now more than ever," Chevalier declared. Unlike "le swing" and "le hot [jazz]," it offered "true melody."[44] The Vichy veterans' organization, the Légion française des combattants, also attacked swing as particularly corrupting.[45] This was the line taken by the Vichy regime and the Germans, although jazz continued to be played and heard by many in Paris.

Chevalier sang his cherished French songs in 1941 not only in Paris but also in the same German prison camp where he had been a prisoner during the First World War.[46] Chevalier's words and songs were broadcast by radio to other camps. "I sang my hits," he told an interviewer, and the French prisoners of war "sang with me. Then I spoke to them like a good buddy [grand copain]. I've known their sadness, their nostalgia, their depression. I told them to have faith in the future and that, once liberated, they will regain, as I did long ago, all their courage, all their reason for living." In that interview he acknowledged having been received by high authorities and artists in Berlin, but he pointedly declared that he had sung only at the camp.[47] He then (and later) glossed over his performances in Paris for German authorities and their French friends.

At the end of the war, it is well known, Chevalier was singled out by some Resistance groups as a collaborator—or at least as a celebrity who adapted too readily to German domination. Chevalier's line of thinking and action was, of course, common among entertainers of the time. They did what they could to cheer people up and did what they had to do to continue their careers. Their role, like Chevalier's, was politically and morally ambiguous. It was—and still is—subject to divergent interpretations. Few songs were as politically clear as "Maréchal, nous voilà!" In any case, the charge of collaboration was not the only one to make. In the 1969 documentary *Le Chagrin et la pitié* director Marcel Ophuls focused more justly on Maurice Chevalier as the leading spokesman for an attitude of willed optimism that long refused to take seriously the difficulties and dangers confronting the nation. In footage from an American newsreel made in late 1944, Chevalier jokes in English about the rumors of his being killed, denies the "propaganda lie" that he had toured Germany during the war, and finally sings (lamely) a verse from "Sweeping the Clouds Away"—lines declaring that no matter what the storm or the weather, he sits on a rainbow and sweeps the clouds away.[48] This was the Chevalier who, amid wartime shortages of everything from food to shoe leather, sang the bouncy "Symphonie des semelles du bois," declaring how he loves the "tap, tap" of the substitute wooden soles: oh how it made him "merry" when he heard that "good rhythm" coming "into his heart like a song!"[49]

Throughout the war, French audiences heard programs full of upbeat songs about love, springtime, vacation, pleasure, and the joys of song: "Il faut varier les plaisirs," "Ça va beaucoup mieux," "Le Printemps nous appelle," "Ça passera," "J'aime l'amour," "La Vie a besoin de chansons." In 1943 "Chantons quand même" repeatedly urged, "Let's sing even so": "Let's rediscover gaiety," and "Let's sing love, hope, and springtime." One of the most successful songs of this sort was a new old-fashioned waltz called "Ah! Le Petit Vin blanc" (1943). The singing narrator begins by hailing springtime and urging the proverbial twenty-year-olds to "leave for vacation"—to go to the old riverside resorts near Paris, to enjoy the old songs and *frites* and the little white wines, and to make love in the woods and meadows near Nogent. "That's not bad," the singer tells us. "That ends all the time in marriage." As long as the sun is in the sky, the song concludes, lovers in spring will go to those woods and meadows. The sheet music sold 1.5 million copies in 1943, making it a best-seller of the war era.[50] Daydreams about spring and love and song filled the air, and the war and violence against French Jews and resisters raged on.[51]

A few hits expressed the widespread sadness that followed the defeat—in particular, songs about separated lovers. Wives and lovers of 1.3 million French prisoners of war in German camps could identify with the melancholy sentiments sung in "Seul(e) ce soir" and "Attend-moi, mon amour." So could the wives, fiancées, and girlfriends of tens of thousands of workers sent to Germany.[52] Another grave love song that became very popular was about a soldier wistfully recalling his young lover Lily Marlène and their all too brief time together (she may have been a professional serving the army camp—her status is not completely clear). The soldier's reminiscence was set to a slow march, sung in a deep heavy voice by Suzy Solidor. That it was originally a German song did not weaken its appeal; it was one of the biggest hits of the occupation period. Many more romantic songs dwelled on intense feelings about a current love. Women anguished about their distant loved one, women on edge from having spent most of the day in lines at the bakery and the *tripier* and the *crémier* listened to the radio playing the mellifluous songs of crooner André Claveau and female crooner Léo Marjane, along with older stars Tino Rossi and Jean Sablon. In cold, dimly lighted rooms across France, men and women alike, anxious and depressed, welcomed the emotional comfort provided by favorite singers.[53] In a time of profound anxieties, hardships, and horrific cruelties, the airwaves were full of soothing voices conjuring up visions of fulfillment in love.

Equivocal Voices

Was mass culture also subtly delivering the Vichy ideological line? Was it serving the cultural hegemony of the new regime even when its products appeared to be nonpolitical? Much of the interpretive problem here is due to the fact that Vichy-era songs and films often continued themes common in the 1930s. There was nothing specifically Pétainist about singing the joys of life in the country, for example. Some songs of the early 1940s, however, seem to go farther and deliver what closely resembles the Vichy message—without Vichy preachiness. Maurice Chevalier's "La Chanson du maçon" (1941) told a happy tale of a France full of singing masons at work on roofs. They pass on their song to others, asking everyone to take to heart the message that working and singing together will build a new France. At first the song was broadcast on Radio-Paris; later in the war the Resistance picked it up (giving it the new meaning of building an anti-Vichy future), and Vichy censors banned it.[54] Another hit attuned to the Pétainist line was Charles Trenet's "Quand Tu reverras ton village" (1942), which addressed listeners as though they were all

Tino (Rossi) and (Charles) Trenet, contrasting faces of sunny Mediterranean France, sang nostalgically of unchanging life in the provinces as though the German military did not occupy the majority of France (1942). Private collection.

provincials at heart longing to rediscover a lost world. The song reassured listeners that "when you'll see your village again, / When you'll see your church tower, / Your house, your parents, the friends of your age / You will say: 'Nothing at home has changed.'"[55] The idyllic village was an antithesis to Paris, formerly the setting of most popular songs as well as the political center of the now scorned republic. Here was the dream of a unified, all-French community, free of alienation and strife and disruptive change—a dream that Vichy ideologists were then promoting in their way.

Through the "black years" a succession of hit songs affirmed the comforting view that despite all the misfortunes besetting France, the country was good and beautiful and enduring: "Ah! Que la France est belle!" (1940), "Ça sent bon la France" (1941), and "Douce France" (1943) were three popular examples. Singing these songs, the cheerful voices of Maurice Chevalier and Charles Trenet soothed and consoled as they proposed the refuge of an idealized rural community. Some verses went on to encourage hope that France would pass through its dark time and rise again. We cannot be sure exactly what listeners heard and understood in those songs. One interpretation is that the new-order visions of a good provincial France played a part in a general surrender to German hegemony. Alternatively, as entertainers like Chevalier insisted, it is possible that those songs were part of a morale-boosting effort to keep alive a French identity—and a patriotic will to resist the powerful Germans, culturally at least. Most likely, the songs had meanings of both accommodation and resistance—with the latter gaining ground as the tide of the war turned against the Germans.

The most popular radio program of the period was similarly ambiguous, blending traditional and Vichy messages into light entertainment. "L'Alphabet de la famille," broadcast Sundays after dinnertime, presented an average French family—mother, father, son, daughter, grandfather, and uncle—continuing their sunny domestic life as though times in France were normal. They visited with their friends, and stars like Raimu and Charles Trenet dropped by. The "alphabet" mentioned in the title referred to letters standing for patriotic and family values that were both traditional and Pétainist: A was for *amour*, B for *bonté* (goodness), C for *compréhension*, D for *dévotion*, and so on.[56]

In the movies, meanwhile, such moralizing and roseate visions of life did not become so popular; certainly they were never dominant. Feature films covered the gamut of long-established genres—comedies, musicals, adventure, detective stories, melodramas. Moviegoers had the choice of seeing French, German, and Italian films in all those genres, but they could no longer see Hollywood's renowned products after the Germans took full control: American films were banned in the occupied zone in September 1940 and banned in the Vichy sector two years later. A fresh wave of German films filled some of the void in the occupied zone (43 percent of the movies shown in Paris in 1941, less in subsequent years), and they drew large audiences—especially German productions that were reminiscent of Hollywood. Still, movie fans remained especially fond of French stars and stories, and French producers and directors did their best to provide them. Hamstrung by wartime disruptions and shortages, French filmmakers were never able to produce at anywhere near the prewar rate, but they continued making movies of all sorts all through the war. And they were able to circulate them freely between the two zones from 1942 on.[57]

Most of the French feature films made during the occupation avoided clear political messages. Film historian Jacques Siclier has found only about 20 movies (out of more than 220 made) to be marked by the new regime's ideology. In contrast, short films ("documentaries") and newsreels were packed with Nazi and Vichy ideology. These evidently did not enjoy much favor with most spectators (though gauging audience reception is particularly problematic here). The famous anti-Semitic film of Veit Harlan, *The Jew Süss*, drew crowds that were mainly curiosity-seekers, witnesses have testified. No more successful were the few French films that vilified the "other"—Jews and Freemasons. Works that blatantly promoted Pétainist ideology also fell flat, particularly after the first year or so of the new order.[58] Most remarkable is that Vichy-era feature movies stayed clear of the anti-Jewish phobia that marked some public discourse. In fact, under the occupation, feature films did not even perpetuate the old anti-Semitic stereotypes that had been commonplace on the screen during the thirties. Nor did they convey anti-British and xenophobic attitudes common in French cinema up to the late 1930s.[59] Yet there is no evidence that this avoidance of such old attitudes was a form of resistance to Vichy and the Germans. The better explanation seems to be that filmmakers were weary of controversial political theses and believed that their audiences were, too.

Most movies made under the new regime featured long-established representations of the ordinary people. Stars from the "bad old days" of the Third Republic continued to show up on movie screens as the good ordinary Frenchman or woman, and almost all the characters they played were familiar pre-Vichy types. Charles Trenet continued to play the nice young fellow who sings happily and loves women. In Jean Boyer's *Romance de Paris* (1941), for example, he was the Parisian "little guy" who, resourcefully dealing with unemployment, sings his way to music-hall stardom and a true-love marriage. Here again was the old myth of Paris as the beautiful city of lovers and joy—without a trace of German soldiers, hardships, and persecutions—once more joined to a tale of the singer whose talent and goodness bring him fame and fortune. In Jacques and Pierre Prévert's *Adieu Léonard* (1943), Trenet was a dreamy innocent who by his naïveté and absurd luck repeatedly escapes a relative's attempts to kill him. He sings blithely, tries learning crafts from happy artisans, and finally takes off for the open road. For the portrayal of a more serious romantic singer and Latin lover there was Tino Rossi, who continued to star in high-grossing movies. In *Fièvres* (1942), for example, he played an opera singer who aroused an irresistible passion in women and caused so much suffering to others (first his wife, later his friend) that he had to give up singing in public and twice sought peace in a monastery, the second time for good. For the role of tough hero, actor René Dary became a replacement for Jean Gabin (now in the United States). Through the occupation years Dary starred regularly as a rebellious working-class fighter, good friend to his buddies, and handsome romantic figure to women. Fernandel continued to play the good-hearted, ridiculously simple Provençal who comes out well in the end, winning the woman of his dreams, for example, in Jean Boyer's light melodrama *La Belle Etoile* (1942). In the years 1940–43 Fernandel appeared in eleven movies and was the nation's favorite comic. People went to see him, regardless of the movie, Jacques Siclier testifies: they delighted in his persona and his broad antics no matter how bad the movie.[60]

Among actresses, Gaby Morlay emerged as a favorite incarnation of the good French woman. Film historian Marcel Oms has argued that she was even a symbol of France under Vichy, suffering yet still smiling. In *Le Voile bleu* (1942) she played a loving, self-sacrificing woman who devoted her life to taking care of other people's children after her husband was killed on the front in 1914 and her own baby died. This melodrama was "the greatest commercial success" of the occupation period, according to Jacques Siclier. Another of her major roles was as a motherly Madelon type who is a small-town telephone operator in Jean Faurez's *Service de nuit* (1943). Hearing every call, she communicates loving concern and vital information to resolve an array of personal problems and crises.[61] With the excep-

Fernandel (*pictured*) starred in the period typically playing the silly, good provincial Frenchman, while Georgius enjoyed continuing fame as the quicksilver Parisian wag. Courtesy of BFI Stills, Posters, and Designs.

tion of Morlay's roles, none of these popular female or male types was Vichy's ideal. In sum, the new order did not come close to establishing itself systematically in feature-length films.

The continuities between the Vichy era and the preceding years are important (as recent film historians have made clear), but the differences are noteworthy, too. One change was that vamps and prostitutes, the longtime foil to good women, almost disappeared from the movies during the Vichy era. Another was the shift away from gritty stories of worker heroes (Gabin's characters, for example) and away from tales of jovial faubouriens. In their place came costume dramas (many of them drawn from nineteenth-century literature) and out-of-time fantasies. Among those that enjoyed the best reception from critics and audiences were *La Nuit fantastique* (1942) and *L'Eternel retour* (1943). Marcel Carné's *Les Visiteurs du soir* (1942), which was also extraordinarily popular, took spectators to an imaginary medieval world of castles and court life into which the devil directs his magical power. The evil one does not bring on food shortages or cruel stormtroopers; rather, he causes emotional distress for the lovers. In the end, however, steadfast and defiant love triumphs over the devil's power and even death, symbolically at least. Audiences liked the movie, and critics praised it highly. It was a classic love story with all the trappings of a fairy tale. There is no solid evidence that spectators read a political message in such tales. Somehow many people in the darkness of 1942 identified with the lovers, storybook nobles of a faraway time who followed their hearts and the siren call of beauty.[62]

More surprisingly, a small number of powerful movies conveyed a harsh, somber view of vaguely contemporary ordinary life, contradicting most songs of the period as well as ideals of the "national revolution." Henri Decoin's *Les Inconnus dans la maison* (1942), based on a Simenon novel, spotlighted the murder of one small-town youth by another. The reviews' disparate readings of the film suggest how spectators could draw quite diverse conclusions about the problems of French society. Some found in the story an indictment of provincial bourgeois life with all its hypocrisy, moral decay, neglect of youth, and failure to offer alternatives to cafés and brothels. Others saw in the film an indictment of some out-of-control prewar youth, or the mixing of young people of different social milieus.[63]

The most remarkable against-the-grain movies of the period appeared in 1943, drawing extraordinary notice from critics and the public. Jacques Becker's *Goupi mains-rouges* presented a portrait of a peasant family that was anything but the warm, generous moral community of Pétainist hopes. Family members were greedy and egoist; one killed and robbed another for money; then they all closed ranks to keep out the gendarmes. That same year audiences for Robert Bresson's *Les Anges du péché* watched nuns in a convent leading lives not of pious calm and saintly harmony, but of conflict, cruelty, and rebellion. With even more disturbing impact director Henri-Georges Clouzot's *Le Corbeau* (a raven or rapacious individual) showed backstabbing, spleen, and fear rampant in a small town. In 1943 when Jews, resisters, and other victims were being denounced by anonymous notes and arrested, Clouzot's dramatization of similar events hit home like "a tornado," as one critic put it. Numerous other dark films dramatized an atmosphere of treachery and suspicion, but ended with the evil force revealed and undone. In the community bedeviled by the Corbeau, there was no single villain; each character was complex and tainted in some way. Tension, sexual frustration, and distrust were rife throughout the town. Some reviewers, after praising the film for its realism, worried that such a "painful" portrayal was inappropriate for such "somber" and "cruel" times, and that spectators would go out and send anonymous accusing letters.[64]

More commonly, from 1943 on, movies contradicted Vichy ideals only in part or in an ambiguous way. Spectators could find subversive (anti-Vichy) messages if they were so inclined—or other messages. In the minds of some viewers *Adieu Léonard* (1943) paid homage to artisanal work; to others it was a derisive treatment of Vichy pieties about the traditional crafts and virtuous family life in the country; to still others (apparently including the censors) the movie was simply a loony comedy. Some spectators hissed a line about money not counting, while others approved of the sentiment that money does not make for happiness. Similarly, Louis Daquin's *Premier de cordée* (1943)—a story of courageous mountaineering youth—was understood in some circles to illustrate Pétainist ideology and in others to refer to the Resistance.

Perhaps the best example of an appealingly ambiguous scenario was Jean Grémillon's *Le Ciel est à vous,* which came out in early 1944. It tells the story of a hardworking married couple named Gauthier, lovable "little people" in the provinces. Garage owner and mechanic Pierre Gauthier is the generous and good-natured humble fellow who, after a hard day, agrees to work half the night repairing a traveling businessman's car. Years after serving in the war as an airplane mechanic for the famous pilot Georges Guynemer, Pierre still loves airplanes and flying, but it is his wife, Thérèse, mother of their two children, who emerges as the heroine by taking up flying and becoming a passionate competitor. She even breaks a distance flight record, flying to the heart of Africa. At last, reviewer Lucien Re-

The crowd acclaims the triumphant pilot, Thérèse Gauthier (played by Madeleine Renaud), the wife and mother in *Le Ciel est à vous* (1944). Courtesy of MoMA Film Stills.

batet (writing as François Vinneuil) exulted, a film presented "true characters, everyday French people," showing off "the finest virtues of our race: its facility for improvisation, its determination, its ready enthusiasm." While the depiction of the family obviously suited Vichy ideology, the home-forsaking adventuresomeness and independent competitiveness of a mother who was also an aviator were clearly in conflict with Pétainist conventions. One uneasy reviewer pointedly complained that the movie should have ended with the woman going back to her everyday life— "cooking, laundry, children, the humble and noble tasks which make daily life."[65] Thérèse Gauthier, like much of the French population, did not fit neatly into manichean political typologies.

To be sure, movies bearing messages that clearly opposed Vichy were exceptional; the censors made sure of that. But one movie often cited in film histories stands out for its blatant expression of anti-government and anti-German feelings: Jean Delannoy's *Pontcarral, colonel d'empire* (1942). Pontcarral is a fiery retired colonel who had fought under Napoleon and later found himself hounded by Restoration authorities and the police. After the 1830 revolution he regains his command and leads troops in the conquest of Algeria, later losing his life in battle there. Audiences responded to the hero's fighting remarks by breaking into applause, reviewers reported. The scenario showed Pontcarral's difficult love life as much as his ardent patriotism and defiant high spirits, but it was the latter that drew special notice and the obvious approval.[66] There is no solid evidence, however, that *Pontcarral* was widely viewed as anti-Vichy at the time, and in any case it was a rarity.

Altogether, the songs and commercial films of the war period can be viewed as a reflection of widely shared wishes and fears and long-standing cultural themes that Vichy adopted. To find the ideology of the new regime in everything produced is to force too much into that political framework. Most filmmakers were not of such a mind, and the same seems to have been true of the majority in the audiences. Some movies that presented such conspicuously ideological, return-to-the-land scenarios as *Monsieur de Lourdines* (1942) and *Port d'attache* (1942) were deprecated by reviewers for the trite censor-pleasing theme but also praised as entertaining and beautiful tales of provincial life, nature, and virtue in another time.[67]

Many spectators probably reacted with similar sentiments. Everyday life presented such worrisome difficulties—getting sufficient food, staying warm, staying alive in wartime—that the desire for a few hours of diversion was understandably strong. For at least a few hours at a time French moviegoers blocked out the war. The German conquerors, for their part, wanted life to go on with a semblance of optimism and cheerfulness. The French press and the radio took a similar position and did yeoman's service maintaining a lighthearted tone, but entertainers did the most to perpetuate the shibboleths of good-humored Frenchness. Millions among the occupied population, trying to keep up their spirits, were receptive to the simple, bright melodies.

At the same time they could not help hearing the complex movements of dissonances and darker tones. Much of what people heard and saw on film, radio, and stage abounded in ambiguities, and public opinion was in flux through the four years. Vichy rule was not a single bloc, recent historians have stressed; it was a succession of political positions, outlooks changing as the circumstances of the war changed. In that fluid context popular responses to the more topical songs and films no doubt shifted as people altered their political views. What is clear is an overall movement of public opinion away from Vichy, particularly its most pro-German and most politically reactionary elements. By 1942–43, spectators were tired of moralizing scenarios and back to the land themes, movie reviewers often noted.[68] The time for Pétainist echoes in feature films had passed. Even right-wing reviewers sympathetic to the regime's moral mission praised *Le Corbeau* and *Goupi mains-rouges* for being more truthful about the French common people. In the last two years of the war, hissing and booing the propagandist newsreels became common practice for many spectators, recalls Jacques Siclier, despite police in the theaters who tried to catch the offenders.[69]

Resistance

As early as 18 June 1940, some French citizens were rejecting any submission to the Nazis. Along with the defiant leader Charles de Gaulle, who called for resistance from his new base in London, a small minority of less prominent people took the view that France was eternal and the German victory was not the end. According to recent historical research, more widespread skepticism toward Vichy set in after only a year. Grateful or simply resigned acceptance of the regime began giving way to a critical spirit and an emergent opposition by the spring of 1941.[70] In the months and years that followed, successive Vichy measures offended a growing part of the population, and Allied advances convinced more and more of the many who wanted to wait-and-see to dare support the Resistance and Gaullism. Specifically, the return to power of Pierre Laval as Pétain's prime minister—perceived as pro-German—in April 1942 contributed to weakening support for Vichy. So did the massive arrests of Jews in July and August, the Allied invasion of North Africa in November, and the German occupation of the Vichy "free zone" shortly thereafter, ending the semblance of independence in the southern zone. The German defeat at Stalingrad early in 1943, the creation of a forced labor organization (Service du travail obligatoire), and the terrorizing police force (the *Milice*) caused further disenchantment. Step by step public opinion shifted away from Vichy.[71]

From the beginning of the new order, singers managed to voice lines that were subversively satirical or ambiguously anti-German and pro-Free French. Implicit allusions helped slip a song by the German censor. In singing "Notre Espoir" nightly at the Casino de Paris when German setbacks were large and obvious, Chevalier had fun with vague nonsense lines suggestive enough to convey hope for a future liberated France.

> To avoid making a mistake, here's what I sing
> Tra la la la la la, tra la la la la la
> Tzim ba poum pa la, tzim ba poum pa la . . . .
> . . . .
> If you want to know
> What my heart thinks this evening
> While singing like that
> Tzim ba poum pa la,
> That's our hope.[72]

In London, French entertainers used the microphones of the BBC to send

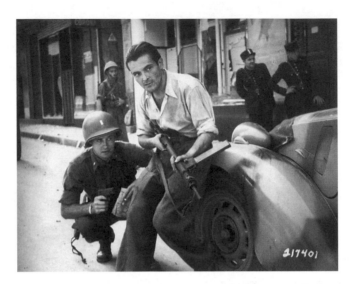

Liberation heroes: a clean-cut French partisan and a supportive American officer take a street fighting stance in August 1944. U.S. National Archives and Record Administration.

out parodies of things German—"Lily Marlène," for example—across the channel to their compatriots. And to the tune of "La Plus Bath' des Javas" word of the approaching Allied victory was conveyed.[73]

Every day from 17 May 1943 to May 1944, radio listeners in France heard a stirring chorus of voices singing a song opposed to all that Vichy represented: "Le Chant des partisans" was broadcast by the BBC as the theme song of a program of the Free French, "Honor and Country." The tune, which was quickly picked up and whistled by Resistance fighters, became known widely in France before the words did. The lyrics begin with low, quiet questions: "Friend, do you hear the black flight of crows over our plains? / Do you hear the muffled cries of the country that is enchained?" Addressing "partisans, workers, and peasants," the narrator explains that those sounds are "the emergency alarm." The rest of the song is a passionate call to arms, urging working people of all sorts to take their rifles, machine guns, grenades, knives, and dynamite and to "kill quickly." The brave resisters will "break the bars of the prisons" for their brothers and end the nightmare of hunger, forced marches and killing by the hated enemy. "Whistle, companions, in the night liberty listens to us." The call to resist and fight was heeded by more and more French people as the prospect of German defeat became clearer. The song was not, however, noticed or heard everywhere; it became a familiar standard only after the Liberation, contrary to postwar recollections.[74]

From 1943 on, filmmakers also joined the Resistance, making movies of the courageous French struggle against the Germans. In Paris from 13 August 1944 on, they turned their cameras on the street fighting that became a large insurrection over the following weeks. Later that month, on the evening of the last day of fighting in Paris, they showed their work, *La Libération de Paris*, on a giant outdoor screen and then sent it on tour around the rest of France. As Jacques Siclier has pointed out, that film and others showing Nazi-fighting Frenchmen (most notably René Clément's *La Bataille du rail* and Jean-Paul Le Chanois's *Au Coeur de l'orage*) did much to establish the "myth of a France almost unanimously resistant"—the myth of a great majority of Frenchmen heroically struggling against Nazis and a small minority of collaborators.[75]

After the liberation of Paris on 25 August 1944, cultural life resumed with barely a hitch. The ending of every war seemed to make the French need reassurance that they were still themselves, and nostalgia for some prewar "good old days" grew. The Casino de Paris reopened in October 1944 with a splashy revue entitled *En Plein Jazz*. That same month a cheery nostalgic song entitled "Fleur de Paris" quickly became a public favorite. Its lyrics expressed the collective wish that all kinds of ordinary French men and women, now free again, were harmoniously united in their love of a happy old Paris and a tricolor France. It was a hymn of joy for the liberation of the forty million French, as though all were undivided and had shared the same fundamental values through the entire war. Weeks earlier, right after the Liberation, Resistance groups had executed thousands for collaboration with the Germans, and for months to come "purification committees" (Comités d'épuration) and special courts inflicted punishment on thousands more (punished by exclusion from a profession, imprisonment, or death). Yet in "Fleur de Paris" the singer declares that his grocer, the tax collector, the pharmacist, the ex-corporal, the ex-general, the peasant, the old priest, and "all those who fought for our liberties" all cherished the "flower of Paris"—"the old Paris that smiles." The "flower of Paris" is "the flower of the return, the return of the good days." Through four years "in our hearts / It kept its colors / Blue, white, red."[76] Maurice Chevalier, the national representative once more, recorded the song, which became an immediate hit—a mass-culture answer to a continuing civil war.

During much of the war, the country had been culturally divided between Vichy's ideological journey backward in time and a popular culture of smiles and denial. The two did not directly clash, for both the popular culture and the official line were responses of avoidance, a turning away from painful realities. Vichy's

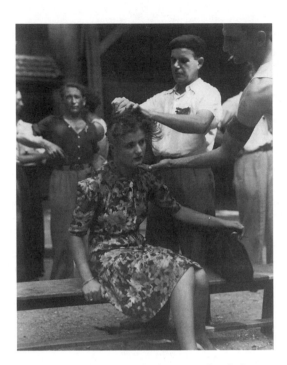

A French victim of the Resistance: a woman who had consorted with Germans is punished and humiliated in the Montélimar area (29 August 1944). Smith, U.S. National Archives and Record Administration.

heavy-handedness ended by discrediting its themes of the virtuous peasant and village artisan. The other extreme, *Le Corbeau*'s disturbingly harsh portrayals, came out of the war even more roundly rejected: after the Liberation the film was banned for its "anti-French intentions."[77] No one could make such a charge against the popular culture that stuck to the prewar folklore of Paris and warm personal themes. Songs and films in the old prewar molds continued to be staples of postwar popular culture.

Timeworn images of the "little people" first reappeared on Parisian screens in a film by Marcel Carné with a screenplay by Jacques Prévert. In March 1945 *Les Enfants du paradis* made its Paris debut, its release timed to make it the first new French film after the Liberation. The "children of paradise" were the good-humored, boisterous populace of mid-nineteenth-century Paris and romantic heroes close to them—notably the actor Frédérick Lemaître, the mime Baptiste Deburau, and the humble woman they love, the beautiful Garance (a red flower)—interspersed with a colorful pègre of thieves and killers. Garance (Arletty), a flower of the faubourgs, is beloved by a variety of men who are masterful at directing their lives and performances, but only the absolute romantic Baptiste wins her love. That is, in a break with populist conventions, the heroine loves not the clever-tongued, exuberant actor or the other wily ones, but rather the passionate dreamer who is neither a bantering débrouillard nor a social superior speaking "fine phrases." Garance herself is a realist. When she gets into trouble, she gives herself to a count who can protect her, and in the end she leaves her beloved Baptiste to his wife and child; she disappears into a carnival crowd as he desperately searches for her. True love does not triumph. Garance is Madelon in a tragic mode, a mysterious siren leaving heartache and misfortune in her wake. Yet as a whole the movie was a welcome reminder of the common people's pleasures, dreams, and personal intrigues back in an age innocent of the twentieth century's atrocities. With its setting and costumes of Romantic Paris and the theater, *Les Enfants du paradis* was a big theatrical production that bespoke classical quality. It won exceptional acclaim from critics and audiences alike.[78]

In songs even more than films, much of the old standard fare came back. Although the peasant myth promoted by Vichy did not survive the war, populist songs about Parisians certainly did. New songs about the people of Paris and their simple pleasures continued a long tradition without a hint of the nightmare just passed. After the Liberation the commercial folklore of Paris once more served as a mainstay of collective memory, which was then working to reconstitute France's

An imaginative view of the Liberation: the people rise up to free themselves in the grand historic manner—with Charles de Gaulle as leader. Documentation Française.

cultural identity. More than nostalgia for prewar life kept that folklore alive. The old themes also persisted because the underlying social realities in the capital remained the same after 1945 much as before (for at least a decade). Other cities came out of the war in ruins, but Paris escaped virtually intact in its physical structure with a full complement of prewar social types, the many living in modest conditions—unfortunately even more modest than before.

On 20 April 1945 *Paris-Soir* reported that Maurice Chevalier was coming back to the ABC and would sing his old hit "Valentine." He also sang "La Chanson populaire," which was a virtual breviary of the populist tradition. The "populo" of the faubourgs, the lyrics declare, ever fill the air with popular songs. "The apprentice with laughing eyes," "the joking worker," the poet and the *midinette* sing "a song of happiness," glad that, with the return of peace, "better days" are ahead.

Many of the old images and fables remained dear to a large public because they seemed current, indeed eternal: in particular the myths of Paris, song, love, and "the good people." They now helped block out the horrors of the recent war and the difficulties of postwar recovery. The country had been plundered by the enemy and ravaged by war; the economy was in critical condition, but spring always returned, and young people fell in love. Even in the wake of the most destructive war in history, lovers still saw "La Vie en rose," as Edith Piaf put it in a song she wrote in 1945. Paris was still beautiful and full of people who loved its rich past as an integral part of their lives ("Paris est à nous" of 1945).

Personal misfortunes and heartbreak were also constants—in life and Piaf's songs. Piaf herself was then nearing the height of her stardom as an incarnation of the tragically suffering faubourienne, living only for love. Like Chevalier decades earlier, she was a flesh-and-blood representation of the traditional *petit peuple*. She endlessly celebrated love, and she cried out the heartaches. "It's always the same story," one of her postwar songs acknowledged. The *fille de joie* found the love of her life, but he went away as a soldier and did not come back ("L'Accordéoniste," copyright 1942). "Without love one has nothing," Piaf sang, but love again and again failed to live up to the dream and the initial ecstasy. Piaf cried out the disappointment, and she also chanted the traditional antidotes to anxiety and regret: "je m'en fous [I don't care] / ça m'est égal"—a response climaxing in her life- and love-affirming hit "Je ne regrette rien" (1960). Continuity with a folkloric past was renewed.[79]

There were also some new touches. The young singer Yves Montand, son of an Italian immigrant worker and a former metalworker himself, updated the populist tradition with his songs of such proletarians as the machinist and the lathe operator. Marcel Mouloudji and Francis Lemarque, both sons of Belleville, added fresh songs about the poor quarters of Paris and the truck drivers and factory workers, secretaries and clerks, who dance Saturday nights at neighborhood bals musette, *filles* who pace the sidewalk and men who sleep beside the Seine, the "little people" who look for fun in Luna Park and live around Pigalle and stroll in banal streets, say, from the Place Maubert to Les Halles.[80]

At the same time France once more opened up to the latest in foreign culture. The cosmopolitanism that cultural conservatives had decried from the Great War through the Vichy era was revived. For decades the public had enjoyed heavy doses of foreign cultures—above all, American movies, music, and cartoons. A return to those sources was part of a return to normal. Besides, who wanted to dwell on France's painful recent past?—the 600,000 French killed in the war (two-thirds of them civilians), the complicity of many in the Third Reich's occupation of France, the sending of 75,000 Jews from France to Polish death camps. With the new peace, fresh alternatives to bad memories and the old French offerings flooded in once more from outside. Yves Montand was one beneficiary. Before the war he had performed as a cowboy singing lyrics about the American West; after the war he rose to stardom singing American jazz rhythms. American swing, bebop, and the samba found new fans. French feet once more tapped and danced openly to a foreign beat. French young people once more embraced cultural importations with gusto, causing others to worry anew about the future of French culture. The strong, deep currents that Vichy had attempted to block now resumed their course.

CONCLUSION

En France, tout finit par des chansons.

[In France, everything ends in songs.]

—*Proverb, from Beaumarchais,* Le Mariage de Figaro

Les feuilles mortes se ramassent à la pelle,
Les souvenirs et les regrets aussi.

[Dead leaves pile up by the bucketful,
Memories and regrets also.]

—*Jacques Prévert, "Les Feuilles mortes" (1947)*

THROUGH THE CRISIS-RACKED YEARS from one world war to another, France's media-fed national culture put a steady limelight on such characters as the "p'tit Parigot" and the Parisian shop girl, the neighborhood singer and the pretty florist, Camille, who worked the streets around the Bastille, and her mean lover, Jules, along with sports stars and entertainers—the likes of Georges Carpentier, Mistinguett, and Maurice Chevalier. One representation of the ordinary people stands out as the most multi-faceted: the idealized poilu of the Great War. Constructed under wartime pressures, the poilu was a remarkable composite of appealing traits understood to be French, traits commanding support from almost all sectors of society. He was the "little guy" who was affable and fun-loving yet tough and combative. He was attached to home and hometown, yet he was also fiercely patriotic and entrenched in a community of comrades drawn from diverse classes. The poilu, the model fighting Frenchman, long remained a revered figure even though glorified versions of that image drew fire from critics of the war and of propaganda.

That older icon of the people, the Parisian faubourien, had the advantages of being less obviously ideological and unburdened by the painful issues of the war.

It also had an apparent disadvantage: those "little people" of Paris were far from being representative in a population of forty million, most living far from the capital. Yet from the vantage point of the Paris-based producer there were strong reasons for casting the faubouriens as the common French people. They lived modest lives, depicted in film and song as essentially simple and stable, with which a maximum number of spectators could identify, especially the big Parisian market. The rest of the nation could not agree on any alternative urban or regional version as a common denominator. Further, the faubouriens were a relatively safe choice for a strife-ridden era. Skirting controversial political theses, populist folklore perpetuated a timeless model of contented work- and family-centered patriots, leading lives unscathed by postwar disillusionment and social dislocations. During a period of deep divisions and conflicts, myths of the simple faubouriens were conciliatory and utopian resolutions of real-life tensions. These were also nostalgic myths whose appeal grew apace with structural changes in French society and daily life. As more and more of the "little people" were losing the old social texture of their work and leisure (the close-knit human scale celebrated in populist works), the old ways lived on in songs, stories, and films. The mass media regularly featured them as models, and the public followed them fondly.

In discussing the reasons for France's defeat in 1940, Marc Bloch has charged that the French bourgeoisie failed or "refused to take the masses seriously"—particularly, the hardships and grievances of the masses. "The bourgeoisie lived completely separated from the people," he maintained, and "made no attempt to reach that understanding which might have led to sympathy."[1] Anyone familiar with the history of the period treated by this book has reason to question that description of the bourgeois as "completely separated" culturally: like "the people," they were consumers of a commercial culture that gave them a kind of sympathetic understanding of the many—as light-hearted and content or as woeful victims of drugs and alcoholism, sickness, conflicts over lovers, and bad luck. In film and song the characters eliciting the greatest sympathy were "women of the people" in standard roles—the broken prostitute of the realist genre, the sweet ingénue (Madelon, Annabella), and the good mother (Gaby Morlay, Madeleine Renaud)—all set off against the femme fatale (Mireille Balin, Viviane Romance). Such depictions, while capturing some semblance of familiar people, left out a great deal. They surely did not teach those who were better off to understand the difficulties and grievances of the masses during the last decades of the Third Republic. Comprehending certain old-fashioned or melodramatic types, the public remained uncomprehending of much more that was current. The entertainment industry's stories did little or nothing to foster understanding of common interests in dealing with national problems, such as structural economic weaknesses.

France's entertainers produced much that can be characterized as calming and diverting, avoiding divisive and contentious issues. They regularly portrayed the representative French man and woman as a natural débrouillard or a stalwart with a ready (dismissive) defense of *je m'en fous*. Popular songs never ceased urging people not to worry: smile, sing, and things will work out. That insouciance was accompanied by a focus on personal fulfillments and pleasures—love and enjoyment of nature and the charms of Paris. In fact, the focus was even more selective than that: it was on youthful love and the enjoyment of springtime and the charms of certain parts of Paris. Such a positive attitude can have its benefits, according to psychologists. The cheer provided by popular culture may well have helped the French endure their adversities without falling into the hatred and rage that waxed strong in Germany. In French culture the simple pleasures of song, wine, and Paris held a place that a "heroic nihilism" took in the land of the Nazis. Whatever the benefits of cheerfulness, however, hindsight makes clearer than ever that there was plenty to worry about and to act on. The calming and consoling message in critical times was deceptive, we now know well. By largely ignoring the society's economic and political problems and the danger of Nazi aggression, popular songs and films contributed to the French failure to understand the difficulties facing them.

To that kind of indictment of popular culture—which French intellectuals (and others) have elaborated for decades[2]—I would add two qualifying comments. First, the producers of popular culture did not bear primary responsibility for addressing the nation's difficulties; that lay with political, military, and religious leaders. Second, it is worth recalling the variety of models and messages that the culture offered simultaneously. They ranged from cheery clichés and images of the past to tearful tales of downfall and a forlorn fatalism ("Adieu la vie, adieu l'amour"). They included both novelties and familiar traditions. Songs and films featured alternately life in the faubourg and life in exotic locales. During the 1930s images of the people as militant crowds became prominent at the same time as stories of men and women fleeing Paris and the hexagon. The common people in the era between the wars considered many scenarios. They contemplated both defensive entrenchment and getting away (fight and flight), vacation and struggle, a new beginning "elsewhere," and also the possibility of defeat. The films, songs, and stories that millions consumed were not so all-controlling and repressive a system as the Frankfurt School theorists maintained.[3] Nor were they all so empty and es-capist. Mass culture set out varied scenarios demonstrating responses to problems, an assortment of stories about French men and women dealing with difficulties.

While French people vicariously experienced the fates of fictional charac-ters, they wrestled with decision making in their personal and collective lives. Some of them, but never the clear majority, committed themselves to exclusive posi-tions—to fight on the revolutionary Left or the Right, to seek personal escape far from familiar French surroundings, or to rebuild an old-fashioned rural society ex-cluding all types of the "other." In the face of an extraordinarily dangerous and un-certain future, a greater number remained unsure and searching. They were in agreement on only a few matters, notably such familiar good experiences and hopes as love, song, spring, and Saturday night at a favorite *petit bal*—experiences and hopes that mass culture highlighted.

Today those themes and the images discussed in these pages continue to be common references for many—and not just the French. Foreigners from Heming-way and Brassaï to current tourists and lovers of film classics (or to Peter Mayle and his readers) have shared the French fascination with the "little people." Accor-dionists playing old javas and organ grinders belle-époque tunes often place them-selves in locations dear to tourists—near Beaubourg and the Eiffel Tower, for ex-ample. In a fast-changing society, almost everyone wants to find something in Paris life that has not changed. It was that way when the personages and songs of Mau-rice Chevalier and Edith Piaf first gained popularity and when the characters played by Jean Gabin and Arletty first grabbed attention. They catered to nostalgia from the very beginning.

For the French today, collective memories and dreams of the village of yes-teryear or the *quartier d'autrefois* endure not only as the stuff of nostalgia, but also as emotional wellsprings of national debates about immigrants and how multicul-tural France should be. Memories of old songs and movies about small French worlds underlie current political attacks on foreign (mostly American) music, tele-vision programs, movies, and even words. Today the question of what should con-stitute a French cultural identity and how to maintain it makes for unending debate and political scuffling. The common idioms of French experience discussed above have contributed to that sense of identity, I think, more than is usually recognized. They now form only a part of an eclectic mass culture, but—for good or ill—they are a special, distinctly French part, affixed in the national memory and imagination like old family photographs in a cherished album.

NOTES

INTRODUCTION

1. On the identity process see Fernand Braudel's final book, *L'Identité de la France*, Vol. I: *L'Espace et histoire* (Paris, 1986), p. 17. For the idea of focusing on an "ongoing argument" in a society, I am indebted to Natalie Zemon Davis's "Toward Mixtures and Margins," *American Historical Review* 97, no. 5 (December 1992), p. 1415.

2. See Pierre Birnbaum, *Le Peuple et les gros: Histoire d'un mythe* (Paris, 1979). On myth, representation, and spectacle in modern society my thinking owes much to Roland Barthes, *Mythologies* (Paris, 1957), and Guy Debord, *La Société du spectacle* (Paris, 1967). See also Pierre Laborie, "Enjeux: De l'opinion publique à l'imaginaire social," *Vingtième siècle* 18 (April 1988), pp. 101–117; the last several pages offer a summary discussion of the question of social representations in relationship to public opinion.

3. For the view that Joan of Arc is the key to understanding the French, see the book entitled *Dieu est-il Français?* (Paris, 1930) by an astute German writer—not an academic historian—named Friedrich Sieburg. For a succinct, telling treatment of the meaning of Joan of Arc in an earlier period of the Third Republic, see Rosemonde Sanson, "La 'Fête de Jeanne d'Arc en 1894': Controverse et célébration," *Revue d'histoire moderne et contemporaine* 20 (July–September 1973), pp. 444–463. For a later period, see Martha Hanna, "Iconology and Ideology: Images of Joan of Arc in the Idiom of the Action française, 1908–1931," *French Historical Studies* 14, no. 2 (Fall 1985), pp. 215–239; for the role of Joan in the important period after the fall of France, see the books on Vichy culture cited in notes to chapter 9. Other works giving background on representations of the French people include Albert Soboul, *The Sans-Culottes: The Popular Movement*

and Revolutionary Government, 1793–1794 (Garden City, N.Y., 1972), and Maurice Agulhon's studies of Marianne, beginning with *Marianne au combat: L'imagerie et la symbolique républicaines de 1789 à 1880* (Paris, 1979). For more general background, see Gérard Fritz, *L'Idée de peuple en France du XVIIIe au XIXe siècle* (Strasbourg, 1988).

4. See Louis Chevalier's *Classes laborieuses et classes dangereuses à Paris pendant la première moitié du XIXe siècle* (Paris, 1958).

5. The character types and myths, which are of main interest here, often appeared in novels and plays before showing up as screenplays (Marcel Pagnol's works, *Le Quai des brumes, Gueule d'amour,* and *Hôtel du nord,* to mention only a few). For my purposes what counts most is not the media or genres and their history, but rather the characters and stories and their role in French life. In this book I have written primarily about the movie versions because they reached the largest audience.

 By images I mean the several "systems of images" that Pierre Sorlin has identified in his study of film: "words, sounds, and pictures." In some succinct statements Sorlin has also helped clarify the working of images: "The notion of 'image' makes us get over the opposition between actuality and representation. Images are not the reality but they are our only access to reality. Our relationship with events and people is mediated by images; some we produce for ourselves but most are assigned to us by the society we live in and are therefore common to virtually all members of the group." See Pierre Sorlin, *European Cinemas, European Societies, 1939–1990* (London, 1991), pp. 6, 19.

6. I use the term *popular culture* as Lawrence Levine has defined it: "popular culture is culture that is popular; culture that is widely accessible and widely accessed; widely disseminated, and widely viewed or heard or read." He adds the important point that "not all mass culture was popular." Many films were hardly seen or noticed by the majority of people; many songs were flops. See Lawrence W. Levine, "The Folklore of Industrial Society: Popular Culture and Its Audiences," *American Historical Review* 97, no. 5 (December 1992), p. 1373.

 The number of films and songs produced during the period is enormous. In the 1920s the number of films produced each year varied widely from around 50 to over 170; in the 1930s a total of more than 1,000 new French feature films were released; even during the difficult period of the Second World War more than 200 French films were made. Hundreds of new songs also appeared each year. While trying to examine and present as much of that primary material as possible, I have obviously had to select a sample for my commentary. First, my theme—representations of the contemporary French people—has guided the selection. Second, I have given most attention to what audiences evidently found most appealing (and not to what critics or film historians have considered the best). Thus this book does not attempt to treat avant-garde films such as Luis Buñuel and Salvador Dali's *Un Chien andalou* (1929) and Jean Vigo's *Zéro de conduite* (1933), which very few people saw or liked during the period. For that kind of specialized film history as well as other kinds of "high" culture (literature, theater, music) there are many good books available. One noteworthy book that covers a particularly wide range is Olivier Barrot and Pascal Ory, eds., *Entre Deux Guerres: La création française entre 1919 et 1939* (Paris, 1990).

 Unfortunately for historians (who generally like quantification), there are no systematic statistics available on box-office receipts for particular movies and royalties for particular songs. In this book I have used the statistics that are available. For example, the relative popularity of competing movies in the 1930s is indicated by occasional local reports (of receipts and weeks of showings) and (unscientific) surveys published in the film industry journal, *La Cinématographie française.* For popular songs, such works as Anne-Marie Duverney and O. d'Horrer's *Mémoire de la chanson française depuis 1900* (Neuilly-sur-Seine, 1979) and Pierre Saka's *La Chanson française à travers ses succès* (Paris, 1988) give some indication of popularity. Scattered reports in contemporary periodicals and memoirs also provide information about certain songs. For the purposes of this book, however, what matters most is not individual movies and their commercial success; it is rather the popularity of recurrent themes and narrative motifs in movies as well as songs.

7. Among the many recent commentaries on Antonio Gramsci's thought and popular culture, Stuart Hall's "Notes on Deconstructing the Popular" is particularly cogent and helpful; it is found in Raphael Samuel, ed., *People's History and Socialist Theory* (London, 1981), esp. pp. 233–235. T. J. Jackson Lears has developed the point that "cultural hegemony"—the power of dominant groups "shaping the values and attitudes of a society"—is power exercised not just by political authorities, but by "entertainment promoters, popular musicians, sports figures, and 'celebrities'"; see Lears, "The Concept of Cultural Hegemony: Problems and Possibilities," *American Historical Review* 90 (June 1985), pp. 567–593.

CHAPTER 1. FRENCH IDENTITIES IN THE CRUCIBLE OF WAR

1. *Le Temps,* 2 Aug. and 3 Aug. 1914, p. 1; *Le Petit Parisien,* 3 Aug. 1914, p. 2.

2. Robert Nye, *Crime, Madness, and Politics: The Medical Concept of National Decline* (Princeton, 1984). Koenraad W. Swart, *The Sense of Decadence in Nineteenth-Century France* (The Hague, 1964). Charles Rearick, *Pleasures of the Belle Epoque: Entertainment and Festivity in Turn-of-the-Century France* (New Haven, 1985), ch. 2.

3. On novelists see I. F. Clarke, *Voices Prophesying War, 1763–1984* (London, 1966), pp. 89, 131–136. No novelist imagined a drawn-out trench war. On the boredom of the long nineteenth-century peace in industrializing Europe and the "itch for chaos," see George Steiner, *In Bluebeard's Castle: Some Notes Toward the Redefinition of Culture* (New Haven, 1971).

4. Jean-Jacques Becker, *1914: Comment les Français sont entrés dans la guerre* (Paris, 1977).

5. *Le Petit Parisien,* 3 Aug. 1914, p. 2. *Le Temps,* 3 Aug. 1914, p. 1. Paul Cazin, *L'Humaniste à la guerre: Hauts de Meuse* (Paris, 1920), p. 7, reporting on villages in Burgundy.

6. Raymond Seris and Jean Aubray, *Les Parisiens pendant l'état de siège* (Paris, 1915), p. 167.

7. "La Marseillaise," *L'Illustration,* 12 Dec. 1914, p. 465. It was not just theatergoers who had been deprived. Thousands of show-business workers had been thrown out of work, and the state had lost revenue from the tax on tickets.

8. On the cinema see Richard Abel, *French Cinema: The First Wave, 1915–1929* (Princeton, 1984), pp. 9–10. Michel Vovelle, "'La Marseillaise,' la guerre ou la paix," in *Les Lieux de mémoire,* ed. Pierre Nora, Vol. I: *La République* (Paris, 1984), p. 125.

9. Many patriotic songs and poems may be consulted in the Bibliothèque de documentation internationale contemporaine at Nanterre University; "Mourir en chantant" is there under the catalog number 4Δ1509. Others are available in the Archives of the Paris Préfecture de Police (hereafter PPA) ("Meurs pour la patrie," for example—BA 716). See also Alain and Nicole Lacombe, *Les Chants de bataille: La chanson patriotique de 1900 à 1918* (Paris, 1992).

10. Gaston Esnault, *Le Poilu tel qu'il se parle* (Paris, 1919), pp. 427–429. Esnault maintains that the usage did not clearly appear before 15 January 1915.

11. Marc Bloch, *Memoirs of War,* trans. Carole Fink (Ithaca, 1980), p. 133.

12. *Le Troglodyte* was the title of a trench paper published in the 44th regiment of artillery. See Stéphane Audoin-Rouzeau, *14–18: Les combattants des tranchées à travers leurs journaux* (Paris, 1986), p. 10.

13. "Le vocabulaire de la guerre," *L'Echo des marmites,* 15 Feb. 1915, p. 6.

14. *Le Miroir*, 20 Sept. 1914, p. 9. "Un Hamman dans la tranchée," *L'Illustration*, 14 Nov. 1914, p. 364.

15. *Le Miroir*, 6 Dec. 1914, p. 2; 14 Feb. 1915, p. 10.

16. The illustrated weekly *Le Miroir* reported regularly with high optimism on front-line activities: 27 Dec. 1914, p. 2, on the soldiers as "big children"; 14 Feb. 1915, p. 13, on songs and newspapers; 10 Jan. 1915, p. 2, on skittles; 20 June 1915, p. 15, 1 Aug. 1915, p. 15, on sports played.

17. *Lectures pour tous*, 15 Feb. 1916, p. 49; "Le Carnaval au front," 1 Mar. 1916, p. 826.

18. A. M., "Vincent Scotto," *Paris qui chante*, 1 Dec. 1915, p. 1.

19. Police Visa, 13 Jan. 1917. Lyrics by P. Albert and E. Joullot.

20. Maurice Barrès, "Le Gai courage," *Les Annales*, 4 Apr. 1915, p. 4; see also his famous article in *L'Echo de Paris*, 17 Dec. 1914: "Gaiety reigns in the trenches," quoted in Audoin-Rouzeau, *14–18*, p. 120. Journalist E. Gomez-Carillo, *Le Sourire sous la mitraille* (Paris, 1916), p. 81; on p. 272 he quotes Poincaré's remark about the soldiers' gaiety being "one of the most charming forms of *la crânerie française*." Note also writer Emile Faguet's calling the soldiers the "Princes of French gaiety" (p. 274). See also G. Vidal's preface in *Les Auteurs de la tranchée* (Paris, 1917), p. 9.

21. *L'Echo des Marmites*, 1 Jan. 1915, p. 2. Article signed "P. C. C. Ajax."

22. Albert Thierry, "Carnets de guerre," *La Grande Revue*, July 1918, p. 86.

23. Audoin-Rouzeau, *14–18*, p. 11.

24. Charles Cost, *La Psychologie du combat* (Nancy, 1928), p. 214. See also Doctors Louis Huot and Paul Voivenel, *La Psychologie du soldat* (Paris, 1918), pp. 114, 144.

25. Gérard Canini, *Combattre à Verdun: Vie et souffrance quotidienne du soldat, 1916–1917* (Nancy, 1988), pp. 117–130, for descriptions of leisure activities. Thierry describes the quarreling and singing in his carnets of March and April 1915; "Carnets de guerre," pp. 88, 95.

26. Guillot de Saix, "Le Théâtre aux Armées," in *Le Théâtre pendant la guerre: Notices et documents, publiés par Adolphe Aderer, G. Astruc, et al.* (Paris, 1916), pp. 53–54. See also Jacques Meyer, *La Vie quotidienne des soldats pendant la Grande Guerre* (Paris, 1966), pp. 347–348. Regina Sweeney has written a dissertation on singing during the period: "Harmony and Disharmony: French Singing and Musical Entertainment during the Great War" (Ph.D. diss., University of California at Berkeley, 1992).

27. Henri Chapron, "Les Chansons composées au front," *Bulletin de l'Ile de France*, July–September 1962, pp. 582–583. Chapron was there on the front and witnessed the revues; for this article he has relied not on memory but on notes he took at the time. The lines quoted—about the *petits* and *obscurs*—were taken from Edmond Rostand's play *L'Aiglon* (1900), II, 8–9.

28. See examples in Pierre Chaffrange, *L'Humour au front: Chansons de poilus* (Paris: Joubert, no date—after the battle of Verdun—1917 or 1918). In 1919 the magazine *Le Théâtre* published photographs of the costumed poilus I have just described.

29. Bloch, *Memoirs of War*, p. 161.

30. On "gueule de civil" see the trench paper *Rigolboche*, 1 June 1915, p. 3, cartoon by Pepin. Cazin, *L'Humaniste à la guerre*, p. 163.

31. On *le cafard*, see Eddy, "Le Cafard," *Les Annales*, 19 Sept. 1915, pp. 343–344. For criticisms of rosy reports of front life, see, for example, the remarks of "un groupe de poilus" writing to *Les Annales*, 8 Aug. 1915, p. 173. On the mood of "gravity" see Henri Lavedan, "La maturité de la guerre," *L'Illustration*, 10 Apr. 1915, p. 362. On the need for more recreation, see Eddy, "Le Cafard," *Les Annales*, 19 Sept. 1915, p. 344, and "En permission," *Le Crapouillot*, no. 6 (no date—January or February 1916), p. 2.

32. Lyrics by Charles Forge, music by J. Dorin and E. Bouquette; Smith Editeur, 1915. See José

Germain, *Une Heure de musique avec les chansons de guerre* (Paris, 1930), pp. 24–28. In French: "un goss' sans pose et sans manières, toujours joyeux."

33. Louis Mairet, *Carnet d'un combattant* (Paris, 1919), pp. 38, 41.

34. Raymond Lefèbvre and Paul Vaillant-Couturier, *La Guerre des soldats* (Paris, 1919), p. 143.

35. See, for example, André Gaucher, "Le Combat à la baïonnette," *La Revue* (June–September 1915), p. 341, and Joseph Bédier, "L'Effort français," *Revue des deux mondes*, 1 May 1919, p. 68, on the debate about the French and the offensive. See also Marc Ferro, *La Grande Guerre, 1914–1918* (Paris, 1969), p. 62.

36. Théodore Botrel, "Les Chants du Bivouac," *L'Echo des Armées* (March 1915), p. 1. At the end of August Botrel had been designated a delegate of the minister of war to perform his patriotic works before "the troops of all the depots and cantonments."

37. Emile Fabre, Administrateur général de la Comédie-Française, "Le Théâtre aux Armées," *Le Théâtre* 17, no. 348 (September 1919), p. 10.

38. According to newspaper interviews of Bach in the 1920s, he sang for front-line troops early in the war on at the request of General Gallieni. See in particular Henri Jeanson's "L'Histoire de 'La Madelon,' racontée par Bach, son créateur," *Belgique Spectacles*, 18 June 1926. War veteran José Germain remarks on the beginnings at Fontenay-sous-Bois in his *Une heure de musique*, p. 7. On this famous song see my article "Madelon and the Men—In War and Memory," *French Historical Studies* 17, no. 4 (Fall 1992), pp. 1001–1034, in which I reproduce and analyze the complete lyrics both in French and in English translation.

39. See Germain, *Une Heure de musique*, p. 49. Lyrics and music by Vincent Scotto; Vincent Scotto Editeur, 1915.

40. Lyrics by Roger Myra and Robert Dieudonné, music by A. Chantrier; Laurent Halet Editeur, 1917.

41. Stéphane Audoin-Rouzeau, "Les Soldats français et la nation de 1914 à 1918, d'après les journaux de tranchées," *Revue d'histoire moderne et contemporaine* (January–March 1987), p. 70. Audoin-Rouzeau, *14–18*, pp. 37, 145–146. This historian has found that the theme most frequently discussed in the papers was daily life in the trenches; women and family came in second.

42. Audoin-Rouzeau, *14–18*, pp. 107–124. The magazine *Le Crapouillot* offered frequent critiques of Parisian entertainments: see, for example, "En permission," issue 6 (no date, early 1916); "Notes d'un permissionaire" by Jean Galtier-Boissière (August 1917), and his column in the February 1918 issue.

43. The censored songs, marked "non visée," are in the Paris Police Archives in the BA series, many of them mixed in with approved songs. Songs with only some lines censored are in dossiers BA 731–735. "Prêtez-moi donc votre chat," for example, was censored because of sexual references and double entendres (BA 723).

44. Abel, *French Cinema*, pp. 9–11. Blaise Cendrars, "La Naissance de Charlot," written in 1926, in Cendrars's *Oeuvres complètes*, Vol. 4 (Paris, 1960), pp. 234–235.

45. The remark about Chaplin's "marvelous vitality" is from Philippe Soupault, *The American Influence in France* (Seattle, 1930), p. 16.

46. For the full songs see Germain, *Une Heure de musique*, pp. 29–33, 55–60.

47. *Le Petit Parisien*, 14 Dec. 1916, p. 1.

48. "La Galerie des Poilus civils" may be found in the Bibliothèque de l'Arsenal, Ro 15254, article dated 24 Feb. 1918. Montéhus's song "La Poilue" was given a police visa 17 Mar. 1917 (PPA BA 722). On Séverine's expression see Françoise Thébaud, *La Femme au temps de la guerre de 1914* (Paris, 1986), p. 242.

49. Gabriel Perreux, *La Vie quotidienne des civils en France pendant la Grande Guerre* (Paris, 1966), p. 254.

50. Barbusse, *Le Feu*, chapter 12. The character is Volpatte.

51. Audoin-Rouzeau, *14–18*, pp. 107–124. "Parmi les héros de Verdun," *Le Petit Parisien*, 21 Dec. 1916. Historian Jean Nicot's research on the "psychology" of the soldiers in the late years of the war supports these characterizations; see Jean Nicot, "Psychologie du combattant français de 1918," *Revue Historique de l'Armée*, no. 2 (1972), pp. 61–74; note esp. p. 67.

52. Adolphe Brisson, "Le Soldat au théâtre," *Journal de l'Université des Annales*, 1 Apr. 1916, pp. 235–236. *Images de 1917, Catalogue* (Paris: Le Musée d'histoire contemporaine et la Bibliothèque de documentation internationale contemporaine, 1987), pp. 150–151.

53. Lyrics by L. Bousquet, music by Camille Robert; L. Bousquet, Editeur, 1914; ©1916 WB Music Corp (Renewed). For background, see Rearick, "Madelon and the Men."

54. Thébaud, *La Femme au temps de la guerre*, p. 137.

55. Audoin-Rouzeau, *14–18*, p. 151. Mathilde Dubesset, Françoise Thébaud, and Catherine Vincent, "Les Munitionnettes de la Seine," in Patrick Fridenson, ed., *1914–1918, l'autre front* (Paris, 1977), pp. 194, 216.

56. Jean Rabaut, *L'Antimilitarisme en France, 1810–1975* (Paris, 1975), pp. 110–111, 126–127. The song was chosen for inclusion in a collection of all-time hits, *La Chanson française à travers ses succès*, ed. Pierre Saka (Paris, 1988), p. 76.

57. Irenée Manget, *En Chantant La Madelon!* (Paris, 1930), pp. 224–226. The author was a soldier in the war and relates his own observations.

58. PPA BA 716, marked "non visée," undated. The word *gobée* [swallowed or wildly desired—by the men] was used to describe the men's reaction to her. On women's attitudes, see Rearick, "Madelon and the Men," pp. 1015–1017.

59. *La Rampe*, 22 Nov. 1917. "La Chanson du pinard" was by the poet-brancardier Damien. The *chansons filmées* were directed and produced by Georges Lordier.

60. Perreux, *La Vie quotidienne des civils*, pp. 329–339.

61. Pierre MacOrlan, *Aux Lumières de Paris* (Paris, 1925), pp. 189–190.

62. Police reports on conversations overheard in cafés and on the streets testify to these worries about French women and American soldiers. See the PPA BA 1587, for example, for 9 and 16 Dec. 1917. See also André Kaspi, *Le Temps des Américains, 1917–1918* (Paris, 1978), pp. 299–300.

63. MacOrlan, *Aux Lumières de Paris*, pp. 187–190.

64. Huot and Voivenel, *La Psychologie du soldat*, pp. 55, 150.

65. Huot and Voivenel, *La Psychologie du soldat*, pp. 52–55.

66. After the war many traditional festivals and dances were not revived. In their place, demobilized French veterans brought new American dances and songs to the villages. Eugen Weber, *Peasants into Frenchmen: The Modernization of Rural France, 1870–1914* (Stanford, Calif., 1976), p. 451.

67. Jean-Louis Talmard, *Pages de guerre d'un paysan* (Lyons, 1971), p. 36. Talmard's account was written in 1914–1918.

68. David Englander, "The French Soldier, 1914–18," *French History* 1 (March 1987), pp. 6off.

69. Jean-Jacques Becker, *Les Français dans la Grande Guerre* (Paris, 1980).

CHAPTER 2. UNQUIET VICTORY

Note to epigraph: Antoine de Saint-Exupéry, *Vol de nuit* (Paris, 1931), p. xxiii.

1. Maurice Chevalier, *Ma Route et mes chansons: Londres, Hollywood, Paris* (Paris, 1947), p. 20.

2. Richard Abel, *French Cinema: The First Wave, 1915–1929* (Princeton, 1984), pp. 296–302.

3. Abel, *French Cinema*, pp. 296–302.

4. Lyrics by Ch.-L. Pothier, music by Borel-Clerc; the lyrics are reproduced in Roland Erbstein, *Les Chemins de la victoire* (Nancy, 1986), n.p. On Valroger's performance, see Gustave Fréjaville, "Petite Chronique du music-hall," *Comoedia*, 18 June 1919.

5. Fréjaville, "Petite Chronique du music-hall." Robert Brécy, *Florilège de la chanson révolutionnaire de 1789 au Front populaire* (Paris, 1978), p. 240. The song is entitled "On a besoin de rire" (G. Krier Editeur).

6. The story that the song was sung during the retaking of the fort of Vaux in 1916 long appeared in the *Grand Larousse encyclopédique* (Paris, 1975—carried over from the first edition in 1962), n.p. General Gouraud's story about the singing during a counteroffensive of the Fourth Army in Champagne in 1918 appears most recently in Pierre Joubert's *En Marchant avec les Soldats de France* (Fontenay/Bois, 1985), p. 88. The story goes that a German advance made a pocket in the French front and the French troops on the left (three regiments of the 163rd division) sang "Quand Madelon." Those on the right responded and, reunited, they drove out the enemy.

7. Gustave Fréjaville, "Petite Chronique du music-hall," *Comoedia*, 16 July 1919.

8. Paris Police Archives (hereafter PPA), DA 456, 298.

9. Archives Nationales, Ministère de l'Instruction publique et des Beaux-Arts, Renseignements—Lucien Jean Boyer, 67999D, Versement 800035.

10. Jacques Valdour, *De la Popinqu'à Ménilmuch'* (Paris, 1924), p. 120.

11. Valdour, *De la Popinqu'*, p. 150.

12. Antoine Prost, "Les Monuments aux morts: Culte républicain? culte civique? culte patriotique?" in *Les Lieux de mémoire*, ed. Pierre Nora, Vol. I: *La République* (Paris, 1984), p. 196; see also his *Anciens Combattants et la société française, 1914–1939* (Paris, 1977), III, 35, 100–101. Prost studied a sample of 564 monuments and found 224 bare steles and 91 with poilus on them. The others had groups of women, old parents, and female allegorical figures ("Les Monuments," p. 200).

13. David G. Troyansky, "Monumental Politics: National History and Local Memory in French Monuments aux morts in the Department of the Aisne since 1870," *French Historical Studies* (Spring 1987), p. 129.

14. Prost, "Monuments," in Nora, *Lieux de mémoire*, I, 216.

15. See Antoine Prost, "Verdun," in Pierre Nora, ed., *Les Lieux de mémoire*, vol. II: *La Nation* (Paris, 1986), pp. 121–122.

16. Prost, "Monuments," in Nora, *Lieux de mémoire*, I, 216.

17. *La Flamme sous l'Arc de Triomphe au tombeau du Soldat Inconnu* (Paris, 1949), p. 14.

18. Valdour, *Ouvriers parisiens d'après-guerre: Observations vécues* (Paris, 1921), p. 5.

19. Henri Desagneux, *A French Soldier's War Diary, 1914–1918*, trans. Godfrey J. Adams (Morley, England, 1975), p. 108.

20. Valdour, *Ouvriers parisiens*, p. 228.

21. Gary S. Cross, "*Les trois huits*: Labor Movements, International Reform, and the Origins of the Eight-Hour Day, 1919–1924," *French Historical Studies* (Fall 1985), pp. 240–255. Paul Rives, *La Corvée de joie: Notes sur les loisirs ouvriers* (Paris, 1924), p. 77.

22. Valdour, *De la Popinqu'*, p. 222n.

23. Bureau international du travail, Conférence internationale du travail, sixth session, "Rapport sur l'utilisation des loisirs des ouvriers." Geneva, June 1924, p. 14.

24. Ibid., pp. 16–20 (summary of a French Ministère du Travail report).

25. The Labor Ministry survey is cited in the Bureau international du travail report cited above, p. 20. For the later period see Hubert Leroy-Jay, "Loisirs et jardins ouvriers," *Politique* (June 1937), pp. 462–464.

26. Jacques Valdour, *Le Faubourg* (Paris, 1925), p. 194n.

27. Jean Beaudemoulin, *Enquête sur les loisirs de l'ouvrier français* (Paris, 1924), pp. 238–243.

28. Annie Fourcaut, *Femmes en l'usine en France dans l'entre-deux-guerres* (Paris, 1982), pp. 156–159, based on testimony dating from 1928.

29. Valdour, *De la Popinqu'*, p. 52.

30. Valdour, *Ouvriers parisiens*, pp. 69–70.

31. Valdour, *De la Popinqu'*, pp. 150–151.

32. Valdour, *De la Popinqu'*, p. 151.

33. Valdour, *Ouvriers parisiens*, p. 181. Valdour, however, praised the eight-hour day and higher wages for permitting workers to live "a life of a human being and no longer of a brute."

34. Valdour, *De la Popinqu'*, p. 227.

35. George L. Mosse, *Fallen Soldiers: Reshaping the Memory of the World Wars* (New York, 1990).

36. Rosemonde Sanson, "La 'Fête de Jeanne d'Arc' en 1894: Controverse et célébration," *Revue d'histoire moderne et contemporaine* 20 (July–September 1973), p. 458. See also Martha Hanna, "Iconology and Ideology: Images of Joan of Arc in the Idioms of the Action française, 1908–1931," *French Historical Studies* 14, no. 2 (Fall 1985), pp. 227–232. On the "new woman" see James F. McMillan, *Housewife or Harlot: The Place of Woman in French Society, 1870–1940* (New York, 1981), chapter 8; A.-M. Sohn, "*La Garçonne* face à l'opinion publique: Type littéraire ou type social des années 20?" *Le Mouvement social*, no. 80 (July–September 1972), pp. 3–27; Mary Louise Roberts, "Samson and Delilah Revisited: The Politics of Women's Fashions in 1920s France," *American Historical Review* 98, no. 3 (June 1993), pp. 657–684, and Roberts, *Civilization without Sexes: Reconstructing Gender in Postwar France, 1917–1927* (Chicago, 1994).

37. Valdour, *Ouvriers parisiens*, p. 170.

38. Léon Deutsch, "La Chanson sentimentale," *La Revue Française*, 21 Dec. 1924, p. 68.

39. Valdour, *De la Popinqu'*, p. 52.

40. Pierre MacOrlan, *Aux Lumières de Paris* (Paris, 1925), p. 194.

41. André Beucler, "Music-Hall," *Nouvelles littéraires*, 21 Apr. 1928.

42. The songs cited are in the Bibliothèque de documentation internationale contemporaine ("Le Mariage de Madelon"), the Paris Police Archives ("Madelon, c'est dimanche"), and the Bibliothèque nationale music department ("Madelon, j'attends la classe"). In "Madelon, j'attends la classe," the line "I wait and that gives me occupation" suggests that the soldier is taking part in the French occupation of the Ruhr in 1923.

43. Gustave Fréjaville, "Les bons couplets et . . . les pires," *Paris qui chante*, 1 Feb. 1921, p. 1. Fréjaville got his information from "boutiques" where "fervent" song-lovers paid twenty centimes to hear and learn the latest releases on phonograph records. "Lison-Lisette," lyrics by Albert Willemetz and Ch.-L. Pothier, music by Borel-Clerc; Paris: Borel-Clerc Editeur, 1920.

44. *Paris qui chante*, 15 June 1922. Lyrics by Vincent Telly.

45. Lyrics adapted by Georges Millandy, music by André Motsa (Paris, 1922); *Paris qui chante*, 15 Mar. 1922.

46. Gérard Noiriel, *Les Ouvriers dans la société française, XIXe–XXe siècle* (Paris, 1986), pp. 161–163.

47. For "Les Bienfaits" see *Paris qui chante*, 1 Jan. 1920; "Marie! Marie! Marie!" is in the PPA BA 716; "Pour avoir la semaine anglaise" is also in the PPA BA 722.

48. BDIC 4 Δ1508–1509.

49. Abel, *French Cinema*, pp. 121–123, 326–339. Paul Monaco, *Cinema and Society: France and Germany during the Twenties* (New York, 1976), pp. 85, 90, 92.

50. Lyrics by Albert Willemetz and C.-A. Carpentier, music by Maurice Yvain; ©Editions Salabert, 1924.

51. Lyrics by Albert Willemetz and Jacques-Charles, music by Maurice Yvain; ©Editions Salabert, 1921.

52. "Vous avez du pognon," lyrics by Jean Rodor, music by Vincent Scotto. See *Paris qui chante*, 15 Apr. 1922. Valdour, *De la Popinqu'*, p. 74.

53. The song of 1915 mentioned is entitled "Le Chant du retour," lyrics by Willems; PPA BA 704. "Ne Jouez Pas aux Soldats," lyrics by Léo Lelièvre and music by Dalbret; ©Editions Salabert, 1921. Duverney and d'Horrer list it as one of the successes of the period. On "La Butte rouge" see Jean-Claude Klein, *Florilège de la chanson française* (Paris, 1990), p. 166. The lyrics were by the long-time antimilitarist Montéhus, and the music was by Georges Krier. See also Serge Dillaz, *La Chanson sous la Troisième République* (Paris, 1991), p. 206.

54. *Paris qui chante*, 1 Nov. 1922, pp. 8–9. Lyrics by Julsam.

55. The Paris police approved "Le Club des fauchées" in September 1919. On the Casino-Montparnasse audience, see Valdour, *Ouvriers parisiens*, p. 106.

56. *Paris qui chante*, 1 Apr. 1920.

57. André Billy, "La Crise du caf'-conc'," *Le Petit Journal*, 19 Apr. 1923.

58. Gustave Fréjaville, "La Semaine au music-hall," *Comoedia*, 5 May 1927; 16 June 1927. On Polin as the last of the *tourlourous* see Jacques Patin's article in *Le Figaro*, 5 June 1927. The theme was commonplace in obituaries.

59. Gustave Fréjaville, "La Semaine au music-hall," *Comoedia*, 12 Jan. 1928.

60. Gustave Fréjaville, "La Semaine au music-hall," *Comoedia*, 21 and 28 Jan. 1926.

61. Henri Jeanson, "L'Histoire de la 'Madelon,' racontée par Bach," *Belgique spectacles*, 6 June 1926.

62. Marcel Espiau, "'La Madelon,' chanson de guerre et de la victoire," *L'Eclair*, 26 July 1926.

63. *Paris Soir*, 11 Dec. 1926. *Le Matin* and *Paris Soir* reviews were full of high praise.

64. *Candide*, 26 Jan. 1927; *L'Avenir*, 25 Jan. 1927; *Le Journal*, 1 and 2 Mar. 1927.

65. *Le Journal*, 9 Dec. 1926; *La Volonté*, 12 Oct. 1926; ("American puerility") Marcel Espiau, *L'Avenir*, 25 Jan. 1927; *L'Illustration*, 18 Dec. 1926.

66. Arsenal, Rondel Collection, Rk 4859. On protests see *Le Journal*, 20 May 1927.

67. *Foch, par un ancien combattant* (Elbeuf: Paul Duval, 1929), p. 93.

68. Janet Flanner, *Paris Was Yesterday, 1925–1939* (New York, 1972), p. 52.

69. Prost, "Monuments," in Nora, *Lieux de mémoire*, I, 216.

70. Eugène Dabit, *Faubourgs de Paris* (Paris, 1933), p. 151.

71. René Lehmann, "Un Grand Film américain sur la guerre," *Pour Vous*, 27 July 1930. Abel, *French Cinema*, pp. 202–204.

72. Modris Eksteins, *Rites of Spring: The Great War and the Birth of the Modern Age* (New York, 1989), pp. 274–277.

73. M. B., "Dans Une Salle de quartier et le public," *Ciné-Miroir*, 20 Apr. 1931.

74. Joseph Daniel, *Guerre et cinéma* (Paris, 1972), pp. 103–104.

75. Daniel, *Guerre et cinéma*, p. 116.

76. José Germain, "Les Croix de bois," *Cinéa-Ciné*, 18 Mar. 1932.

77. J. V., "Les Croix de bois," *Cinéa-Ciné*, 11 Mar. 1931, with the subtitle: "How I dare make a war film after *Quatre de l'infanterie* and *A l'ouest rien de nouveau*."

78. Daniel, *Guerre et cinéma*, pp. 117–122.

79. Marcel Lapierre, *Le Cinéma et la paix* (Paris, 1932), pp. 51–63, 87.

80. Jacques Perdu, "Pouvons-Nous lutter contre le cinéma asservi?" *Le Monde*, 5 Jan. 1929. Lapierre (*Le Cinéma et la paix*, p. 40) agreed that Poirier's film "insisted on heroism."

81. Lapierre, *Le Cinéma et la paix*, pp. 56–60, 63 (on women and films about pilots). On the children's reactions, see also Georges Altman, *Ça c'est du cinéma* (Paris, 1931), pp. 121–123. Altman was a movie critic for the Communist paper *L'Humanité*. Emile Moussat, "Films de guerre," *Revue de la Gendarmerie*, 15 Mar. 1931, p. 125.

82. Moussat, "Films de guerre," p. 126.

CHAPTER 3. PARISIAN MODERN

Note to epigraph: Philippe Soupault, *The American Influence in France* (Seattle, 1930), p. 7.

1. Gustave Fréjaville, "Petite Chronique du music-hall," *Comoedia*, 13 Oct. 1920.

2. Cocteau quoted by Louis Roubaud, "Le Jazz et Josephine," *Le Petit Parisien*, 17 July 1928. Legrand-Chabrier (André Legrand), "Pistes et Plateaux," *La Presse*, 13 Nov. 1924.

3. Gustave Fréjaville, "Petite Chronique du music-hall," *Comoedia*, 13 Oct. 1920.

4. Jacques Feschotte, *Histoire du music-hall* (Paris, 1965), pp. 99–100.

5. Fréjaville, "Les Attractions de la Quinzaine," *Comoedia*, 7 May 1930.

6. Pierre MacOrlan, *Aux Lumières de Paris* (Paris, 1925), pp. 134, 137, 141–142.

7. "Ça, C'est Paris!"—lyrics by Lucien Boyer and Jacques-Charles, music by José Padilla; ©Editions Salabert. The copyright on the sheet music is given as both 1926 and 1927. The hit song came out of a Jacques-Charles revue by the same title at the Moulin Rouge.

8. Pierre Scize, "Maurice Chevalier," in *Bonsoir*, 24 June 1922.

9. Maurice Chevalier, "L'Art de plaire," *Paris-Soir*, 3 July 1926.

10. Max Viterbo, "L'Avenir de la chanson au théâtre," *Paris qui chante*, 1 Apr. 1922.

11. Scize, "Maurice Chevalier."

12. Fréjaville, "Petite Chronique du music-hall," *Comoedia*, 31 Mar. 1921.

13. "Oh! Maurice"—lyrics by A. Trébitsch, music by H. Christiné; ©Editions Salabert, 1919.

14. Scize, "Maurice Chevalier."

15. Lyrics by Albert Willemetz, music by Henri Christiné; ©Editions Salabert, 1925.

16. Maurice Chevalier, "Le Théâtre moderne et le problème sexuel," *Paris-Midi*, 15 Aug. 1928.

17. Auguste Bailly, reviewing Chevalier's book, in *Candide*, 20 June 1927.

18. *L'Intransigeant*, 3 July 1927.

19. Louis Léon-Martin, *Le Music-hall et ses figures* (Paris, 1928), pp. 66–67.

20. Fréjaville, "Chronique de la semaine," *Comoedia*, 8 Oct. 1925. The story of the Revue nègre is well told in Phyllis Rose's biography *Jazz Cleopatra: Josephine Baker in Her Time* (New York, 1989), pp. 6–18.

21. See Rose, *Jazz Cleopatra*, chapter 1.

22. Gus Bofa, reviewing Josephine Baker's memoirs, in *Le Crapouillot*, October 1934, p. 14.

23. Eugène Dabit, *Faubourgs de Paris* (Paris, 1933), pp. 149–150.

24. Jacques Valdour, *Ouvriers parisiens d'après guerre: Observations vécues* (Paris, 1921), p. 69.

25. Richard Abel, *French Cinema: The First Wave, 1915–1929* (Princeton, 1984), pp. 210–220.

26. Jacques Valdour, *De la Popinqu'à Ménilmuch'* (Paris, 1924), p. 98.

27. Valdour, *Ouvriers parisiens*, pp. 101, 104. Dabit, *Faubourgs*, p. 211.

28. Fréjaville, "Petite Chronique du music-hall," *Comoedia*, 11 Aug. 1921.

29. Dabit, *Faubourgs*, p. 199.

30. Jacques Valdour, *Le Faubourg* (Paris, 1925), p. 64. The cafés were on corners of the boulevard de Charonne and the rue d'Avron.

31. Charles Lejay, "Le Théâtre chantant de Georgius à la Scala," *La Volonté*, 3 Mar. 1928.

32. *Le Journal*, 31 Mar. 1927.

33. *Le Petit Parisien*, 29 Apr. 1928.

34. *La Volonté*, 11 Feb. 1926.

35. Eugène Dabit, *Journal intime, 1928–1936*, new edition, ed. Pierre Edmond Robert (Paris, 1989), pp. 253–254.

36. Louis Roubaud, "Une enquête de 'Petit Parisien' sur le music-hall," *Le Petit Parisien*, 14 July 1928, reprinted in Roubaud, *Music-hall* (Paris, 1929), pp. 11–13.

37. The comments on American dancing appeared in *Paris qui chante*, 1 Aug. 1919. The song "Kiss Me" (lyrics by W. Burtey, music by Dick Stone) is in the same magazine, 15 Jan. 1922.

38. Valdour, *Le Faubourg*, p. 185.

39. *Paris qui chante*, 1 Aug. 1922, p. 1.

40. Maurice Hamel, *Nos artistes de café-concert, de music-hall et de cabaret* (Paris: Encyclopédie du café-concert, n.d. [ca. 1919], p. 3. *Paris qui chante*, 15 Oct. 1919, p. 1; "La Chanson se meurt, par un amateur de café-concert," *Paris qui chante*, 15 Sept. 1921, p. 1. Pierre Fontaine, "Est-ce l'agonie de la chanson française?" *Comoedia*, 15 Nov. 1926.

41. Pierre Lazareff, "Des projecteurs à la Rampe, Une fougue de Bach," *Le Soir*, 10 Feb. 1926.

42. "La mort de la chanson ce serait un peu la mort de l'esprit français." Yvonne Moustiers, "Deux époques," *L'Ami du peuple du soir*, 18 May 1929.

43. Gustave Fréjaville, "La Semaine au music-hall," *Comoedia*, 14 Jan., 10 and 24 June 1926. "Mon Paris"—lyrics by Lucien Boyer, music by Jean Boyer and Vincent Scotto; ©Editions Salabert, 1925.

44. See Ralph Schorr, *L'Opinion française et les étrangers, 1919–1939* (Paris, 1985), pp. 471–476.

45. André Warnod, "Montparnasse," *Le Figaro artistique illustré*, June 1931, p. 23.

46. Lucie Derain, "La Faune de Plaisir," *Vu*, 31 Dec. 1930, p. 145.

47. Sisley Huddleston, *Paris Salons, Cafés, Studios* (Philadelphia, 1928) p. 25.

48. Francis Carco, *Montmartre à vingt ans* (Paris, 1938), p. 40.

49. Louis Chevalier, *Montmartre du plaisir et du crime* (Paris, 1980), pp. 315, 322–324.

50. Bibliothèque de l'Arsenal, Ro 15254. Program for the Colisée.

51. Adolphe Aderer, "Chronique," *L'Echo de Paris*, 10 Dec. 1919. José Germain, "Les Danses modernes," *La Revue mondiale*, 1 Mar. 1922, pp. 25–26. For the comment on the *Revue française* editor, see Germain, "Les Danses modernes," *La Revue mondiale*, 15 Mar. 1922, p. 275.

52. Adolphe Aderer, "Chronique," *L'Echo de Paris*, 10 Dec. 1919. Germain, "Les Danses modernes," *La Revue mondiale*, 1 Mar. 1922, pp. 5, 8, 19, 31; 15 Mar. 1922, p. 275.

53. Dominique Desanti, *La Femme au temps des années folles* (Paris, 1984), pp. 198–200.

54. José Germain, "L'Appel du sexe," *Le Parisien*, 19 May 1931. The article begins in English: "Sex appeal! Le mot fait fureur." See also Francis Rohl, "Sex Appeal," *Cinémagazine*, June 1932, p. 35.

CHAPTER 4. FOLKLORE OF THE PEOPLE'S PARIS

Note to epigraph: "Mon Paris," lyrics by Lucien Boyer, ©Editions Salabert, 1925.

1. On commercialism see Georges Coulonges, *La Chanson en son temps: De Béranger au Juke Box* (Paris, 1969), pp. 89–91.

2. In a garment shop in Ménilmontant, for example, worker and reporter Jacques Valdour found ten hours a day the announced standard, but an extra hour was also required, on penalty of dismissal. During his first night in a cheap rooming house (a room for 3F50 a day) he killed 640 *punaises* (bedbugs). Other nights were interrupted by loud fights in a nearby room. Jacques Valdour, *De la Popinqu'à Ménilmuch'* (Paris, 1924), pp. 53, 124, and Valdour, *Le Faubourg* (Paris, 1925), p. 64.

3. "Les Midinettes," lyrics by René de Buxeuil and Virgile Thomas, music by Léon Montagne. No date. Paris Police Archives (hereafter PPA) BA 716.

4. Maurice Chevalier, *Ma Route et mes chansons* (Paris, 1946), p. 193.

5. Lyrics by Albert Willemetz and Jacques-Charles, music by Maurice Yvain. ©Editions Salabert, 1921.

6. "Dans la vie faut pas s'en faire. / Moi, je n'm'en fais pas. / Ces petites misères sont passagères. / Tout ça s'arrangera." Lyrics by Albert Willemetz, music by Henri Christiné; ©Editions Salabert, 1921.

7. *Paris qui chante*, 1 Nov. 1922, pp. 6–7. Lyrics by Alex Trébitsch.

8. Lyrics by Albert Willemetz and Jacques-Charles, music by Maurice Yvain; ©Editions Salabert, 1922.

9. Lyrics by Phylo, music by Gabroche and Red Pearly. *Paris qui chante*, 1 Jan. 1921. No copyright date.

10. Gustave Fréjaville, "La Semaine au music-hall," *Comoedia*, 14 Jan., 10 and 24 June 1926. "Viva Mussolini," copyright 1923. Lyrics by Lucien Boyer.

11. Steven M. Zdatny, *The Politics of Survival: Artisans in Twentieth-Century France* (New York, 1990), pp. 6, 9, 29, 69–70.

12. Gustave Fréjaville, "La Semaine au music-hall," *Comoedia*, 28 Jan. 1926.

13. Lyrics and music by Jean Lenoir; ©SEMI, 1930. Pierre Saka, *La Chanson française à travers ses succès* (Paris, 1988), p. 98. Jean-Claude Klein, *Florilège de la chanson française* (Paris, 1990), p. 168.

14. Lyrics by A. Decaye and Lucien Carol, music by Vincent Scotto; ©Fortin, 1925. Lyrics reprinted in Saka, *La Chanson française*, p. 87.

15. Eugène Dabit, *Faubourgs de Paris* (Paris, 1933), p. 211.

16. "Plaisir qui tue, Chanson vécue," lyrics by J. Lysère. PPA BA 722. "Le Marchand de cocaïne" may be found in PPA BA 715. Copyright 1915.

17. Lyrics by Stolle and Haldy, music by Emile Spencer; ©Editions Paul Beuscher, 1918.

18. "La Misère" (PPA BA 716) was censored in October 1915.

19. Legrand-Chabrier, "Pistes et plateaux," *La Presse*, 13 Nov. 1924. For the song "Dans les Fortifs" (lyrics by R. Champigny and F. L. Benech, music by Henri Piccolini), see *Paris qui chante*, 15 May 1922, pp. 8–9.

20. Lyrics by Charles-Louis Pothier, music by Léon Raiter; L. Raiter, Editeur, 1925. See C. Brunschwig, L.-J. Calvet, and J.-C. Klein, *Cent ans de chanson française* (Paris, 1981), p. 335.

21. Lyrics by P. Goupil, music by M. Zimmermann; ©SEMI, 1927.

22. Paul Monaco, *Cinema and Society: France and Germany during the Twenties* (New York, 1976), pp. 84–111. Richard Abel, *French Cinema: The First Wave, 1915–1929* (Princeton, 1984), pp. 103–130, ch. 2, "The Commercial Narrative Film," particularly the section on "realist" films. Abel notes that relatively few so-called realist films were about the urban poor that were featured in songs. Evidently moviegoers, particularly urban ones, preferred to *see* stories with less familiar settings, mostly glamorous, exotic, or old-fashioned rural. "Perhaps many people are happy, thanks to cinema, to look at what happens in places where they don't usually go," observed the author of an article entitled "Bouges, Bars, Dancings, Boîtes de nuit," which appeared in *Mon Ciné*, 12 Feb. 1928, p. 12.

23. Gustave Fréjaville, "La Petite Chronique du Music-Hall," *Comoedia*, 6 Aug. 1919.

24. Seymour S. Weiner, *Francis Carco: The Career of a Literary Bohemian* (New York, 1952), p. 243. The play's co-author was André Picard. On "Mon homme" see Klein, *Florilège de la chanson française*, p. 164. The lyrics were by Jacques-Charles and Albert Willemetz, and the music was by Maurice Yvain; ©Editions Salabert, 1920.

25. Valdour, *Le Faubourg*, p. 182.

26. Music by Vincent Scotto, lyrics by Jean Rodor; Editions Fortin, 1919.

27. Pierre MacOrlan, *Aux Lumières de Paris* (Paris, 1925), p. 86.

28. Pierre MacOrlan, *Nuits aux bouges* (Paris, 1929), pp. 31–32. "Après les représentations d'Aristide Bruant," *Paris qui chante,* 1 Sept. 1921. Bruant bitterly contrasts the old and the postwar new.

29. Lyrics by Georgius, music by Jean Rit; Editions Marcel Labbé, n.d.

30. Lyrics by Georgius; Editions Marcel Labbé, 1920.

31. On Georgius's sketches and songs, see Fréjaville's columns in *Comoedia*—e.g., 1 June 1928 and 8 Nov. 1928; P. V., "A l'Européen," *Paris-Soir,* 17 Nov. 28; and Legrand-Chabrier's weekly column "Pistes et plateaux" in *La Volonté* ("Cinq Minutes chez les Juifs" mentioned 22 Oct. 1929). Several volumes of articles on his shows and songs may be found in the Bibliothèque de l'Arsenal in Paris (Ro 16052 bis).

32. Gustave Fréjaville, "La Contre-offensive du caf' conc'," *Comoedia,* 1 Feb. 1923. Legrand-Chabrier, "Le Vingt-septième Spectacle Georgius," *La Volonté,* 30 May 1930. A compendium of press reviews appears in admirer Charles Lejay's *Du café-concert au Théâtre-chantant de Georgius* (Paris, 1928).

33. "Attache-toi . . . il y a du vent!" lyrics by Georgius, music by Trémolo; ©Marcel Labbé Editeur, 1927. "Mon Paris," lyrics by Lucien Boyer, music by Jean Boyer and Vincent Scotto; ©Editions Salabert, 1925.

34. "Gosse de Paris," lyrics by Léo Lelièvre fils and Henri Varna and De Lima, music by René Sylviano; ©Editions Salabert, 1929.

35. Dabit, *Faubourgs,* pp. 146–147.

36. Léon Lemonnier, *Le Populisme* (Paris, 1931). A rival movement was the proletarian literary "school" of Henry Poulaille. See Henri Chambert-Loir, ed., *Henry Poulaille et la littérature proletarienne* (Rodez, 1974). The populists awarded Eugène Dabit the first Populist Novel prize for *L'Hôtel du nord* in 1931. See Pierre-Edmond Robert, *D'un Hôtel du nord l'autre: Eugène Dabit, 1898–1936* (Paris, 1986), p. 103.

37. Ford Madox Ford, *A Mirror to France* (New York, 1926), p. 14.

38. Gustave Fréjaville, "Les Attractions de la semaine," *Comoedia,* 12 Mar. 1930.

39. Louis Le Sidaner, "Le Populisme au cinématographe," *Le Nord artistique,* 15 Feb. 1930, p. 41.

40. Jean Oberlé, "Films parlants et sonores," *Le Crapouillot,* June 1930, p. 42.

41. "Répugnante"—Emile Vuillermoz, *Le Temps,* 24 May 1930. "Sous les Toits," *Nouvelles littéraires,* 2 May 1930. L. Borgex, "Le Succès de 'Sous les Toits de Paris,'" *Comoedia,* 24 Apr. 1930. Jean Oberlé, *Le Crapouillot,* June 1930, p. 42. "True slice of life"—Carmelo Puglionisi, *Paris-Soir,* 13 June 1930.

42. Louis Le Sidaner, "Le Populisme," *Le Nord artistique,* 15 Feb. 1930, p. 41.

43. François Ribadeau Dumas, "14 Juillet," *La Revue mondiale,* February 1933.

44. Georges Simenon and Paul Bringuier, "Les Films policiers," *Pour Vous,* 11 Sept. 1932, p. 9. Michael B. Miller's *Shanghai on the Métro: Spies, Intrigue, and the French between the Wars* (Berkeley and Los Angeles, 1994) provides much fascinating background on public interest in sensational crime and spy stories and the press that fed that interest.

45. "Les Films policiers," *Pour Vous,* 11 Sept. 1932, p. 9, a caption about *Au Nom de la loi.* On differences between the United States and France and the *films policiers* see, for example, Daniel Abric, "Le Cinéma," *L'Européen,* 13 Nov. 1929, and Maurice Mairgance, "Le Film policier français," *L'Ami du peuple du soir,* 7 June 1932, praising *Au Nom de la loi* in particular.

46. Eugène Dabit, *Journal intime, 1928–1936,* new edition, ed. Pierre Edmond Robert (Paris, 1989), p. 254. Entry for 23 Oct. 1933. What I have translated as "beastly" is the word *vaches.*

CHAPTER 5. HEROES FOR HARD TIMES

Note to epigraph: Eugène Dabit, *Faubourgs de Paris* (Paris, 1933), p. 47.

1. Pathé-Nathan went out of business in 1936 and Gaumont-France/Film Aubert in 1938. See chapter 1, "Les Bases économiques," in Jean-Pierre Jeancolas, *15 ans d'années trente* (Paris, 1983). Colin Crisp, in *The Classic French Cinema, 1930–1960* (Bloomington, 1993), argues against the established view of the cinema industry in crisis, but the figures on film production are contradictory. Much of the difficulty in using the figures given in the sources and drawing conclusions is due to differences in definition of "French film," as Crisp notes on p. 7. On Hollywood's success in Europe, see Victoria de Grazia, "Mass Culture and Sovereignty: The American Challenge to European Cinemas, 1920–1960," *Journal of Modern History* 61, no. 1 (March 1989), pp. 53–87.

2. *Vu,* 7 Oct. 1936, p. 1198.

3. "Lucien Boyer," interview article by Roger Ducret, in *L'Ami du peuple du soir,* 16 Aug. 1931.

4. Albert Fournier, "Les Chansons préférées du public dans les salles d'audition," *La Rampe,* 1 Oct. 1931, pp. 26–28.

5. Pierre MacOrlan, "Disques," *Le Crapouillot,* May 1930, p. 43.

6. After the war, demographically weak France had needed a large infusion of foreign manpower: more than a million new foreign workers had found work there from 1921 to 1931. Gérard Noiriel, *Les Ouvrières dans la société française, XIXe–XXe siècle* (Paris, 1986), pp. 133, 172. Noiriel adds that after foreign workers, women were laid off in large numbers.

7. As noted in Henry Rousso, *Le Syndrome de Vichy, 1944–198 ?* (Paris, 1987), p. 76.

8. For enthusiastic reports of Chevalier's Paramount deal, see, for example, "Le plus formidable contrat du monde," *La Volonté,* 20 June 1928; "Le plus gros cachet du monde," *La Rumeur,* 20 June 1928. Lucien Farnoux-Reynaud, "Un événement," *Candide,* 18 Oct. 1928. At the time of Chevalier's departure, unfavorable press came from critics of the "bad taste" of praising the entertainer when the poet Paul Claudel was France's real ambassador to the United States and such other worthy heroes as aviators Costes and Le Brix were overlooked; see, for example, "De Chevalier à Costes et Le Brix," *Aux Ecoutes,* 13 Oct. 1928, and Emile de Vireuil, "Le Type même du Français!" *Marsalia,* 20 Oct. 1928.

9. The comment on the $25,000 a week came from Robert Dieudonné in "Paradoxe sur les gros cachets," *Paris-Soir,* 26 Dec. 1928. "Avalanche de dollars," *Le Carnet de la semaine,* 9 Mar. 1930.

10. René Wisner, "L'Arrivée de Chevalier," *La Volonté,* 21 Aug. 1930.

11. Gustave Fréjaville, "Les Attractions de la Quinzaine," *Comoedia,* 21 May 1930.

12. *L'Echo de Paris,* 28 June 1929.

13. La Meilleraye, "La Chanson de Paris," *Pour Vous,* 27 May 1929.

14. Paul Reboux, "Conseils de modestie à Maurice Chevalier," *Paris-Soir,* 2 Oct. 1930.

15. Georges Altman, *Ça, c'est du cinéma* (Paris, 1931), p. 77.

16. "Maurice Chevalier vu par Pomiès," *L'Intransigeant,* 24 Aug. 1930.

17. "Maurice Parle à 'Paris-Soir' de Maurice," *Paris-Soir,* 4 Oct. 1930.

18. Jean Marguet, "Bravo! Chevalier," *Excelsior,* 28 June 1929.

19. "Un nouveau jeu," *Pour Vous,* 10 Oct. 1929, p. 2.

20. *Le Matin,* 24 Aug. 1930.

21. Candide, *Aux Ecoutes,* 26 July 1930.

22. Altman, *Ça, c'est du cinéma,* pp. 25–26, 76.

23. "'La Chanson de Paris' qui nous vient d'Hollywood," *Pour Vous,* 27 May 1929.

24. *Pour Vous,* 10 Oct. 1929, p. 2. Maurice Huet, "Le Dernier Maurice," *Le Petit Parisien,* 5 July 1929. Pierre de Lacretelle, *Gringoire,* 5 July 1929.

25. "Costes et Chevalier," *Oeil de Paris*, 20 Sept. 1930.

26. J. C. Auriol, "La Chanson de Paris," *L'Ami du peuple du soir*, 20 June 1929.

27. J. E. C., "Doit-on le dire," *Le Temps*, 26 June 1930.

28. "Chevalier for ever" (title in English), *Oeil de Paris*, 27 Sept. 1930.

29. Philippe Soupault, "'Parade d'amour' avec Maurice Chevalier," in *Philippe Soupault, Ecrits de cinéma, 1918–1931*, ed. Odette and Alain Virmaux (Paris, 1979), p. 94, originally published in *L'Europe Nouvelle*, 22 Mar. 1930, pp. 505–506.

30. Michel Murray, "Georgius et son théâtre chantant," *Le Quotidien*, 21 Sept. 1930.

31. Gustave Fréjaville, "Les Attractions de la semaine," *Comoedia*, 23 Sept. 1930. Fernand Léger, "Georgius et le théâtre populaire," *Candide*, 4 Jan. 1934.

32. "Carnet d'un optimiste," *Aux Ecoutes*, 30 Aug. 1930.

33. J.-M. Aimot, "Der 'beau garçon' von Paris," *Le Carnet de la semaine*, 31 Aug. 1930.

34. Altman, *Ça, c'est du cinéma*, p. 76.

35. The comment on Chevalier portraits appeared in Lopès, "Quelques types," *Avant-scène*, 5 June 1932. Pierre Loiselet, *Le Soir*, 31 Jan. 1932. Michel Doran, "Maurice Chevalier," *Marianne*, 9 Apr. 1932.

36. Mairgance, *L'Ami du peuple du soir*, 25 Dec. 1930.

37. Lyrics by René Pujol and Pierre Colombier, music by Ralph Erwin; ©Editions Salabert, 1930.

38. *Le Journal*, 14 Nov. 1930.

39. Philippe Soupault, "Milton, le nouveau 'Roi de Paris,'" in *Philippe Soupault, Ecrits de cinéma*, pp. 192–193, originally published in *Bravo*, June 1931, p. 35.

40. *Paris-Midi* (29 Dec. 1930) called Milton a new type. Aimot in *Le Carnet de la semaine*, 23 Nov. 1930. Soupault, "Milton, le nouveau 'Roi de Paris,'" p. 192.

41. François Vinneuil, "Le Film populaire," *L'Action française*, 12 Dec. 1930. Paul Reboux, *Paris-Midi*, 18 July 1931.

42. Puc in *Charivari*, 29 Nov. 1930.

43. H. Frédéric Pottecher, "Crise de héros," *Comoedia*, 24 Dec. 1931.

44. See Adrian Rifkin, *Street Noises: Parisian Pleasures, 1900–1940* (Manchester, 1993), for fascinating commentary on the magazine and the lowlife of Paris. For another excellent treatment see Michael B. Miller's *Shanghai on the Métro: Spies, Intrigue, and the French between the Wars* (Berkeley and Los Angeles, 1994), esp. pp. 227–233.

45. Paul Morand, "Réflexions sur le roman détective," *La Revue de Paris*, April 1934, p. 491.

46. François Guérif, *Le Cinéma policier français* (Paris, 1981). Jean-Jacques Tourteau, *D'Arsène Lupin à San-Antonio* (Tours, 1970). Michel Carrouges, "Les Derniers de la chance," *Cahiers du Sud* (July 1951), pp. 390–405. In Gramsci's terms the cultural producers of policiers worked in oppositional themes, which helped win popular consent for an order satisfying the powerful above all.

47. Marcel Berger, "Le Sport et le sentiment de la beauté," *Miroir du Monde*, 12 Sept. 1931.

48. Theodore Zeldin, *France, 1848–1945*, Vol. II: *Intellect, Taste and Anxiety* (Oxford, 1977), pp. 561, 687–88. Richard Holt, *Sport and Society in Modern France* (Hamden, Conn., 1981), pp. 74, 77. Georges Vigarello, "Les Premières Coupes du monde ou l'installation du sport moderne," *Vingtième siècle* 26 (April–June 1990), pp. 5–8. Alfred Wahl, ed., *Les Archives du football: Sport et société en France, 1880–1980* (Paris, 1989), pp. 209, 223–224.

49. Gustave Fréjaville, "Music-halls, cirques et cabarets," *Comoedia*, 9 Sept. 1931.

50. Bernard Champigneulle, "Spectacles et spectateurs," *Mercure de France*, February 1934, pp. 570, 572.

51. Pierre-Henry Proust, "Le Goût d'une époque: Pourquoi le public aime les films sportifs," *Comoedia*, 15 Nov. 1931, n.p.

52. Proust, "Le Goût d'une époque."

53. Another cycling hero of the period was France's great stayer Georges Paillard, the champion of France six times (1928–34) and world champion twice (1929, 1932), winning middle-distance (*demi-fond*) races on a cycle track. See François Terbeen, *Les Grandes Heures du cyclisme* (Paris, 1982), p. 47. On the Tour winners see Henri Quiquère, *Des Géants et des hommes: 1903–1987, Les vainqueurs du Tour de France* (Paris, 1988), pp. 71, 81, 114–115. Wahl, *Les Archives du football*, p. 209.

54. Rigoulot's weightlifting came to an end in 1931 after an accident, but he went on to new glory in wrestling and automobile racing. Ladoumègue's racing career ended when he was disqualified for the 1932 Olympics because he was found to be not fully amateur. Lucien Dubech, *Où Va le Sport* (Paris, 1930), p. 73.

55. Wahl, *Les Archives du football*, p. 205.

56. Proust, "Le Goût d'une époque."

57. Marcel Carné, "Sport et cinéma," *Cinémagazine*, October 1931, pp. 3–6, 8.

58. Marcel Huret, *Cinéactualités* (Paris, 1984), pp. 55, 87.

59. Pierre Barlatier, "Music-Hall XYZ à l'ABC," *Comoedia*, 24 Oct. 1934.

60. Robert Chenevier, "L'Essor prodigieux de la radiodiffusion nationale," *L'Illustration*, 28 Sept. 1935, p. 104. From 31 July 1933 to 30 June 1935, the number of officially declared radios (on which a tax was imposed) nearly doubled, rising from 1,087,147 to 1,996,999. Chenevier estimated at least three listeners per radio. Technical progress made it possible for stations like Radio-Paris and Lyon-PTT to send stronger signals and reach more listeners.

61. Georges Coulonges, *La Chanson en son temps: De Béranger au juke-box* (Paris, 1969), pp. 127, 131–132.

62. André Coeuroy, "Le Phonographe et l'actualité," *La Revue de Paris*, 15 Jan. 1934, p. 419. Another new singer of note was Marlene Dietrich, who made records in French ("Assez," "Je m'ennuie") for the first time in 1933. See Coeuroy article cited above, p. 418.

63. R. de Thomasson, "'Je ne suis pas pour le mariage, moi,' s'exclame Maurice Chevalier," *Pour Vous*, 20 Sept. 1934, p. 3.

64. Marcel Carné, "Jean Gabin un chic type," *Cinémagazine*, January 1933.

CHAPTER 6. THE WISH TO BE ELSEWHERE

1. France's movie producers and directors were still overwhelmingly Parisian and still put the capital at the center of most of their works, but the proportion of films set outside Paris was significantly higher during the thirties.

2. Lyrics by Jean Nohain, music by Mireille; ©Raoul Breton Editeur, 1932. The lyrics appear in Pierre Saka, *La Chanson française* (Paris, 1988), p. 100. The song became popular in the United States under the title "Lying in the Hay."

3. *Kriss* (1931) was directed by F. W. Murnau and Robert Flaherty. *Tabou* (1931) was directed by André Roosevelt and Armand Denis.

4. Gaston Mortier, *Le Tourisme* (Grenoble, 1941), pp. 68–69.

5. *L'Illustration*, October 1923, p. 306.

6. Mortier, *Le Tourisme*, p. 93. The number was more than two million in 1937.

7. Lucien Dubech, "Le Nouveau Paris," *Le Figaro illustré*, June 1931, p. 12.

8. Charles Epry, "Le Tourisme et nos paysages," *Revue hebdomadaire* 9 (September 1916), p. 211.

9. Gaeton Fouquet, *Les Auberges de la jeunesse* (Paris, 1944), p. 365.

10. Arnold Brémond, *Une Explication du monde ouvrier* (Paris, 1927), p. 112. The American engi-

neer Frederick Winslow Taylor's name was attached to just about any "modernizing" changes designed to increase workers' production.

11. Jacques Valdour, *Les Puissances de désordre: Vers la Révolution, ouvriers de la Plaine Saint-Denis, Aubervilliers, Paris-Belleville* (Paris, 1934), p. 30.

12. Dubech, "Le Nouveau Paris," p. 14.

13. Fouquet, *Les Auberges,* pp. 9, 38–42.

14. C., "Jeux d'été, joie, santé, jeunesse," *L'Illustration,* 29 Aug. 1931, p. 593.

15. On the "function" of song as "collective dream," see Yvonne Bernard, "La Chanson, phénomène social," *Revue française de sociologie* 5 (April–June 1964), pp. 171–172.

16. "Sur la Route un beau dimanche," lyrics by Léo Lelièvre, music by Albert Chantrier. "Ce Petit Chemin," lyrics by J. Nohain, music by Mireille. On the songs of Jean Nohain and Mireille and Jean Tranchant, see Lucienne Cantaloube-Ferrieu, *Chanson et poésie des années 30 aux années 60* (Paris, 1981), pp. 55–65.

17. René Ginet, "La Mort du documentaire," *Critique cinématographique* 6 (September 1931), pp. 21–22.

18. Thiébaut Flory, *Le Mouvement régionaliste français* (Paris, 1966), pp. 2–18.

19. Blaise Cendrars, "Au Hasard des rencontres," *Excelsior,* 26 Apr. 1934, reproduced in Cendrars's *Panorama de la pègre* (Paris, 1986), p. 58.

20. On movies set in the provinces and the quoted directors, see Louis Saurel, "Des horizons," *Ciné-monde,* 7 July 1932, p. 552. On *Poil de carotte* and other provincial realist films see Richard Abel, *French Cinema: The First Wave, 1915–1929* (Princeton, 1984), pp. 103–114. *La Glu* was based on a novel (1881) by Jean Richepin.

21. Serge Dillaz, *La Chanson française sous la Troisième République* (Paris, 1991), pp. 179–181, 212. Christian Plume and Xavier Pasquini, *Tino Rossi* (Paris, 1983).

22. P. H., "Les Projets de Marcel Pagnol," *Critique cinématographique* 13 (March 1933).

23. On films see the excellent study by Claudette Peyrusse, *Le Cinéma méridional: Le Midi dans le cinéma français (1929–1944)* (Toulouse, 1986).

24. See in particular the review of Pierre Wolff in *Paris-Soir,* 31 Nov. 1932: "There is an essentially French film, which has not been directed by a German, and which will please all publics." Pagnol himself stressed that *Fanny* was a "Marseilles film . . . a film that will have nothing American about it" (*Petit Provençal,* 18 June 1932).

25. Geneviève Guillaume-Grimaud, *Le Cinéma du Front populaire* (Paris, 1986), p. 195, reproducing lists from *La Cinématographie française* for 1936, 1937, and 1938.

26. *Le Figaro,* 7 Apr. 1935. Notably, high praise came from Pierre Wolff in *Paris-Soir* and *Comoedia,* in addition to *Le Figaro.* Qualified praise came from Jean Fayard writing in *Candide.* François Vinneuil in *L'Action française* was critical of the characters as morally abhorrent and, in several cases, badly cast.

27. Peyrusse, *Le Cinéma méridional,* pp. 96, 110–115.

28. Guillaume-Grimaud, *Le Cinéma du Front populaire,* pp. 78, 211. *La Terre qui meurt* was one of the first color movies made in France.

29. Françoise Cachin, "Le Paysage du peintre," in *Les Lieux de mémoire,* ed. Pierre Nora, Vol. II, *La Nation* (Paris, 1986), pp. 481–482.

30. Maurice Dide (medical director of public insane asylums), *L'Hystérie et l'évolution humaine* (Paris, 1935), p. 61.

31. "Quand on s'promène au bord de l'eau / Comm' tout est beau . . . / Quel renouveau . . . / Paris au loin nous semble une prison, / On a le coeur plein de chansons." Lyrics by Louis Poterat and Julien Duvivier, music by Maurice Yvain and Jean Sautreuil; ©1936 Editions

Joubert-Royalty, rights transferred to Editions et Productions Théâtrales Chappell. Alain La-combe, *La Chanson dans le Cinéma français* (Paris, 1984), pp. 32–34.

32. See Herman Lebovics, *True France: The Wars over Cultural Identity, 1900–1945* (Ithaca, N.Y., 1992), chapter 2.

33. H. T., "Le Cinéma et la vie moderne," *Le Petit Parisien*, 13 Aug. 1927.

34. Charles-Robert Ageron, "L'Exposition coloniale de 1931, mythe républicain ou mythe impér-ial?" in *Les Lieux de mémoire*, ed. Pierre Nora, Vol. I: *La République* (Paris, 1984), p. 573.

35. Guillaume-Grimaud, *Le Cinéma du front populaire*, p. 121.

36. Jean Tedesco, "Films africains," *Cinéa*, 20 Apr. 1923, p. 7.

37. Abel, *French Cinema*, pp. 154–159. The novel was by Pierre Benoît. Jean Tedesco, "Films africains," *Cinéa*, 20 Apr. 1923.

38. Raymond Asso wrote the lyrics of "Le Fanion de la Légion" especially for young Edith Piaf in the wake of her hit "Mon Légionnaire." On Fernandel's legionnaire epic see Joseph Daniel, *Guerre et cinéma* (Paris, 1972), pp. 185, 163. Jean-Pierre Jeancolas, *15 ans d'années trente: Le cinéma des français, 1929–1944* (Paris, 1983), pp. 250–258.

39. Lyrics by Raymond Asso, music by Marguerite Monnot; ©SEMI, 1936.

40. Guillaume-Grimaud, *Le Cinéma du Front populaire*, p. 122.

41. According to the ratings of *La Cinématographie française*, *Le Quai des brumes* was the second most commercially successful movie of 1938, after the American animated movie *Blanche-Neige* (Snow White); see Guillaume-Grimaud, *Le Cinéma du Front populaire*, p. 197. Paul Achard's review appeared in *Ordre*, 15 June 1938. For more on critical and public reaction, see Guillaume-Grimaud, *Le Cinéma du Front populaire*, pp. 118–121.

42. J.-R. Money, *Le Démocrate*, 30 Nov. 1937. Shanny Peer has a full-length study forthcoming (State University of New York Press) entitled "France on Display: Peasants, Provincials, and Folklore in the 1937 Paris International Exposition."

43. I have summarized materials in the Archives Nationales, F12 12120—a collection of memos, brochures, and newspaper clippings on the Rural Center.

44. For a theoretical discussion of this "dynamic" role of social fictions, see Raymond Ledrut, "So-ciété réelle et société imaginaire," *Cahiers internationaux de sociologie* 82 (Special issue, 1987), pp. 41–56.

CHAPTER 7. BONHOMIE AND MILITANCY

1. The fullest cultural history of the Popular Front period is Pascal Ory's *La Belle Illusion: Culture et politique sous le signe du Front populaire, 1935–1938* (Paris, 1994). In rich detail (1,033 pages) it tells a great deal about the programs of the state and of Popular Front associations. It does not tell much about the commercial productions that my work emphasizes.

2. On fêtes see my "Festivals in Modern France: The Experience of the Third Republic," *Journal of Contemporary History* 12 (1977), pp. 435–460. On postwar workers see Gérard Noiriel, *Les Ouvriers dans la société française, XIXe–XXe siècle* (Paris, 1986), pp. 132–133, 145–150, 154–170.

3. Antoine Prost, *Les Anciens Combattants et la société française, 1914–1939* (Paris, 1977), III, 1. For a recent discussion identifying the Croix de Feu as fascist, see William D. Irvine, "Fascism in France and the Strange Case of the Croix de Feu," *Journal of Modern History* 63 (June 1991), pp. 271–295.

4. See Robert Soucy, *French Fascism: The First Wave, 1924–1933* (New Haven, 1986). The pio-neering "proto-fascist league" (Soucy's words) called the Action française underwent a decline as other extreme-right movements emerged after 1924. The pope's condemnation in 1926 also

weakened the organization that had long attracted Catholic conservatives. Eugen Weber's *Action Française: Royalism and Reaction in Twentieth-Century France* (Stanford, Calif., 1962) is (still) an excellent full treatment.

5. Danielle Tartakowsky, "Front populaire et renouvellement des cultures politiques," *Mouvement Social* 153 (October–December 1990), p. 4. Julian Jackson, *The Popular Front in France Defending Democracy, 1934–38* (Cambridge, England, 1988), pp. 23–27.

6. Aline Coutrot, "Youth Movements in the 1930s," *Journal of Contemporary History* 5, no. 1 (1970), pp. 23–35. By the mid-thirties the strongest youth hostel organization was the CGT-sponsored Centre laïque des Auberges de Jeunesse. It claimed more than 400 auberges, compared to about 200 for the Ligue française des Auberges de Jeunesse.

7. Robert Wohl, *The Generation of 1914* (Cambridge, Mass., 1979). See also Antoine Prost, "Jeunesse et société dans la France de l'entre-deux-guerres," *Vingtième Siècle* 13 (January–March 1987), pp. 35–43. E. and Georges Lefranc, *Le Syndicalisme devant le problème des loisirs* (Paris, Librairie syndicale, n.d., ca. 1936), p. 18. Perhaps the most notable sports organization was the CGT-sponsored Fédération sportive et gymnique du Travail, which organized regional and international athletic competitions.

8. *Le Crapouillot*, July 1934, pp. 29, 34.

9. Serge Berstein and Pierre Milza, *Histoire de la France au XXe siècle*, II: *1930–1945* (Paris, 1991), pp. 130–135.

10. See Jamet's journal, *Notre Front populaire: Journal d'un militant, 1934–1939* (Paris, 1977).

11. Danielle Tartakowsky, "Stratégies de la rue," in Jean-Charles Asselain et al., *La France en mouvement, 1934–1938* (Paris, 1986), p. 32.

12. Tartakowsky, "Stratégies," p. 46.

13. Archives Nationales, F7 13305. Police reports.

14. Tartakowsky, "Stratégies," p. 54.

15. Georges Lefranc, *Histoire du Front populaire (1934–1938)* (Paris, 1965), pp. 82–84.

16. Emmanuel Mounier, "Court Traité de la mythologie de gauche," *Esprit*, 1 Mar. 1938, p. 896. On the Buffalo assembly, see the booklet *14 Juillet 1935*, edited by the Comité national du Rassemblement populaire (Paris, 1935).

17. Tartakowsky, "Stratégies," p. 56.

18. Georges Dauger, "Les Fêtes de la Creuse," *Vingtième Siècle* 27 (July–September 1990), pp. 77–78, gives detailed examples of Popular Front fêtes, as I have described them, in small towns in the Creuse. Other examples are found in Noëlle Gérome, "Les Loisirs populaires de Poitiers," in the same issue of *Vingtième Siècle*, pp. 81–87.

19. Antoine Prost, "Les Manifestations du 12 février 1934 en province," *La France en mouvement*, pp. 25–27.

20. Jean Touchard and Louis Bodin, "L'Etat de l'opinion au début de l'année 1936," in *Colloque sur Léon Blum, Chef de gouvernement, 1936–1937* (Paris, 1967), pp. 61–62.

21. Pierre Birnbaum, *Le Peuple et les gros: Histoire d'un mythe* (Paris, 1979), pp. 27, 29–35, 58. Touchard and Bodin, "L'Etat de l'opinion au début de l'année 1936," pp. 57, 64.

22. Jonathan Buchsbawm, *Cinéma engagé: Film in the Popular Front* (Urbana, Ill., 1988), pp. 28–29.

23. Geneviève Guillaume-Grimaud, *Le Cinéma du Front populaire* (Paris, 1986), p. 121.

24. On the lack of success of "nonconformist" films, see the Marxist film critic Léon Moussinac, "The Condition of International Cinema" (1933), reprinted in Richard Abel, *French Film Theory and Criticism: A Historical Anthology, 1907–1939*, Vol. II (Princeton, 1988), p. 110.

25. Alexander Sesonske, *Jean Renoir: The French Films, 1924–1939* (Cambridge, Mass., 1980), pp. 166–168. Guillaume-Grimaud, *Le Cinéma du Front populaire*, pp. 53–55.

26. Guillaume-Grimaud, *Le Cinéma du Front populaire*, pp. 55–56.

27. Guillaume-Grimaud, *Le Cinéma du Front populaire*, p. 197. The listing first appeared in *La Cinématographie française* 96 (26 Mar. 1937).

28. Ferdinand Lot, "Grand Courant populiste," *Comoedia*, 29 Jan. 1937. Germaine Decaris, review of *Ménilmontant*, in *La Lumière*, 30 Jan. 1937.

29. The hostile critic was A. de Montgon, writing in *Le Petit Bleu*, 6 Dec. 1936. The favorable reviewer was G. Bernard, writing in *Le Matin*, 6 Dec. 1936. The movie had only moderate success at the box office, Chevalier himself observed in his memoirs (*Tempes grises* [Paris, 1948], p. 28). Chevalier's luster as a movie actor had faded as rivals rose; he was no longer young nor the leading man most in demand.

30. The dark comedy *L'Homme du jour* met with a lukewarm response. See John W. Martin, *The Golden Age of French Cinema, 1929–1939* (Boston, 1983), pp. 86–87.

31. "Au Lycée Papillon," *Comoedia*, 6 Apr. 1936.

32. Other songs in this vein include "Qu'est-ce qu'on attend pour être heureux?" (lyrics by André Hornez, music by Paul Misraki; ©CIMG, 1937). The lyrics are reproduced in Saka, *La chanson française*, pp. 129–130. The snappy foxtrot "Pourquoi se biler pour rien" (1935) offered more cheery advice for the anxious and troubled: don't worry or feel bad today; there'll be time tomorrow; just say, "everything's fine."

33. Simone Weil, "Journal d'usine" (written in May 1935), in *La Condition ouvrière* (Paris, 1951), p. 83; see also pp. 106–107.

34. On cultural activities of the Popular Front era, see Pascal Ory's monumental work *La Belle Illusion*. See also Buchsbawm, *Cinéma engagé*, pp. 42–54.

35. "Y a trop de tout" was written by Paul Vaillant-Couturier and Maurice Marc, members of a worker-theater group that was a branch of the AEAR; see Serge Dillaz, *La Chanson française de contestation de la Commune à Mai 68* (Paris, 1973), p. 81.

36. On "Le Pain, la Paix et la Liberté," see Robert Brécy, *Florilège de la chanson révolutionnaire de 1789 au Front populaire* (Paris, 1978), pp. 268–286. Lyrics by Roger Duvert, music by Jean-Claude Simon. A similar song is Eugène Bizeau's "La Chanson de Paris," the text of which is also found in Brécy.

37. Sesonske, *Jean Renoir*, chapter 15; Buchsbawm, *Cinéma engagé*, chapter 2. Michel Fauré, *Le Groupe Octobre* (Paris, 1977), pp. 315–318. A memo for the minister of national education dated 17 June 1936 (Archives Nationales, F21 4695 [3]) explains that the film was not to be shown in public halls during the electoral period because the Action Française and the Croix de Feu "would present propaganda films which would provoke disorders in the movie theaters of Paris and the departments."

38. Jean-Pierre Rioux, *Révolutionnaires du Front populaire* (Paris, 1973), p. 119.

39. Antoine Prost has emphasized this view of the strikes as fêtes in "Les Grèves de juin 1936," in *Colloque sur Léon Blum, Chef de gouvernement, 1936–1937* (Paris, 1967), pp. 81–82. Michel Collinet had made the same point in *L'Ouvrier français, esprit du syndicalisme* (Paris, 1952).

40. *Sport*, 17 June 1936, p. 1.

41. *Sport*, 10 June 1936.

42. Lyrics by Paul Misraki, Bach, and Laverne, music by Paul Misraki; Editions Ray Ventura, 1936.

CHAPTER 8. STRUGGLE AND VACATION

1. Most notably, the Croix de Feu was transformed into the Parti Social Français, which became the biggest political party in France. On the historians' debate about whether the Croix de

Feu was fascist, see William D. Irvine, "Fascism in France and the Strange Case of the Croix de Feu," *Journal of Modern History* 63 (June 1991), pp. 271–295. See also Julian Jackson, *The Popular Front in France Defending Democracy, 1934–38* (Cambridge, England, 1988), pp. 253–254.

2. Rosemonde Sanson, *Les 14 juillet: Fête et conscience nationale, 1789–1975* (Paris, 1976), pp. 118–119. See also Roger Bordier, *36, la fête* (Paris, 1985), pp. 60–61 and photos following p. 78.

3. Maurice Savin, "'Le 14 Juillet' de Romain Rolland," *Nouvelle Revue Française*, 1 Aug. 1936, pp. 396–398. Pascal Ory, *La Belle Illusion: Culture et politique sous le signe du Front populaire, 1935–1938* (Paris, 1994), pp. 400–404.

4. Marc Boyer, "1936 et les vacances des Français," *Le Mouvement social* (July–September 1990), pp. 35–44, esp. p. 44.

5. Jacques Valdour, *Le Faubourg* (Paris, 1925), p. 20.

6. Madame Gaston Etienne, *Utilisation des loisirs des travailleurs* (Paris, 1935), p. 50. Comité national d'études sociales et politiques (session of 2 Mar. 1931), pp. 15, 22.

7. Lyrics by Jeanne Perret (1933), music by Dmitry Shostakovich (1932). The French lyrics are reproduced in Bénigno Cacérès, *Allons au-devant de la vie: La naissance du temps des loisirs en 1936* (Paris, 1981), pp. 74–75. I have translated and paraphrased some excerpts: "Ma blonde, entends-tu dans la ville / Siffler les fabri's et les trains? / Allons au-devant de la brise, / Allons au-devant du matin. / Debout ma blond', chantons au vent, / Debout amis! / Il va vers le soleil levant / Notre pays. / La joie te réveille, ma blonde / Allons nous unir à ce choeur; / Marchons vers la gloire et le monde, / Marchons au-devant du bonheur. / Et nous saluerons la brigade / Et nous sourirons aux amis. / Mettons en commun, camarades, / Nos plans, nos travaux, nos soucis. / Dans leur triomphale allégresse / Les jeunes s'élancent en chantant, / Bientôt une nouvelle jeunesse / Viendra au-devant de nos rangs."

8. Boyer, "1936 et les Vacances des Français," pp. 35–44, esp. p. 44. The exact number of vacationers is unknown. Some 560,000 people quickly took advantage of special reduced-fare train tickets for August trips; many others went by car and bicycle.

9. *Le Petit Dauphinois*, 18 Aug. 1937. On Popular Front cultural programs, see Pascal Ory, "La Politique culturelle du premier gouvernement Blum," *La Nouvelle Revue socialiste* 10–11 (1975), pp. 75–93, and Ory, *La Belle Illusion*.

10. In *La Belle Illusion*, Ory devotes hundreds of pages to the history of the cultural programs I have the space only to summarize. See also Jackson, *The Popular Front*, chapter 4, "The Cultural Explosion."

11. *Le Petit Dauphinois*, 18 Aug. 1937.

12. Henri Noguères, *La Vie quotidienne au temps du Front populaire* (Paris, 1977), pp. 150–154. Henri Dubief, *Le Déclin de la IIIe République, 1929–1938* (Paris, 1976), p. 208. On the economic problems, see Jackson, *The Popular Front*, pp. 169–177.

13. Valérie Colin-Simart and Laurence Benaïam, "Music-Hall 1938: La France chante sur un volcan," *Historama* 29 (July 1986), p. 81.

14. "Tout le jour, mon coeur bat, chavire et chancelle / C'est l'amour qui vient avec je ne sais quoi / C'est l'amour, bonjour bonjour les demoiselles / Y'a d'la joie, partout y'a d'la joie." Lyrics by Charles Trenet, music by Charles Trenet and Michel Emer; ©Raoul Breton Editeur, 1937.

15. Charles Trenet, *Boum! Chansons folles* (Paris, 1988), pp. 21–23. Lyrics by Charles Trenet, music by Charles Trenet and Paul Misraki; ©Editions Raoul Breton, 1937.

16. Lyrics and music by Charles Trenet; ©Editions Raoul Breton, 1938.

17. Geneviève Beauvarlet, *Trenet* (Paris, 1983), p. 59.

18. *Paris qui chante*, 1 Apr. 1939, p. 13.

19. See Lucienne Cantaloube-Ferrieu, *Chanson et poésie des années 30 aux années 60* (Paris, 1981), pp. 35–38.

20. *Paris qui chante*, 1 Apr. 1939, p. 12. The lyrics of "Ça . . . c'est d'la bagnole" appear in Pierre Saka's *La Chanson française* (Paris, 1988), pp. 131–132; lyrics by Georgius, music by Henri Poussigue; ©Editions Paul Beuscher, 1938.

21. Serge Dillaz, *La Chanson sous la Troisième République* (Paris, 1991), pp. 235–236. "Amusez-vous," lyrics by Albert Willemetz, music by W. R. Heymann; ©Editions Salabert, 1934.

22. Lyrics by André Hornez, music by Johnny Hess; ©CIMG, 1938. Saka, *La Chanson française*, pp. 134–135.

23. Pierre Varenne, "Tino Rossi dans 'Plaisirs de Paris,'" *Paris-Soir*, 16 Oct. 1936.

24. Merry Bromberger, "Est-ce un Record?" *L'Intransigeant*, 17 June 1939. Reportedly, Rossi had a machine that opened 200 letters in a morning.

25. Cantaloube-Ferrieu, *Chanson et poésie*, pp. 29–33. Pierre Duclos et Georges Martin, *Piaf* (Paris, 1993), pp. 93–97. "Sans lendemain" (1938) was sung by Fréhel at the end of the film *L'Entraineuse* (lyrics by Michel Vaucaire, music by Georges Van Parys; ©Editions Filmatone, 1938, rights transferred to Intersong Paris SA, rights transferred to Warner Chappell Music France). On "La Java bleue" (lyrics by Géo Koger and Noël Renard, music by Vincent Scotto; ©Paul Beuscher éditeur, 1938) see Jean-Claude Klein, *Florilège de la chanson française* (Paris, 1990), p. 194. Important songs of the realist repertory during this period included Fréhel's "Je n'attends plus rien" and "Comme un Moineau," and Piaf's "Les Mômes de la cloche" and "Mon Coeur est au coin de la rue."

26. Louis Chevalier, *Montmartre du plaisir et du crime* (Paris, 1980), p. 451.

27. René Rémond and Janine Bourdin, eds., *La France et les Français en 1938–1939* (Paris, 1978), p. 16.

28. Pierre Miquel, *Histoire de la radio et de la télévision* (Paris, 1984), p. 46, comparing radio's lulling effect to the notoriously dull speeches given at agricultural fairs.

29. Marie-Geneviève Chavignard and Nicole Faure, "Système de valeurs et de références dans la presse féminine," in Rémond and Bourdin, eds., *La France et les Français*, pp. 43–50.

30. Rémond and Bourdin, eds., *La France et les Français*, p. 16.

31. For a particularly vivid discussion of "communion" in the cinemas see René Vincent, "Les Horizons du cinéma," *Les Cahiers de combat* 5 (1939), p. 3.

32. Norman King, "Patrie et nation: Fictions populistes dans le *Napoléon* d'Abel Gance et *La Marseillaise* de Jean Renoir," *Europe* (November–December 1988), pp. 68–75.

33. Geneviève Guillaume-Grimaud, *Le Cinéma du Front populaire* (Paris, 1986), pp. 94–112.

34. John W. Martin, *The Golden Age of French Cinema, 1929–1939* (Boston, 1983), pp. 95–98. Ginette Vincendeau has shown how the scenarios and camera techniques made Jean Gabin the clear hero with whom both men and women could identify. See her article "Community, Nostalgia, and the Spectacle of Masculinity," *Screen* 26 (November–December 1985), pp. 18–38. On women in film see Véronique Sefani and Pierre Sefani, "L'Image de la femme dans quelques films de 1930 à 1939," *Cahiers de la Cinémathèque* 23–24 (Christmas 1977), p. 60—a study of 47 films. See also Susan Hayward, *French National Cinema* (London, 1993), pp. 171–172. Arletty played similar legend-building roles in *Fric-Frac* (1939) and *Circonstances atténuantes* (1939).

35. Cacérès, *Allons au-devant de la vie*, p. 256.

36. For the film scripts of the different endings, see Guillaume-Grimaud, *Le Cinéma du Front populaire*, pp. 179–184. Renoir's *Les Bas Fonds* (adapted from a Gorky play), which came out in December 1936, offered a similar dialogue of optimism and pessimism. As its characters were not so clearly French, and space not permitting encyclopedic treatment of similar films, I have had

to slight it. See Alexander Sesonske, *Jean Renoir: The French Films, 1924–1939* (Cambridge, Mass., 1980), chapter 17.

37. Vincendeau, "Community, Nostalgia, and the Spectacle of Masculinity." Vincendeau's analysis of the Gabin myth offers some excellent new perspectives on the appeal of Gabin and the workings of community, although to my mind she has overstated the male protagonist's regression and passivity.

38. Guillaume-Grimaud, *Le Cinéma du Front populaire*, pp. 153–154. Joseph Daniel, *Guerre et cinéma* (Paris, 1972), pp. 137–142.

39. Chantal's review appeared in *Le Journal de la femme*, 27 May 1938.

40. For the classification of leading actors and movies (lists taken from *La Cinématographie française*) see Guillaume-Grimaud, *Le Cinéma du Front populaire*, pp. 195, 197.

41. For lists (taken from *La Cinématographie française*) of the most successful films of 1936–1938 see Guillaume-Grimaud, *Le Cinéma du Front populaire*, p. 197.

42. René Bizet, *Le Jour-Echo de Paris*, 8 May 1938.

43. The screenplay may be found in *L'Avant-scène du cinéma* 374 (October 1988). In the same issue see the important interpretive article by Michel Marie, "Les cent sous de Nazarède (*Hôtel du Nord*, Marcel Carné, 1938)," pp. 7–12.

44. Pierre Birnbaum, *Un Mythe politique: "La République juive"* (Paris, 1988), pp. 267–292. Jean-Pierre Jeancolas, *15 ans d'années trente: Le cinéma des Français, 1929–1944* (Paris, 1983), pp. 129–130.

45. Guy Bourde, "La Grève du 30 novembre 1938," *Le Mouvement social* 55 (April–June 1966), pp. 87–91.

46. Daniel, *Guerre et cinéma*, pp. 149–164. Jeancolas, *15 ans d'années trente*, pp. 243–247.

47. Sanson, *Les 14 juillet*, pp. 122–124.

48. Guillaume-Grimaud, *Le Cinéma du Front populaire*, pp. 75–76 (on the film and its reception). The film script was by Jacques Prévert and Jacques Viot.

49. Jeancolas, *15 ans d'années trente*, p. 296.

50. André Braun-Larrieu, *Le Rôle social du cinéma* (Paris, 1938), p. 26.

51. Charles William Brooks, "Jean Renoir's *The Rules of the Game*," *French Historical Studies* 7, no. 2 (Fall 1971), p. 281. Jean Doucet and Gilles Nadeau, *Paris Cinéma: Une ville vue par le cinéma, de 1895 à nos jours* (Paris, 1987), p. 136.

52. *Les Cinq Sous de Lavarède*, directed by Maurice Cammage, was released in March 1939. The débrouillard becomes a sports hero as well as a rich heir and successful suitor of his girlfriend. Toward the end of the story, as Lavarède makes his way back to Paris, he takes a fisherman's car (which runs out of gas) and then steals a bicycle and, after being pulled at top speed by a passing truck, slips into the Tour de France race with crowds cheering him as a winner.

53. *Match*, 24 Aug. 1939, pp. 5–7.

54. Pierre Ducrocq, *L'Ordre*, 18 Mar. 1939.

55. Pierre Guillen, "Opinion publique et politique extérieure en France, 1914–1940," in *Opinion publique et politique extérieure* (Rome, 1984), pp. 52–53.

CHAPTER 9. CULTURAL STRATEGIES IN A NEW WAR

1. Georges Sadoul, *Journal de guerre* (Paris, 1977), pp. 55–56. Entry for 13 Oct. 1939. "J'attendrai," lyrics by Louis Poterat, music by Dino Olivieri; Paris: P. Leonardi Editeur, 1938.

2. On public opinion see J. L. Crémieux-Brilhac, "L'Opinion publique française, l'Angleterre et la Guerre (Sept. 1939–Juin 1940)," in Comité d'histoire de la deuxième guerre mondiale, *Français et Britanniques dans la drôle de guerre* (Paris, 1979), pp. 4–8.

3. *Le Petit Parisien*, 25 Sept. 1939, p. 2.

4. See, for example, *L'Ether dechainé* and *Le Reveil de Beauséjour* in the archives of the Armée de Terre, Vincennes, Témoignage 104. On the gaiety of the younger men resembling their elders, see Roland Dorgelès, *La Drôle de guerre, 1939–1940* (Paris, 1957), pp. 50–51 (observations made in December 1939). See also Guy Rossi-Landi, *La Drôle de guerre: La vie politique en France, 2 septembre 1939–10 mai 1940* (Paris, 1971), p. 175, n. 35, quoting *Le Temps*, 25 Nov. 1939, and Henri Amoureux, *La Grande Histoire des Français sous l'Occupation*, Vol. I: *Le Peuple du désastre* (Paris, 1976), pp. 176, 232, 244–245, 288–289, 294.

5. *Match*, 19 Oct. 1939. See also Hervé Le Boterf, *Le Théâtre en uniforme* (Paris, 1973), pp. 54–55.

6. Maurice Chevalier, *Tempes grises* (Paris, 1948), pp. 50–51.

7. *L'Illustration*, 25 Nov. 1939, p. 335.

8. Rossi-Landi, *La Drôle de guerre*, pp. 175–176.

9. Dorgelès, *La Drôle de guerre*, pp. 50, 97–98, 187. On wine and home-front activities for the soldiers, see Philippe Richer, *La Drôle de guerre des Français, 2 septembre 1939–10 mai 1940* (Paris, 1990), pp. 277–284.

10. *Le Canard enchaîné*, 6 Dec. 1939.

11. Lyrics by Jean Boyer, music by Georges Van Parys; ©Editions Salabert, 1939.

12. War correspondent and former poilu Roland Dorgelès, for example (in *La Drôle de guerre*, pp. 100–101), testified that the men shared a mood of optimism. For a balanced account of reports about morale, see Rossi-Landi, *La Drôle de guerre*, p. 177.

13. Sadoul, *Journal de guerre*, pp. 100–101, 106–107, 123. On attitudes toward the officers, see also Charles Rist, *Une saison gâtée: Journal de la guerre et de l'occupation (1939–1945)*, ed. Jean-Noël Jeanneney (Paris, 1983), p. 88, entry for Aug. 7, 1940, and Philippe Masson, "Moral et propagande," in Comité d'histoire de la deuxième guerre mondiale, *Français et Britanniques dans la drôle de guerre*, pp. 164–165.

14. Rossi-Landi, *La Drôle de guerre*, pp. 171–173.

15. English lyrics by Jimmy Kennedy, music by Michael Carr. See Georges Coulonges, *La Chanson en son temps: De Béranger au jukebox* (Paris, 1969), p. 147. See also Dorgelès, *La Drôle de guerre*. According to Gilles Ragache and Jean-Robert Ragache (*La Vie quotidienne des écrivains et des artistes sous l'occupation, 1940–1944* [Paris, 1988], p. 143), it was Ray Ventura's rendition of "On ira pendre notre linge sur la ligne Siegfried" that "put balm in hearts" in November 1939.

16. Rossi-Landi, *La Drôle de guerre*, p. 176.

17. Jean-Pierre Jeancolas, *15 ans d'années trente: Le cinéma des français, 1929–1944* (Paris, 1983), p. 280. René Noëll reports, however, that *La Bête humaine* played in Perpignan during this period. Some movie theater managers ignored the government's ban. National as well as local censorship on moral and political grounds had been at work since the First World War—under Popular Front governments as well as rightist governments. Any film offensive to the army, government officials, or teachers could be banned, or approved only after cuts were made. See Jean Bancal, *La Censure cinématographique* (Paris, 1934), and Paul Leglise, *Histoire de la politique du cinéma français: Le Cinéma et la IIIe République* (Paris, 1970), esp. chapter 21.

18. Rossi-Landi, *La Drôle de guerre*, p. 174.

19. *Match*, 7 Dec. 1939. "Paris sera toujours Paris," lyrics by Albert Willemetz, music by Casimir Oberfeld; ©Editions Salabert, 1939.

20. Chevalier, *Tempes grises*, pp. 50–52.

21. Le Boterf, *Le Théâtre en uniforme*, pp. 28–29.

22. Amoureux, *Peuple du désastre*, pp. 288–294.

23. Pierre Laborie, "Vichy et ses représentations dans l'imaginaire social," in *Le Régime de*

Vichy et les Français, ed. Jean-Pierre Azéma and François Bédarida (Paris, 1992), pp. 500–503, and Jean-Marie Fonneau, "L'évolution de l'opinion publique de 1940 à 1944," in the same volume, p. 507.

24. Alphonse de Parvillez, "L'Assault des forces invisibles" (Paris, 1939), pp. 34, 57.

25. Lucien Rebatet, *Les Tribus du cinéma et du théâtre* (Paris, 1941), p. 87. Rebatet, under the pseudonym François Vinneuil, had long been the movie critic for the newspaper *Action Française.*

26. Pierre Birnbaum, *Le Peuple et les gros: Histoire d'un mythe* (Paris, 1979), pp. 61–62. See Hervé Le Boterf, *La Vie parisienne sous l'occupation* (Paris, 1975), II, 207–211, for a survey of anti-Semitic writings of the period.

27. Rebatet, *Les Tribus,* pp. 12, 16–17, 48, 51, 86–87.

28. Rebatet, *Les Tribus,* pp. 108–109.

29. Rebatet, *Les Tribus,* pp. 87, 97, 120–122. On Vichy's anti-Semitic policies and actions see Michael R. Marrus and Robert O. Paxton, *Vichy France and the Jews* (New York, 1981).

30. François Bédarida, "Vichy et la crise de la conscience française," in *Le Régime de Vichy et les Français,* ed. Azéma and Bédarida, p. 82. Marrus and Paxton make it clear that the Vichy government ordered the internment of "foreign" Jews (in October 1940) before the Germans took such a step in the occupied zone; see *Vichy France and the Jews,* p. 12. On Jews and the cinema, see Evelyn Ehrlich, *Cinema of Paradox: French Filmmaking under the German Occupation* (New York, 1985), chapter 4.

31. Laborie, "Vichy et ses représentations dans l'imaginaire social," p. 502. Pierre Servent, *Le Mythe Pétain* (Paris, 1992).

32. Bédarida, "Vichy et la crise," p. 85.

33. Serge Berstein and Pierre Milza, *Histoire de la France au XXe siècle,* II: *1930–1945* (Paris, 1991), p. 325. On the song "Maréchal, nous voilà!" see Jean-Claude Klein, *Florilège de la chanson française* (Paris, 1990), p. 197.

34. Christian Faure, *Le Projet culturel de Vichy* (Lyons, 1989). Faure stresses that this social ideology dominated Vichy until late 1942, when all of France was occupied by the Germans. For the contributions of anthropology and folklore studies to that ideology about a narrow, essential French identity, see Herman Lebovics, *True France: The Wars over Cultural Identity, 1900–1945* (Ithaca, N.Y.: 1992).

35. Christian Faure, "Le Film documentaire sous Vichy," *Ethnologie française* (July–September 1988), p. 284.

36. W. D. Halls, *The Youth of Vichy France* (Oxford, 1981), chapter 11.

37. Jean-Louis Gay-Lescot, "La Politique sportive de Vichy," in *Politiques et pratiques culturelles dans la France de Vichy,* ed. Jean-Pierre Rioux (Paris, 1988), pp. 57–77. After the Liberation, Nakache returned alive but alone.

38. André Halimi, *Chantons sous l'occupation* (Paris, 1976), p. 10.

39. Ragache and Ragache, *La Vie quotidienne des écrivains et des artistes,* p. 143.

40. Ragache and Ragache, *La Vie quotidienne,* p. 143. On the general migration of film personnel, see Colin Crisp, *The Classic French Cinema, 1930–1960* (Bloomington, Ind., 1993), pp. 186–196.

41. *La Semaine à Paris,* 16–23 Sept. 1941.

42. Edward Behr, *The Good Frenchman: The True Story of the Life and Times of Maurice Chevalier* (New York, 1993), pp. 260–278, emphasizing the relationship with Radio-Paris as the source of Chevalier's later troubles with the Resistance.

43. "Maréchal, nous voilà!" March, lyrics by A. Montagard, music by A. Montagard and C. Courtioux; ©Editions Musicales du Vert luisant, 1941.

44. *La Semaine à Paris,* 16–23 Sept. 1941.

45. Robert O. Paxton, *Vichy France: Old Guard and New Order, 1940–1944* (New York, 1972), p. 147. Paxton cites *La Légion* 9 (February 1942).

46. *Le Petit Parisien,* 25 Nov. 1941.

47. *Le Petit Parisien,* 1 Dec. 1941.

48. The documentary had its commercial première in 1971. For the full text see Marcel Ophuls, *Le Chagrin et la pitié* (Paris, 1980); the Chevalier interview appears on pp. 195–196.

49. "La Symphonie des semelles du bois," recorded in 1943. Lyrics by Albert Willemetz and Maurice Chevalier, music by Vincent Scotto.

50. Pierre Saka, *La Chanson française à travers ses succès* (Paris, 1988), p. 152.

51. Halimi, *Chantons,* pp. 145–146.

52. Klein, *Florilège de la chanson française,* p. 198. For a full history, see Sarah Fishman, *We Will Wait: Wives of French Prisoners of War, 1940–1945* (New Haven and London, 1991).

53. On women's lives, see Dominique Veillon, "La Vie quotidienne des femmes," in *Le Régime de Vichy et les Français,* ed. Jean-Pierre Azéma and François Bédarida (Paris, 1992), pp. 631–632, 635–638.

54. Serge Dillaz, *La Chanson française de contestation de la Commune à Mai 68* (Paris, 1973), p. 90 n. 32.

55. Lyrics and music by Charles Trenet; ©Editions Salabert, 1942.

56. Hervé Le Boterf, *La Vie parisienne sous l'occupation,* Vol. II (Paris, 1975), pp. 338–339.

57. The number of movies showing during the "black years" was at a historic low, considerably lower than before the war, but French production increased every year until 1944. François Garçon, *De Blum à Pétain: Cinéma et société française, 1936–1944* (Paris, 1984), pp. 33, 43–44. Ehrlich, *Cinema of Paradox,* pp. 11, 20, 27–28. The debate about how French spectators reacted to German films goes on unresolved; see Jeancolas, *15 ans d'années trente,* pp. 312–314. See also Jacques Siclier, *La France de Pétain et son cinéma* (Paris, 1981), pp. 19–20. Siclier, who was a lycée student during the occupation, draws on his personal notes and memories of audiences and movies in Troyes.

58. Jacques Siclier, "The Psychology of the Spectator, or the 'Cinema of Vichy' Did Not Exist," in Mary Lea Bandy, ed., *Rediscovering French Film* (New York, 1983), pp. 142–146. See also Siclier's *La France de Pétain et son cinéma,* chapter 3 ("Le Domaine limité de la propagande politique") and p. 88. Two notable vilifying French "documentaries" (both produced in Paris by the Germans) were *Les Corrupteurs* (1942) and *Forces occultes* (1943); see Jeancolas, *15 ans d'années trente,* pp. 354–358. One of the most patently ideological fiction films was Jean-Paul Paulin's Nativity story set in Provence, *La Nuit merveilleuse,* which came out in 1941; see Siclier, ibid., p. 83.

59. Garçon, *De Blum à Pétain,* pp. 180, 183–184.

60. Siclier, *La France de Pétain et son cinéma,* on Trenet and Tino, pp. 186–188; on Fernandel, pp. 185–186; on René Dary, chapter 7. On types see also Jean-Pierre Bertin-Maghit, *Le Cinéma français sous Vichy: Les films français de 1940 à 1944* (Paris, 1980).

61. Marcel Oms (on Gaby Morlay), "Le Charme discret du cinéma de Vichy," *Les Cahiers de la cinématographie* (Winter 1973), p. 68. Siclier, *La France de Pétain et son cinéma,* on Gaby Morlay, chapter 6.

62. On the "fantastic" movies (including Marcel L'Herbier's *La Nuit fantastique,* Carné's *Les Visiteurs du soir,* and Jean Delannoy's *L'Eternel retour*), see Siclier, *La France de Pétain et son cinéma,* chapter 9. Siclier dismisses as "nonsense" the political interpretation of *Les Visiteurs du soir*—the "rumor" that the devil represented the Nazis and that the beating heart in the stone statue represented undying France. Jean-Pierre Jeancolas strongly agrees; see his *15 ans d'an-*

nées trente, p. 328. The difficult methodological question here is how close to the evidence should the historian stay? In an elaborate psychoanalytic and semiological analysis, Jean-Pierre Bertin-Maghit has argued that films of the period did "mirror" the concerns (even the unconscious) of most people and did serve Vichy's cause. Unfortunately, he cannot demonstrate that his complex schemata corresponded to what the people in the audiences thought and felt. See Bertin-Maghit, *Le Cinéma français sous Vichy*.

63. Jean Laffray in *L'Oeuvre* (26 May 1942) saw the story as an indictment of bourgeois society. Georges Champeaux in *Le Cri du peuple* (3 June 1942) saw therein a portrayal of some prewar youth. Maurice Rousseau du Gard in *Voix françaises* saw immorality in "this strange association of diverse social milieus."

64. On *Goupi mains-rouges, Le Corbeau,* and other dark films, see Siclier, *La France de Pétain et son cinéma,* pp. 62–63, 214–217. The script of *Les Anges du péché* was by Jean Giraudoux, whose literary fame brought special attention to the film. Critics gave the movie highest praise, especially for its refreshing break with sanctimonious depictions of Catholic life. The tornado image came from Roger Régent in his review in *Les Nouveaux temps,* 9 Oct. 1943. The worries were expressed in reviews by Audiberti, writing in *Comoedia* (9 Oct. 1943) and André Le Bret in *Paris-Soir,* 6 Oct. 1943. Some reviews pointed out that some years previously a wave of anonymous letters hit Tulle, causing great distress. *Le Corbeau,* like *Les Inconnus dans la maison,* was produced by the German-owned company Continental Films, which made 30 of the 220 films released during the war. Continental's films did not have to obtain preliminary approval by German censors as French-produced movies did, and they also passed immediately into the Vichy zone without being subject to French censorship. The Resistance and Vichy attacked *Le Corbeau* as German anti-French propaganda, but the evidence is strong that the Germans had no significant role in shaping the film; see Ehrlich, *Cinema of Paradox,* pp. 177–183.

65. Yves Malestroit in *Nouvelles continentales* (2 Oct. 1943) found *Adieu Léonard* confusing but asked if the makers had wanted to "demonstrate pleasantly that the little crafts were honorable and that money does not make happiness." Hélène Garcin in *Aujourd'hui* (6 Sept. 1943) treated the movie as a zany comedy. The spectators' "protest" against the line about money was reported by Pierre Maurice in *La Gerbe* (9 May 1943), among others. On *Premier de cordée* see Siclier, *La France de Pétain et son cinéma,* pp. 201–202. François Vinneuil's review of *Le Ciel est à vous* appeared in *Le Petit Parisien,* 5 Feb. 1944. The last review cited (author unnamed) appeared in *La Révolution nationale,* 5 Feb. 1944.

66. Paul-Louis Thirard, "Eloge de *Pontcarral,*" *Cahiers de la Cinématographie,* 8 (Winter 1973), p. 30. Reviewers described audience reactions; see Pierre Ducrocq's review in *L'Appel,* 17 Dec. 1942, and François Vinneuil's in *Je suis partout,* 18 Dec. 1942.

67. On Pierre de Hérain's *Monsieur des Lourdines,* see Siclier, *La France de Pétain et son cinéma,* pp. 136–138. In *Nouvelles continentales* (26 June 1943), Yves Malestroit effusively praised the beautiful photography without dwelling on the contemporary political themes. Reviews of Jean Choux's *Port d'attache* were more dismissive of the political message while appreciating the action and landscapes. See, for example, P. Michaut's review in *Information musicale,* 19 Feb. 1943. The reviews were overall less favorable than those for *Monsieur des Lourdines.*

68. In praising Robert Bresson's *Les Anges du péché,* for example, the reviewer for *Je suis partout* (9 July 1943) noted that in a large boulevard hall the diverse audience's close, respectful attention to the difficult film was another "proof that this public was up to more than . . . all the sanctimonious weak tea that the Vichy beadles have given us to drink under the pretext of edification." Similar comments appeared in reviews of *Goupi mains-rouges;* see, for example, *La Gerbe,* 22 Apr. 1943.

69. Siclier, *La France de Pétain et son cinéma*, p. 36, recounts his memories of audience reactions in Troyes in 1944.

70. René Rémond, introduction, in Azéma and Bédarida, eds., *Le Régime de Vichy et les Français*, pp. 16; Bédarida, "Vichy et la crise," p. 82.

71. See the public opinion studies by Jean-Marie Flonneau, John Sweets, and others in Azéma and Bédarida, eds., *Le Régime de Vichy et les Français*, part seven.

72. Dillaz, *La Chanson française*, p. 89. Lyrics by Maurice Chevalier, music by Henri Betti; ©Editions Salabert, 1941.

73. Dillaz, *La Chanson française*, p. 91.

74. Dillaz, *La Chanson française*, pp. 91–92, 216–217. Klein, *Florilège de la chanson française*, p. 203. The first set of lyrics by Anna Marly were replaced at the end of May 1943 by new ones by Maurice Druon and Joseph Kessel. The second version became famous.

75. Siclier, *La France de Pétain et son cinéma*, pp. 241–243.

76. Lyrics by Maurice Vandair, music by Henri Bourtayre; ©Beuscher, 1944; see Pierre Saka, *La Chanson française à travers ses succès* (Paris, 1988), p. 158. On the purification committee's decisions on individual entertainers, see the list of names and sanctions in Jean-Pierre Bertin-Maghit, *Le Cinéma sous l'occupation* (Paris, 1989), pp. 430–436.

77. Jeancolas, *15 ans d'années trente*, pp. 341–342.

78. Jean-Pierre Jeancolas, "Beneath the Despair, the Show Goes on: Marcel Carné's *Les Enfants du paradis* (1943–1945)," in Susan Hayward and Ginette Vincendeau, eds., *French Film Texts and Contexts* (London and New York, 1990), pp. 117–125. For a fuller treatment see Edward Baron Turk, *Child of Paradise: Marcel Carné and the Golden Age of French Cinema* (Cambridge, Mass., 1989).

79. I refer to the following of Piaf's songs: "Paris est à nous" (1945) by Anna Marly; "C'est toujours la même histoire" (1944), lyrics by H. Contet and music by D. J. White; "J'm'en fous pas mal" (1946), lyrics and music by M. Emer; "L'Hymne à l'amour" (1949), lyrics by Piaf; "L'Accordéoniste" (1947), music and lyrics by M. Emer. See Lucienne Cantaloube-Ferrieu, *Chanson et poésie des années 30 aux années 60* (Paris, 1981), pp. 296–298, 328.

80. On Montand, Lemarque, and Mouloudji, see Cantaloube-Ferrieu, *Chanson et poésie*, pp. 304–307. Cantaloube-Ferrieu stresses the influence of the surrealists and the freshness of postwar songs.

CONCLUSION

Note to epigraph: Pierre-Augustin Caron de Beaumarchais, *Le Mariage de Figaro*, X, xix.

1. Marc Bloch, *Strange Defeat*, trans. Gerard Hopkins (New York, 1968), p. 167.

2. Brian Rigby, *Popular Culture in Modern France: A Study of Cultural Discourse* (London, 1991), provides a clear, perceptive discussion of French critiques of popular culture.

3. See, for example, the classic essay by Theodor Adorno, "The Culture Industry: Enlightenment as Mass Deception" (written in 1944), in Max Horkheimer and Theodor W. Adorno, *Dialectic of Enlightenment* (New York, 1972), pp. 120–167.

SELECTED
BIBLIOGRAPHY

A NOTE ON SOURCES

The Rondel Collection in the Bibliothèque de l'Arsenal in Paris has given me access to an organized mass of materials from newspapers and magazines on singers, actors, music halls, songs, and films. I have also used the invaluable resources of the Bibliothèque nationale, the Bibliothèque de documentation internationale contemporaine at Nanterre, the archives of the Paris Préfecture de Police, and the Archives nationales.

One of the delights of studying the era of the world wars was discovering and rediscovering many songs and films that are still enjoyable. The successful songs of the period are readily available in Paris on cassette and compact disc. I have found much of the sheet music in the department of music of the Bibliothèque nationale, in the Paris Police Archives (for songs of the First World War), and in Parisian flea markets. Many movies are now more easily accessible thanks to videocassettes. In Paris one can see the old films not only at the Cinémathèque, but also at the Vidéothèque de Paris in the Forum des Halles, as I did when I lived near there in 1988–89. In the United States one can find the films of Marcel Pagnol and Jean Renoir and some of Marcel Carné's in many larger video stores. Less famous films may be rented by mail from specialty video stores like Paname Video in Baldwin, New York, and Facets Multimedia in Chicago. The screenplays of important films are also readily available; a number appeared in *L'Avant-scène du Cinéma* (for example, *La Grande Illusion* in the December 1962 issue, *Les Enfants du paradis* in the July 1967 issue, *A*

Nous la liberté in November 1968, *Pépé le Moko* in June 1981, and *Hôtel du Nord* in October 1988).

BOOKS AND ARTICLES

Abel, Richard. *French Cinema: The First Wave, 1915–1929.* Princeton: Princeton University Press, 1984.

————. *French Film Theory and Criticism: A Historical Anthology, 1907–1939.* 2 vols. (Vol. II: 1929–1939). Princeton: Princeton University Press, 1988.

Andrew, Dudley. *Mists of Regret: Culture and Sensibility in Classic French Film.* Princeton: Princeton University Press, 1995.

Asselain, Jean-Charles, et al. *La France en mouvement, 1934–1938.* Paris: Seyssel, 1986.

Audoin-Rouzeau, Stéphane. *14–18: Les Combattants des tranchées à travers leurs journaux.* Paris: Armand Colin, 1986.

Azéma, Jean-Pierre, and François Bédarida, eds. *Le Régime de Vichy et les Français.* Paris: Fayard, 1992.

Barrot, Olivier, and Pascal Ory, ed. *Entre Deux Guerres: La création française entre 1919 et 1939.* Paris: Editions François Bourin, 1990.

Barthas, Louis. *Les Cahiers de guerre de Louis Barthas, tonnelier (1914–1919).* Paris: François Maspero, 1978.

Becker, Jean-Jacques. *1914: Comment les Français sont entrés dans la guerre.* Paris: Presses de la Fondation nationale des sciences politiques, 1977.

————. *Les Français dans la Grande Guerre.* Paris: Robert Laffont, 1980.

Behr, Edward. *The Good Frenchman: The True Story of the Life and Times of Maurice Chevalier.* New York: Random House, 1993.

Berstein, Serge, and Pierre Milza. *Histoire de la France au XXe siècle.* Vol. II: 1930–1945. Paris: Editions Complexe, 1991.

Bertin-Maghit, Jean-Pierre. *Le Cinéma français sous Vichy: Les films français de 1940 à 1944.* Paris: La Revue du cinéma et Editions Albatross, 1980.

————. *Le Cinéma sous l'occupation.* Paris: Olivier Orban, 1989.

Birnbaum, Pierre. *Le Peuple et les gros: Histoire d'un mythe.* Paris: Grasset, 1979.

————. *Un Mythe politique: La "République juive."* Paris: Fayard, 1988.

Bloch, Marc. *Memoirs of War.* Trans. Carole Fink. Ithaca, N.Y.: Cornell University Press, 1980.

————. *Strange Defeat.* Trans. Gerard Hopkins. New York: Norton, 1968.

Bordier, Roger. *36, la fête.* Paris: Editions Messidor, 1985.

Brécy, Robert. *Florilège de la chanson révolutionnaire de 1789 au Front populaire.* Paris: Editions Hier et demain, 1978.

Brunschwig, Chantal, Louis-Jean Calvet, and Jean-Claude Klein. *Cent ans de chanson française.* Paris: Seuil, 1981.

Buchsbawm, Jonathan. *Cinéma engagé: Film in the Popular Front.* Urbana: University of Illinois Press, 1988.

Cacérès, Bénigno. *Allons au-devant de la vie: La naissance du temps des loisirs en 1936.* Paris: François Maspero, 1981.

Calvet, Louis-Jean. *Chanson et société.* Paris: Payot, 1981.

Canini, Gérard. *Combattre à Verdun: Vie et souffrance quotidienne du soldat, 1916–1917.* Nancy: Presses Universitaires de Nancy, 1988.

Cannavo, Richard. *Trenet, le siècle en liberté.* Paris: Hidalgo Editeur, 1989.

Cantaloube-Ferrieu, Lucienne. *Chanson et poésie des années 30 aux années 60*. Paris: A. G. Nizet, 1981.

Cazin, Paul. *L'Humaniste à la guerre: Hauts de Meuse*. Paris: Plon, 1920.

Cendrars, Blaise. *Panorama de la pègre* [1934] *et autres reportages*. Paris: Union générale d'Editions, 1986.

Charpentreau, Jacques, and France Vernillat. *Dictionnaire de la chanson française*. Paris: Larousse, 1968.

Chevalier, Louis. *Montmartre du plaisir et du crime*. Paris: Editions Robert Laffont, 1980.

Chevalier, Maurice. *Ma Route et mes chansons*. Paris: Julliard, 1946.

———. *Ma Route et mes chansons: Londres, Hollywood, Paris*. Paris: Julliard, 1947.

———. *Ma Route et mes chansons: Tempes grises*. Paris: Julliard, 1948.

Chirat, Raymond. *Le Cinéma français des années 30*. Paris: Hatier, 1983.

Crisp, Colin. *The Classic French Cinema, 1930–1960*. Bloomington: Indiana University Press, 1993.

Dabit, Eugène. *Faubourgs de Paris*. Paris: Gallimard, 1933.

———. *Journal intime, 1928–1936*. New edition, ed. Pierre Edmond Robert. Paris: Gallimard, 1989.

Daniel, Joseph. *Guerre et cinéma: Grandes illusions et petits soldats, 1895–1971*. Paris: A. Colin, 1972.

De Grazia, Victoria. "Mass Culture and Sovereignty: The American Challenge to European Cinemas, 1920–1960," *Journal of Modern History* 61, no. 1 (March 1989), 53–87.

Desanti, Dominique. *La Femme au temps des années folles*. Paris: Stock, 1984.

Dillaz, Serge. *La Chanson française de contestation de la Commune à Mai 68*. Paris: Seghers, 1973.

———. *La Chanson sous la Troisième République*. Paris: Tallandier, 1991.

Dorgelès, Roland. *La Drôle de guerre, 1939–1940*. Paris: Editions Albin Michel, 1957.

Dubois, Raoul. *Au soleil de 36*. Paris: Editions de Messidor, 1986.

Duclos, Pierre, et Georges Martin. *Piaf*. Paris: Seuil, 1993.

Duval, René. *Histoire de la radio en France*. Paris: Editions Alain Moreau, 1979.

Duverney, Anne-Marie, and O. d'Horrer. *Mémoire de la chanson française depuis 1900*. Neuilly-sur-Seine: Musique et Promotion, 1979.

Ehrlich, Evelyn. *Cinema of Paradox: French Filmmaking under the German Occupation*. New York: Columbia University Press, 1985.

Eksteins, Modris. *Rites of Spring: The Great War and the Birth of the Modern Age*. New York: Doubleday, 1989.

Englander, David. "The French Soldier, 1914–1918." *French History* 1 (March 1987): 49–67.

Faure, Christian. *Le Projet culturel de Vichy: folklore et révolution nationale*. Lyons: Presses Universitaires de Lyon, 1989.

Fauré, Michel. *Le Groupe Octobre*. Paris: C. Bourgois, 1977.

Ferro, Marc. *La Grande Guerre, 1914–1918*. Paris: Gallimard, 1969.

Fieschi, Jean Toussaint. *Histoire du sport français de 1870 à nos jours*. Paris: Editions PAC, 1983.

Fishman, Sarah. *We Will Wait: Wives of French Prisoners of War, 1940–1945*. New Haven: Yale University Press, 1991.

Fléouter, Claude. *Un Siècle de chansons*. Paris: Presses Universitaires de France, 1988.

Garçon, François. *De Blum à Pétain: Cinéma et société française, 1936–1944*. Paris: Les Editions du Cerf, 1984.

Guerrand, Roger-Henri. *La Conquête des vacances*. Paris: Les Editions ouvrières, 1963.

Guillaume-Grimaud, Geneviève. *Le Cinéma du Front populaire*. Paris: Lherminier, 1986.

Halimi, André. *Chantons sous l'occupation*. Paris: Olivier Orban, 1976.

Halls, W. D. *The Youth of Vichy France*. Oxford: Clarendon Press, 1981.

Hayward, Susan. *French National Cinema*. London: Routledge, 1993.

Hayward, Susan, and Ginette Vincendeau, eds. *French Film, Texts and Contexts*. London: Routledge, 1990.

Hewitt, Nicholas, and Brian Rigby, eds. *France and the Mass Media*. London: Macmillan, 1991.

Hirschfeld, Gerhard, and Patrick Marsh, eds. *Collaboration in France: Politics and Culture during the Nazi Occupation, 1940–1944*. Oxford: Berg Publishers, 1989.

Holt, Richard. *Sport and Society in Modern France*. Hamden, Conn.: Archon Books, 1981.

Jackson, Julian. *The Popular Front in France Defending Democracy, 1934–38*. Cambridge: Cambridge University Press, 1988.

Jacques-Charles [pseud.]. *Cent ans de music-hall*. Paris: Jeheber, 1956.

Jamet, Claude. *Notre Front populaire: Journal d'un militant (1934–1939)*. Paris: La Table Ronde, 1977.

Jeancolas, Jean-Pierre. *15 ans d'années trente: Le cinéma des Français, 1929–1944*. Paris: Stock, 1983.

Kedward, Roderick, and Roger Austin, eds. *Vichy France and the Resistance: Culture and Ideology*. Totowa, N.J.: Barnes & Noble, 1985.

Klein, Jean-Claude. *Florilège de la chanson française*. Paris: Bordas, 1990.

Le Boterf, Hervé. *La Vie parisienne sous l'occupation*. 2 vols. Paris: Editions France-Empire, 1974–1975.

Lebovics, Herman. *True France: The Wars over Cultural Identity, 1900–1945*. Ithaca, N.Y.: Cornell University Press, 1992.

Leed, Eric. *No Man's Land: Combat and Identity in World War I*. New York: Cambridge University Press, 1979.

Lefranc, Georges. *Histoire du Front populaire, 1934–1938*. Paris: Payot, 1965.

Leglise, Paul. *Histoire de la politique du cinéma française*. Vol. I: *Le Cinéma et la IIIe République*. Paris: Librairie générale de droit et de jurisprudence, 1970.

Leprohon, Pierre. *L'Exotisme et le cinéma*. Paris: J. Susse, 1945.

Lequin, Yves, ed. *Histoire des Français, XIXe-XXe siècles*, Vol. 3. Paris: Armand Colin, 1984.

MacOrlan, Pierre. *Aux Lumières de Paris*. Paris: Les Editions G. Crès, 1925.

Mairet, Louis. *Carnet d'un combattant*. Paris: Editions Georges Crès, 1919.

Martin, John W. *The Golden Age of French Cinema, 1929–1939*. Boston: Twayne Publishers, 1983.

Mayer, Jacques. *La Vie quotidienne des soldats pendant la Grande Guerre*. Paris: Hachette, 1966.

Miller, Michael B. *Shanghai on the Métro: Spies, Intrigue, and the French between the Wars*. Berkeley and Los Angeles: University of California Press, 1994.

Miquel, Pierre. *Histoire de la radio et de la télévision*. Paris: Perrin, 1984.

Monaco, Paul. *Cinema and Society: France and Germany during the Twenties*. New York: Elsevier, 1976.

Noguères, Henri. *La Vie quotidienne au temps du Front populaire*. Paris: Hachette, 1977.

Noiriel, Gérard. *Les Ouvriers dans la société française, XIXe–XXe siècle*. Paris: Seuil, 1986.

Ory, Pascal. *La Belle Illusion: Culture et politique sous le signe du Front populaire, 1935–1938*. Paris: Plon, 1994.

———. "La Politique culturelle du premier gouvernement Blum," *La Nouvelle Revue socialiste* 10–11 (1975), pp. 75–93.

———. "Vers une Culture démocratique" and "Une Culture nationale à son apogée," chapters 4 and 5, Livre II, in Yves Lequin, ed., *Histoire des Français, XIXe–XXe siècles*, Vol. 3. Paris: Armand Colin, 1984.

Paxton, Robert O. *Vichy France: Old Guard and New Order, 1940–1944*. New York: Knopf, 1972.

Perreux, Gabriel. *La Vie quotidienne des civils en France pendant la Grande Guerre*. Paris: Hachette, 1966.

Peyrusse, Claudette. *Le Cinéma méridional: Le Midi dans le cinéma français (1929–1944)*. Toulouse: Eché, 1986.

Prost, Antoine. *Les Anciens Combattants et la société française, 1914–1939*. Paris: Presses de la Fondation nationale des sciences politiques, 1977.

Rémond, René, and Janine Bourdin, eds. *La France et les Français en 1938–1939*. Paris: Presses de la Fondation nationale des sciences politiques, 1978.

Richer, Philippe. *La Drôle de guerre des Français, 2 septembre 1939–10 mai 1940*. Paris: Olivier Orban, 1990.

Rieger, Dietmar, ed. *La Chanson française et son histoire*. Tubingen: Gunter Narr Verlag, 1988.

Rifkin, Adrian. *Street Noises: Parisian Pleasures, 1900–1940*. Manchester, England: Manchester University Press, 1993.

Rigby, Brian. *Popular Culture in Modern France: A Study of Cultural Discourse*. London: Routledge, 1991.

Ringgold, Gene, and Dewitt Bodeen. *Chevalier: The Films and Career of Maurice Chevalier*. Secaucus, N.J.: Citadel Press, 1973.

Rioux, Jean-Pierre, ed. *Politiques et pratiques culturelles dans la France de Vichy*. Cahiers de l'Institut d'histoire du Temps present, no. 8 (June). Paris, 1988.

Rives, Paul. *La Corvée de la joie: Notes sur les loisirs ouvriers*. Paris: Presses Universitaires de France, 1924.

Roberts, Mary Louise. *Civilization without Sexes: Reconstructing Gender in Postwar France, 1917–1927*. Chicago: University of Chicago Press, 1994.

Romi [Robert Miquel]. *Gros succès et petits fours: La Chanson du café-chantant au microsillon*. Paris: SERG, 1967.

Rose, Phyllis. *Jazz Cleopatra: Josephine Baker in Her Time*. New York: Doubleday, 1989.

Rossi-Landi, Guy. *La Drôle de guerre: La vie politique en France, 2 septembre 1939–10 mai 1940*. Paris: Armand Colin, 1971.

Sadoul, Georges. *Journal de guerre*. Paris: Les Editeurs Français réunis, 1977.

Saka, Pierre. *La Chanson française à travers ses succès*. Paris: Larousse, 1988.

Sesonske, Alexander. *Jean Renoir: The French Films, 1924–1939*. Cambridge, Mass.: Harvard University Press, 1980.

Siclier, Jacques. *La France de Pétain et son cinéma*. Paris: Editions Henri Veyrier, 1981.

Soucy, Robert. *French Fascism: The First Wave, 1924–1933*. New Haven: Yale University Press, 1986.

———. *French Fascism: The Second Wave, 1933–1939*. New Haven: Yale University Press, 1995.

Talmard, Jean-Louis. *Pages de guerre d'un paysan*. Lyons: Emmanuel Vitte, 1971.

Thébaud, Françoise. *La Femme au temps de la guerre de 1914*. Paris: Stock, 1986.

Turk, Edward Baron. *Child of Paradise: Marcel Carné and the Golden Age of French Cinema*. Cambridge, Mass.: Harvard University Press, 1989.

Valdour, Jacques [Louis Martin]. *De la Popinqu'à Ménilmuch'*. Paris: Editions Spes, 1924.

———. *Le Faubourg*. Paris: Editions Spes, 1925.

———. *Le Flot montant du socialisme, ouvriers de Lyon et Troyes*. Paris: Nouvelles Editions Latines, 1934.

———. *La Menace rouge: Ouvriers d'après guerre en Touraine*. Paris: Editions de La Gazette française, 1926.

———. *Ouvriers catholiques et royalistes: Romans-sur-Isère et Decazeville*. Paris: Flammarion, n.d. [1928].

———. *Ouvriers parisiens d'après guerre: Observations vécues*. Paris: Arthur Rousseau, 1921.

————. *Les Puissances de désordre: Vers la Révolution, ouvriers de la Plaine-Saint-Denis, Aubervilliers, Paris-Belleville*. Paris: Nouvelles Editions Latines, 1935.

Vincendeau, Ginette, and Keith Reader, eds. *La Vie est à nous: French Cinema of the Popular Front, 1935–1938*. London: British Film Institute, 1986.

Wahl, Alfred, ed. *Les Archives du football: Sport et société en France, 1880–1980*. Paris: Julliard, 1989.

Weber, Eugen, *The Hollow Years: France in the 1930s*. New York: Norton, 1994.

Weil, Simone. *La Condition ouvrière*. Paris: Gallimard, 1951.

Williams, Alan. *Republic of Images: A History of French Filmmaking*. Cambridge, Mass.: Harvard University Press, 1992.

Zdatny, Steven M. *The Politics of Survival: Artisans in Twentieth-Century France*. New York: Oxford University Press, 1990.

INDEX